The
Ceramic
Spectrum

The Ceramic Spectrum

A Simplified Approach to Glaze & Color Development

ROBIN HOPPER

Chilton Book Company · Radnor, Pennsylvania

AAY 7232

PHOTOGRAPHY CREDITS

Special thanks to my photographer, Trevor Mills, for the
twelve color glaze test photographs following page 48 and for
black and white figures (1-13, 1-18, 1-19, 1-22, 1-27, 1-29, 2-
10, 2-11, 3-1, 4-2, 4-3, 4-4, 5-2, 5-3, 7-1, 8-3, 9-4, 11-3, 11-5, 11-
6, 12-1, 12-2, 12-3, 12-4, 13-8, 13-9, 13-10, 13-11, 14-1, 14-3, 18-
1, 18-2, 18-4, 18-7, 19-1, 19-4, 19-6, 20-3, and 20-13). Other
photos by Andley (18-5), Robert M. Aude (2-2), Bengt-Göran
Carlsson (18-10), James A. Chambers (19-5), David Cripps
(18-12), Larry Dixon (2-7), Joan Farano (20-14), Goian
Gustafson (7-3), Don Hall (18-8), Bernard Judge (20-1), Lelkes
Laszlo (18-3), Bill Lorenze (19-2), Robert McNair (20-16), Paul
Morin (2-8, 19-8), Stephen S. Myers (13-6), Marlen Perez (14-
5), Pete Petersen (13-4), Ian Robson (2-6, 11-4), Jochen Schade
(13-12), Schenck and Schenck (20-5), Paul Schwartz (20-4),
Scianamblo/Benzle (2-9), Bill Thomas (7-4, 13-1, 14-2), Robert
Vigiletti (14-4).
All other color and black-and-white photographs by the
artist, except where otherwise noted.

On the dust jacket: Robin Hopper. Feather Basket Bowl (detail). Porcelain, with fluted, three-colored agateware rim;
once fired in oxidation at cone 9. 14″ diameter. Photograph
by Trevor Mills.

Copyright © 1984 by Robin Hopper
All Rights Reserved
Published in Radnor, Pennsylvania 19089, by Chilton Book Company
Designed by Jean Callan King/Metier Industrial, Inc.
Manufactured in the United States of America

Library of Congress Cataloging in Publication Data
Hopper, Robin.
    The ceramic spectrum.

    Bibliography: p. 218
    Includes index.
    1. Glazes.   2. Color.   I. Title.
TP823.H66   1984   738.1′5   83-70777
ISBN 0-8019-7275-2

5 6 7 8 9 0   2 1 0

To my patient, tolerant, and understanding family

Contents

Acknowledgments

I wish to express my gratitude to all of the people who have helped in the development of this book, the many potters, students, collectors and interested people who want to know more about ceramic phenomena. My thanks especially to my wife, Sue, for her careful reading of the manuscript (many, many times!), her helpful suggestions and her tolerance of the extra work load during the process; to Veronica Stewart, who untiringly worked through close to 15,000 glaze and color tests; to Tom and Ginny Marsh who initiated the project; to a number of readers, including Ann Mortimer, Walter Ostrom, Gordon Barnes, Les Manning, John Porter, Judi Dyelle, Jeanne Otis, Allan Crimmins, Pat Forst, Theo Dombrowski, Stuart Holland and Claire Moore; to the many teachers from whom one learns, sometimes directly, sometimes by example, sometimes by their writings and sometimes by osmosis and without their awareness, including Arthur Barnett, Michael Cardew, Mick Casson, Val Cushing, Vivika Heino, Harry Horlock-Stringer, Bernard Leach, Glenn Nelson, John Reeve and Daniel Rhodes; to Frank Boyden for the information on terra sigillatas and their use; to Eileen Lewenstein and Emmanuel Cooper, of *Ceramic Review* magazine, London, who first published some of my material, which is included in this book; to the following companies for their assistance in technical matters: Blythe Colors Limited, England; Pemco Products, U.S.A.; Harshaw Chemical Company, U.S.A.; Pottery Supply House Ltd., Canada; Greenbarn Potters Supply Ltd., Canada; to the staff of museums and art galleries which were so helpful, including The Art Gallery of Greater Victoria, The Royal Ontario Museum,

The Musée des Beaux Arts de Montreal, The Vancouver Museum, all of Canada; The National Museum of Greece (Heraklion); and the Nelson-Atkins Museum of Art, Kansas City, Missouri; to Jane Mahut, Orland Larson, and Robin Skelton for their support; to ceramists from around the world who have generously given support and loaned illustration material; to Tom, the intrepid typist; and to the Canada Council who generously supported the research for this project.

To all, my sincere thanks.

Robin Hopper
Victoria, Canada, 1983

Introduction

No words can convey the excitement and satisfaction that come from the study of glaze and color development. It is a process of personal understanding, and of the development of a sympathetic relationship with the materials which have been used by our ceramic forefathers for millennia.

This book is not intended to be a recipe book, but to de-mystify an extremely complex subject. It aims to make available to the student of ceramics, whether beginner, advanced, or professional, an approach to the study of ceramic glaze and color development which does *not* rely on the use of published formulae, recipes, or mathematics. It goes back to the empirical methods of glaze making, in use for nearly five thousand years before the understanding of glaze formulation by mathematical equation. As a teacher, I came to the conclusion that the vast majority of potters, ceramists, and students of ceramics are totally intimidated by the alien chemical/mathematical methods of glaze making, to the point that that they give up any meaningful exploration of this fascinating aspect of the potter's art. They turn instead to a bewildering array of other people's recipes, readily available in many books, which seldom offer a totally satisfactory solution to the problem in hand.

Unfortunately, this dependency has the effect of dulling the senses to the almost limitless possibilities of the medium. It also tends to fill the potters' marketplaces with an alarming array of stereotyped pottery, coated with boring and overused glazes. I continually ponder how so many so-called artists or craftsmen can accept such boredom, and ask the following question: "Is there life after temmoku, celadon, and high alumina matt?"

I certainly believe so, and the aim of this book

is to encourage the personal exploration of materials for glaze and color, so that anyone can develop his own glazes, without pain or anguish, and with a very exciting learning experience. Although many recipes are included, they are offered only as suggested examples, or parameters to learn from, not necessarily as solutions in themselves.

The material for this book developed from the teaching of glaze chemistry, and the quick realization that the vast majority of people cannot add, subtract, multiply, or divide with any reliable degree of accuracy more than 50 percent of the time. Thus a study that relies on mathematics is fraught with potential problems. Furthermore, if one adds the complexities of understanding chemical symbolism to that of mathematics, the combination often discourages even the most adventurous from experiment. On a global scale, this is tragic for the continued health of a vigorous and longlived art, which through the centuries has served as an important vehicle for man's creative talents.

First, we trace the historical developments in ceramics, later relating these to the use of materials. We follow a path of increasing complexity to gain a wide knowledge of material reactions under heat. From there we find out what is responsible for the development of color, the assisting factors and the inhibiting factors, and how to create specific colors, rather than the usual unsatisfactory approach of accepting what happens. For most colors, it should be possible to work toward a desired goal, in much the same way as one chooses paint from charts in a paint store.

Any course of glaze development study is only as good as the application which is given to it, the degree of accuracy which is used, and the recording of processes, results, and observations. These will be outlined early on, to make sure of maximum benefit. I cover glaze development and coloration at those temperatures most widely used, cones 04–1, 3–6, and 8–10, which will be called *low-fire, mid-fire,* and *high-fire.* There is also coverage of specific temperature areas for colors such as chromium and uranium reds, yellows and oranges, overglaze enamels, and other specialized glazes. The atmospheric variations of oxidation and reduction and their effects, combined with suggestions on how

to relate these to your kiln, are discussed in chapter 3.

Although some might think of this approach as regressive, the material covered in this book is the result of over 25 years of study, much of which dealt with molecular formula, and the resultant commitment that there must be an approach that does not represent an anathema to such an overwhelming number of people. There is a perfectly valid reason for the ceramic industry to use formulae for the development of industrially controlled glazes which can be quickly compared. The studio potter doesn't generally need or want such control in his work; it is too far removed from the actual process and the intimate understanding of ceramic materials. For those who wish to use formulae, and there are many who do, I hope that this book will suggest new approaches, and be of use in determining color development, which formulae cannot do. For those who feel intimidated by mathematical formulae, it is my hope that in the exploration of this book it will be possible for the reader to find a new direction in the search for an individual idiom.

The text can be used as a course outline for either the individual or group, where shared experiences tend to enhance and speed up the learning process. It should also be usable as a research tool for the understanding and development of colors which may have previously seemed beyond reach. The book is a distillation of all that I have read on the subject and a large amount of personal research, in combination with the opportunity, while teaching, of seeing vast numbers of glaze and color tests each year.

Part V is a portfolio of the work of selected potters and ceramists from different parts of the world, who use color in widely differing ways. The captions for these illustrations contain the potters' descriptions of methodology in the creation of the works shown. The portfolio should serve as an inspiration source, and a small view of the incredible wealth of creative potential in the sensitive uses of ceramic materials by experienced artists and craftsmen.

Since the whole concept of this book is to simplify a mystifyingly complex subject, and I have found from personal experience, both as teacher and potter, that one tends to become overanxious and intimidated by both equation and symbol, I have decided to eliminate these from the text. Except for chapters 5, 14, and 17, which include lists of ceramic materials, colorants, and opacifiers, with their chemical symbolism, and any places where chemical symbolism is unavoidable, all reference to materials will be made in the commonly used form. For example, kaolin will be called kaolin, and not china clay or hydrous silicate of alumina, and its formula will only be found in chapter 5; similarly dolomite will be called dolomite, and not calcium-magnesium carbonate; and iron will be red iron, unless stated differently, instead of ferric oxide. Particular types or brand names of various materials, such as feldspar, kaolin, ball clay and so on will be omitted, and only these generic terms will be used. Mathematics will be limited to the addition and subtraction of 1 to 100. All temperatures will be recorded either by Orton cones or degrees Celsius (centigrade). Appendix 1 is a reference chart on cones and temperatures (including a conversion for Celsius to Fahrenheit) for comparison purposes.

This means that anyone, anywhere in the world, can use the information as guidelines, setting out knowing nothing, and in this ignorance or innocence achieve exciting results. This doesn't mean that we should turn our backs on chemistry, since the whole process of glaze and color development is one of chemical reaction. What it does mean, however, is that by eliminating the dogma of chemistry and mathematics, we can concentrate on the actual and observable reaction, and leave the other to the chemists and mathematicians. Glazemaking can and should be an exciting and enjoyable learning experience, as well as an extremely important part of a ceramist's personal development, and the growth of an individual approach to working in clay.

As one learns to develop glazes and colors, it will soon become obvious that one cannot be dogmatic about a great deal of the technical side of things. The nature of the materials and process will suggest a variety of ways to achieve a given result. Explore them all and make decisions accordingly. Don't accept dogma as gospel; there is almost always more than one way to do things and get the required result.

PART ONE

The Basics

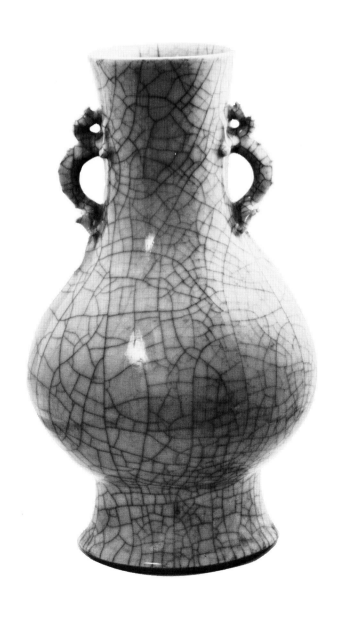

Glaze: A Brief Technical History

To appreciate the gradual development and understanding of ceramic materials which has occurred over the last 8000 years of man's history, it is helpful to know a little of the background which has given birth to the overwhelmingly rich and diverse art form that we have in ceramics. I choose not to follow these developments in any specific chronological order, but more in the order of technological progress, the transition from pit fire to porcelain. This transition has led from the earliest accidents of pottery making to the astounding scientific advances in the use of ceramics in the space programs of the twentieth century. These advances in ceramic technology are already having a profound effect on the potter, and will certainly create new and exciting movements for the future. The illustrations also follow the same zig-zag path as

ceramic history, where one culture has learned from the developments of another.

Archaeologists generally agree that like most of mankind's major discoveries, the earliest pottery probably developed by accident. This may have occurred from observations of the way the earth became baked around fire pits, with the subsequent experiment of firing clay pots. It could have also come from the accidental burning of clay-lined baskets. Baskets woven from reeds, roots, or soft tree branches were the original storage containers. At this time, man was primarily a seed-eating creature who stored his food supplies in baskets. Baskets, of course, are anything but impervious to the loss of small seeds, which easily find their way through the mesh of basket weave. After a while, inner coatings of clay were probably smeared onto

1–1. Round bottomed urn. Red earthenware pottery; moulded criss-cross decoration in relief around base, crosshatched string impressions on body. China, late Zhou, 6th–3rd century B.C. Courtesy of the Royal Ontario Museum, Toronto, Canada: 924.26.32. George Crofts Collection.

the basket to prevent loss. The next development was likely the accidental setting on fire of one of these mud-lined baskets, resulting in the first major step in our technology, that of fired clay, and thus pottery.

The same sort of accident most likely occurred all over the world at different times, creating what is generally referred to as primitive pottery. Because of the early associations with baskets, much of the world's earliest pottery is decorated with simulated basketweave patterns. Over very long periods of time man developed his use for fired clay materials to encompass a wide range of functions, from seed container to sculpture, from votive doll to space capsule. In this book I am not concerned with the most recent developments of space age technology, except where pertinent to some other aspect of the potter's art. I am concerned only with those ceramic developments which fall into the area of impervious coatings of clay, glaze and color.

Clay, when fired in a pit or bonfire, doesn't get hot enough to shrink and fuse into a waterproof solid. Although in many cultures porous clay vessels were and still are used for the storage of water, where loss by evaporation causes the water to be kept cool, it soon became evident that some method for making the surface of clay impervious to water loss would be beneficial. The earliest waterproofing was most likely done by the rubbing of pots, hot from the fire, with some form of resinous material from the leaves of trees, or by smearing the pots with animal fats to seal the pores of the clay. Burnishing the clay with a pebble would also help to develop a very smooth and fairly waterproof surface. These techniques are still very much in use in societies where pottery is made in primitive ways. In fact, a significant amount of the world's pottery is made this way, although it is falling victim to the insidious encroachment of plastics. Unfortunately, the resin and fat coated surfaces are not very resistant to continual use, and other methods of making vessels waterproof were soon looked for.

The next step in the development of an impervious surface came through the use of a refined liquid clay coating, or thin colloidal slip having ultrafine particle size, which formed a glaze-like skin. These slips are mostly reddish brown, dark brown or black in color, and are generally known by the Latin name of *terra sigillata*, meaning sealed earth. They are made by allowing surface clays, usually red clays, to soak in a suspension of water until the heavier particles sink to the bottom. The water and thin slip are then siphoned off and the process repeated until the resultant slip is of a very fine particle size. The slip is sometimes made to liquify and settle more readily by using an alkaline deflocculant such as lye or sodium hydroxide, sodium silicate, sodium carbonate, or even urine.

The waterproof terra sigillata glaze surface was employed by many cultures, some in very colorful ways. Despite its Latin name, its use was particularly developed by the Greeks. It formed the basic decorating medium on classical Greek pottery from very early times, and became the basis for the familiar black and red decorated ware. The black develops from the reduced slip surface (see reduction, chapter 3), and provided the artists in the Greek society an excellent medium in which to record their myths and customs. This pottery was fired in kilns of a more sophisticated nature than the pit-

1–2. Casserole with cover. Burnished earthenware with impressed pattern. Nigeria. Courtesy of the Royal Ontario Museum, Department of Ethnology, Toronto, Canada: 980.279.2.

fired wares, with significant control over the firing. The subtle reduction of the surface slip is achieved without reduction of the underlying clay body. If over-reduced, both would turn black. The fact that there is still so much of this pottery around today points to a very successful methodology of firing, done not by the potters themselves, but by a fireman responsible for only that part of the total process. In fact, the Greeks were the first to develop a factory system of working, where specific jobs were done by designated people. The pot was made by a potter, decorated by a painter, mainly the court painters of the time, and fired by the fireman. The degree of control which each exerted in his particular field allowed interesting ceramics to de-velop. The forms were established along mathematically controlled lines according to the principles of the Golden Mean. The potter did not have much opportunity for self-expression; the vessel was just the ground for the more important painting on the surface. Although we often find that the pot and surface tend to detract from each other, in the hands of sensitive painters the integration of form and surface is delightful. Scenes of mythological heroics and histrionics abound on the vast majority of these pots, done with a combination of brush painting, sgraffito (scratching through the painted surface with a pointed metal implement of some sort), and sometimes post-firing additions of white details. This seemingly small pallette of color

1–3. Vessel and cover. Burnished earthenware with impressed pattern. South Congo. Courtesy of the Royal Ontario Museum, Department of Ethnology, Toronto, Canada: HA2700.

1–4. Gourd shaped vessel. Burnished earthenware with impressions. Congo. Courtesy of the Royal Ontario Museum, Department of Ethnology, Toronto, Canada: HA1383.

1–5. Spouted vessel. Earthenware with decoration in black, red, and white pigments over red-buff clay. Minoan—Palace of Phaistos, Crete, 2000–1700 B.C. Courtesy of the Heraklion Museum, Crete.

painting with a fairly stiff slip to leave a similar raised surface. The piece was subsequently dipped into a thin sigillata slip, and fired in a kiln with no reduction, leaving a reddish satin surface. Roman pottery decoration rarely has the same vigor as that of the earlier Greek wares, and far less is seen in the museums of the world. Many other cultures used terra sigillata techniques for sealing and beautifying the surfaces of their wares, particularly Pre-Colombian cultures of Central and South America. Terra sigillata slips have been in use for thousands of years.

The first actual glazed surface occurred, again probably accidentally, in the area of Egypt approximately five thousand years ago. The usual theory of the first glaze development comes from the probable use of sandstone containing considerable sodium and potassium, called Natron, as the material with which to build a fireplace. Natron has a very low melting point, and the surface of the rock facing the fire would easily develop to a fused glaze. A fairly logical step from this point might have been

1–7. Jar. Lead glaze with copper. China, Eastern Han, 25–220 A.D. Collection of the Musée des Beaux-Arts de Montréal, Quebec, Canada: 962.ED.24. F. Cleveland Morgan Bequest.

1–6. Ewer. Earthenware with painted decoration of reed grasses, in iron pigment on red-buff clay. Minoan—Palace of Knossos, Crete, 2000–1700 B.C. Courtesy of the Heraklion Museum, Crete.

was entirely sufficient to depict the subject matter for these wares.

Terra sigillata was also used to a very large degree by the Romans for the pottery made especially for the patricians, and was known as samian ware. Instead of being painted, however, this ware was generally made in moulds where a decoration was cut into the mould surface. Clay was then pressed into the mould, forming a raised relief pattern. These wares emulated the repoussé decoration of silver and gold vessels that possibly originated in China. Decoration was also made by

to make small statues from this sandstone and heat them, and this is what most likely led to the first glaze on pottery. Natron, sand and clay were mixed, and figurines were made by pressing the mixture into moulds. When the material dried, the soluble sodium materials migrated to the surface, forming a powdery scum. When heated to a low red heat, this scum melted, and combined with the clay to form a glaze. This is, in fact, a self glazing clay, which we now call Egyptian paste. It was often colored by the introduction, natural or fabricated, of metallic compounds of copper, manganese, iron and cobalt.

It is a comparatively small jump from this material to a glaze made from the same materials, put into a solution with water, and subsequently used to coat the pottery form. So we have the first glazes developed for use on pottery. This discovery seems to have had little practical use in functional pottery for quite some time. Egyptian patricians generally used either gold, alabaster or onyx for their functional needs, and the humble peasant potter made use of simple unglazed dishes and storage con-

1–9. Jug. Earthenware, buff clay with copper colored green lead glaze. English, 17th century A.D. Courtesy of the Vancouver Museum Collection, Vancouver, Canada.

1–8. Miniature jug. Buff earthenware, yellow lead galena glaze inside, mottled green with copper outside. English, 14th or 15th century A.D. Courtesy of the Nelson-Atkins Museum of Art, Kansas City, Missouri.

1–10. Jug. Silhouette ware, black slip under clear turquoise alkaline glaze, with sgraffito decoration. Persia, late 12th century A.D. Collection of the Musée des Beaux-Arts de Montreal, Quebec, Canada: 939.DP.10. Gift of Harry A. Norton.

tainers for his daily life, blissfully unaware of the fact that he could have had impermeable glazed surfaces to eat from and store liquids in. Alkaline glazes such as these had certain drawbacks, such as some solubility after firing, particularly when used in cooking. There were also difficulties in application, as well as a strong tendency to craze and chip easily. However, even with their drawbacks, they were a great deal more serviceable than the earlier unglazed wares.

Further developments were needed, and the next important advance in the understanding of materials came with the introduction of lead compounds into materials for use by potters. Lead compounds are fairly common, and it was found that lead sulfide, or galena, when ground up and applied to the surface of the clay, would easily melt and fuse to a shiny smooth glaze. This advance

1-11. Cosmetic box. Earthenware with underglaze brush decoration. Persia, Kubachi ware, 17th–18th century A.D. Courtesy of the Royal Ontario Museum, Toronto, Canada: 974.68.2.

probably occurred in either Babylonia or Syria between 2500 and 2000 B.C. Both lead and alkaline materials were used together in the production of colored glazes.

At this point I should make it clear that neither alkalis nor lead are glazes in themselves, but become so because of the immediate availability of silica and alumina in clay when combined.

A period of ceramic history where one can see the simplest use of lead is in the pottery of medieval England. Damp pots were dusted with powdered galena, which, when the pots dried and were fired, fused with the clay to form a glazed surface.

We now know that these wares were potentially hazardous, but for several centuries simple

1-12. Cosmetic box. Detail of figure 1–11. Courtesy of the Royal Ontario Museum, Toronto, Canada: 974.68.2.

1–13. Bowl. Earthenware, buff clay, white slip and brush pattern in manganese brown slip. Clear glaze. Islamic—Nishapur, 9th–10th century A.D. Courtesy of the Art Gallery of Greater Victoria, B.C., Canada: AGGV.65.171. Fred and Isabel Pollard Collection.

1–14. Bowl. Earthenware, painted in colored slips and oxides under a bluish glaze. Turkey—Isnik, Ottoman period, about 1600 A.D. Collection of the Musée des Beaux-Arts de Montreal, Quebec, Canada: 944.Ea.10. Miss Adaline Van Horne Bequest.

1–15. Bowl. Earthenware, painted in black under turquoise glaze. Persia, probably Kashan, Seljuq period, 1037–1300 A.D. Collection of the Musée des Beaux-Arts de Montreal, Quebec, Canada: 928.Ea.5.

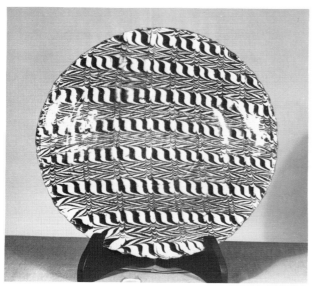

1–16. Combed dish. Slip decorated earthenware, buff clay, cream and brown slip under yellowish lead glaze. English, Staffordshire circa 1700. Courtesy of the Nelson-Atkins Museum of Art, Kansas City, Missouri: B.769.

1–17. Adam and Eve dish. Press moulded earthenware, decorated with cream, orange and brown slip under a yellowish lead glaze. English, Staffordshire, attributed to Samuel Malkin. Courtesy of the Nelson-Atkins Museum of Art, Kansas City, Missouri: B.771.

lead glazes were used for the production of amber, colored, and clear glazes for domestic pottery in many parts of the world. Although the use is diminishing, simple lead glazes are still used in many areas, presumably because of availability and ease of fusion.

The Assyrians learned to make colored glazes by the addition of metallic oxides to the lead glaze, and with these glazes decorated huge architectural edifices with multicolored low relief bricks and tiles. This represented a high development in the process of glazemaking.

Knowledge of the use of lead in glazes spread eventually to China, and much of the pottery of the Han dynasty (25–220 A.D.) used lead for its surface. In many cultures, clay was used as a material to provide an acceptable copy of other more precious materials, and both the form and surface of much Han dynasty pottery emulates bronze. The addition of copper to lead glazes produces colors that closely resemble bronze. Lead glazes later developed into regular use for pottery, and eventually lead to a wide range of colored glazes.

Low temperature earthenware glazes fulfilled the needs of man for many centuries before the next major step in glaze technology occurred. This step depended on the development of a kiln which could be made to fire at considerably higher temperatures than previously obtained. With the discovery of more heat resistant clay materials that could be used for kiln building, the production of a dense, hard form of pottery which we call stoneware became possible. Stoneware clays had very great advantages over the red burning low temperature clays in use at the time; when fired, they were considerably harder, and thus more durable.

These new developments in ceramic technology occurred in China as long ago as 1500 B.C., and represented a great technical leap forward. With higher temperatures, new forms of glaze were needed. The earliest to appear were those which came from the natural melting of wood ash, as it moved through the kiln from the stoking of the fireboxes, and of the red burning clays which fused to glass.

Wood ash is a material which, at high temperatures, fuses with the clay and forms glazed surfaces with no other materials needed. Another common material which formed the basis of high temperature glazes with no other additions was the

1–18. Jar. Buff stoneware with dark brown glaze. China, Tz'u
Chou type ware, Yuan dynasty, 1269–1368 A.D. Collection of
the Musée des Beaux-Arts de Montreal, Quebec, Canada:
925.Ed.4.

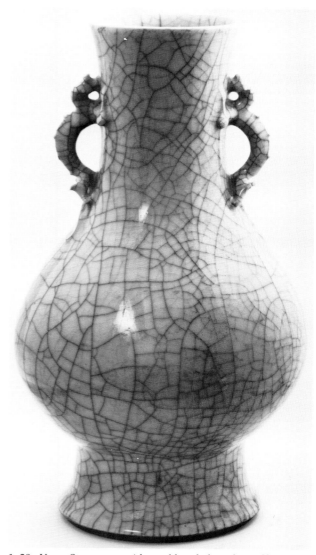

1–20. Vase. Stoneware with crackle celadon glaze. China, 19th century. Courtesy of the Art Gallery of Greater Victoria, B.C., Canada: AGGV.62.223. Gift of Kathleen Graham.

1–19. Vase. Porcellaneous stoneware. China, Yue ware, Chekiang province, 10th century A.D. Collection of the Musée des Beaux-Arts de Montreal, Quebec, Canada: 951.Dp.55.

red earthenware clay which had until this point been the basic material for the production of the pots themselves. These clays contained the basic requirements of flux, alumina and glassformer, to form a glaze. When liquified to a slip, and applied over the stoneware clay, they turned readily into a gloss surface when exposed to a sufficiently hot fire. Combinations of wood ash and clay in varying ratios were used to make a wide variety of glazes.

With the further understanding of their raw materials, the potters toiled for more refinement,

1–21. Tea bowl. Stoneware, with crackle celadon glaze. Japan, probably late 19th century. Collection of the Musée des Beaux-Arts de Montreal, Quebec, Canada: 944.Dp.18. Miss Adaline Van Horne Bequest.

1–22. Pillow. Stoneware, painted in black slip on white slip. China, Tz'u Chou type, Chin dynasty, 1115–1234 A.D. Collection of the Musée des Beaux-Arts de Montreal, Quebec, Canada: 957.Ed.2.

and through the use of rocks ground to powder learned to produce a wide range of glazes at high temperatures. The powdering of a certain igneous rock called petuntze, and the subsequent inter-mixing with a light firing clay called kaolin brought about the development of what was to become the most sought after pottery compound ever produced, porcelain.

The Chinese first produced porcelain during the Tang dynasty (618–906 A.D.) from the refinements of hard firing light colored stoneware clays used in the Han dynasty. These gradual refinements produced a paste material which, when fired properly, had a quality of translucency never seen

1-23. Bowl. Precellaneous stoneware, with mixed brown and white clays, and a transparent glaze. China, Sung dynasty, 11th–12th century A.D. Courtesy of the Royal Ontario Museum, Toronto, Canada: 923.18.1. George Crofts Collection.

1-25. Delftware dish. Tin glazed earthenware with brush painting in cobalt blue. Netherlands (possibly Southwark, England), 1725–1750 A.D. Courtesy of the Art Gallery of Greater Victoria, B.C., Canada: AGGV.80.14.1. Anonymous gift.

1-24. Posset pot. Earthenware, tin opacified glaze with painting in cobalt and manganese. English delftware, possibly Brislington. Courtesy of the Art Gallery of Greater Victoria, B.C., Canada: AGGV.80.14.7. Anonymous gift.

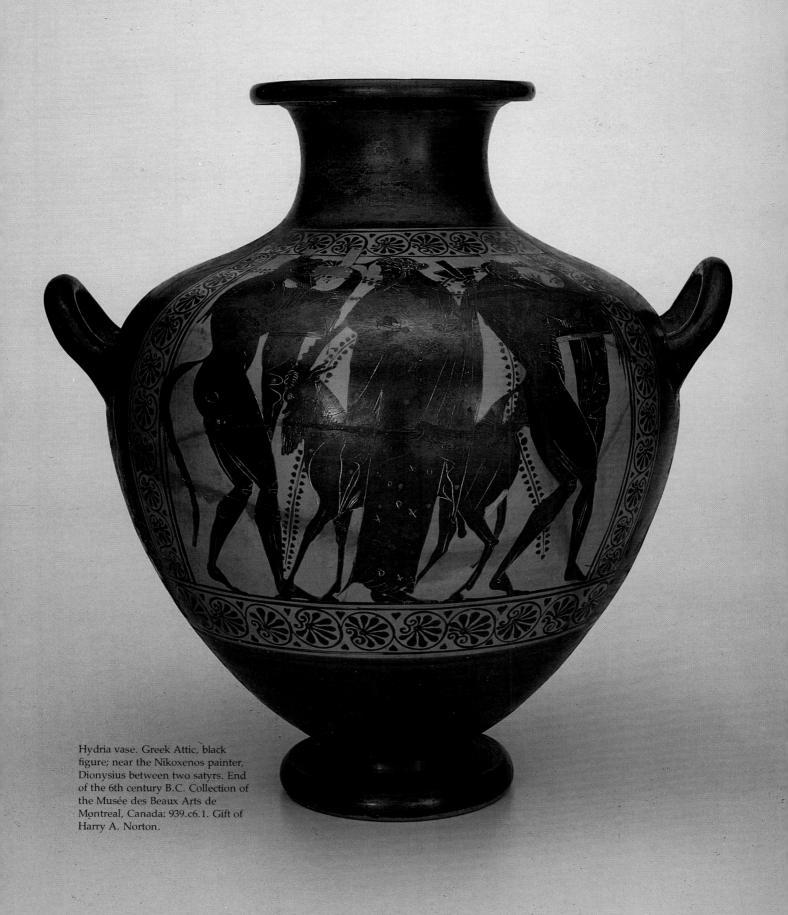

Hydria vase. Greek Attic, black
figure; near the Nikoxenos painter,
Dionysius between two satyrs. End
of the 6th century B.C. Collection of
the Musée des Beaux Arts de
Montreal, Canada: 939.c6.1. Gift of
Harry A. Norton.

Left: Jug and bowl. Earthenware, painted with iron pigment and white slip. Minoan, Kamares style—Palace of Phaistos, Crete, 2000–1700 B.C. Courtesy of the Heraklion Museum, Heraklion, Crete. Photograph: Hannibal, Athens.

Below: Zuni vessel. Earthenware, painted with iron and black pigment on white slip. American—Southwest Pueblo Indian. Courtesy of the Royal Ontario Museum: 901x4.

Facing page: Luster bowl, bird motif. Earthenware with smoked copper luster over cream glaze. Spanish—Hispano Moresque, 17th century. Courtesy of the Art Gallery of Greater Victoria, Canada. Gift of J. J. Mero.

Left: Plate, "Pelican in Her Piety." Slipware: buff brown body, cream base slip, trailed in brown, orange and cream-colored slips, covered with a yellowish lead glaze. English—Staffordshire, 1680-1690; made by Ralph Simpson. Courtesy of the Nelson-Atkins Museum of Art, Kansas City, Missouri: B.784. W. R. Nelson Trust.

Below: Armrest. Buff stoneware with white slip, and mottled amber, green and colorless glazes. Top surface decorated with impressed stylized scroll and floral design. Tang Dynasty (first half 8th century A.D.). Courtesy of the Royal Ontario Museum, Toronto, Canada: 920.10.93. The George Crofts Collection.

Facing page: Dish, Adam and Eve motif. Earthenware with tin opacified glaze, overpainted with cobalt, chromium, iron and antimony pigments. English Delftware—Bristol, ca. 1800–1825. Courtesy of the Art Gallery of Greater Victoria, B.C., Canada. Ann and Joseph Pearson Purchase Fund.

Right: Kogo (incense box). Chubby woman, emblem of happiness, in the form of Ofuku. Minpei style, overglaze enameled decoration on porcelain. Awagi ware, Awagi Island, Hyogo Prefecture, Japan. Collection of the Musée des Beaux Arts de Montreal, Canada: 960.Ee.612. Gift of Joseph Arthur Simard.

Below right: Vase, Famille Rose. Porcelain with overglaze polychrome enamels. Ching Dynasty (1644–1912 A.D.); Ching-Te-Chen, Kiangsi, China. Yung-Chen 1723–1735. Collection of the Musée des Beaux Arts de Montreal, Canada: 962.Ed.45. Gift of N. Phillips, I. Phillips, and Horsley and Annie Townsend Bequest.

Below: Ewer. Turquoise alkaline glaze; grey areas due to devitrification. Islamic—13th century A.D. Courtesy of the Art Gallery of Greater Victoria, B.C., Canada. Fred and Isabel Pollard Collection.

1–26. Decorative plate. Earthenware with copper and silver smoked luster decoration. England, Maw and Co., Shropshire, 1886. Collection of the Musée des Beaux-Arts de Montreal, Quebec, Canada: 1976.Dp.3.

1–27. Lusterware pitcher. Earthenware, buff clay, clear glaze with reduced copper luster. English, Staffordshire, early 19th century. Collection of the author.

1–28. Polychrome bowl. Earthenware, decorated with overglaze enamels. Persia, early 13th century. Collection of the Musée des Beaux-Arts de Montreal, Quebec, Canada: 934.Ea.4. Gift of Harry A. Norton.

before. The refinements reached their peak during the Song dynasty (960–1220 A.D.), although further developments were made in later dynasties. The new material was more or less half clay and half glass, and retained some of the qualities of both materials. Not only was it translucent, it also rang like a bell when tapped. It was so close to glass in its makeup that when glazes were developed for its surface, the materials fused together so completely that the body and its skin were integrated as never before. The resultant material was so pure and fine that the Venetian merchant explorer Marco Polo dubbed it *porcellana* after the quality of the smooth glossy sea shell.

The development of this wonderful new material represented the ultimate achievement of the potter's art. The subsequent export of wares made from porcelain across the Asian trade routes, and later in large volume by ship, brought about great changes in pottery styles in the areas it touched.

The world of Islam was the first to experience this change. Pottery production in the Islamic cities on the trade routes was at this time limited to earthenware. The new imports from China were highly prized and sought after. The net effect of this trade was to put the livelihood of the local potter in jeop-

1–29. Salt glazed pitcher. Stoneware, impressed with roulette pattern, fired in a combination wood–salt firing. English, possibly Liverpool, late 18th or early 19th century. Collection of the author.

the port cities such as Delft, in Holland, Bristol and Lowestoft in England, and others in various parts of the world at a considerably later date. However, the hunt was on for the secret of the wondrous material in centers of pottery making all over Europe, and this in itself led to other technical developments. The secret was eventually found in Germany in the eighteenth century, but the search had already led to the invention of both soft-paste porcelain and bone china. Since glaze chemistry at this time was purely an empirical affair, the developments were slow in coming. This is not surprising, particularly when one remembers that the secrets were passed through generations of families, and little change might occur in a single lifetime.

Islam saw the growth of many different styles of pottery within its borders, particularly of surface embellishment using the wide range of color available with low temperature glazes. Two processes of decorating on top of an already fired glaze were used. The first, smoked luster, was made by fusing a thin layer of metal to the slightly softened glaze surface by heavy reduction of metallic salts, creating an iridescent sheen. The second, using a highly colored, very low temperature glaze led to what we call overglaze enamel. Wares from Islam travelled across the trade routes to China, and soon the decorative use of enamels was seen in great abundance, although they may well have been independently developed there. The new Chinese wares were exported in great volume to the Middle East, to Europe, and to Japan in the seventeenth and eighteenth centuries. This led to the production on a massive scale of wares of an oriental flavor in factories throughout Europe, and was itself responsible for the great surge of growth of industrially produced wares of the eighteenth and nineteenth centuries. The cycles of growth, alteration, refinement and further growth continue to the present day.

One particular development which seems to have no associations with other cultures was that of salt glaze, which occurred in Germany during the fifteenth and sixteenth centuries. This seemingly autonomous discovery of the reaction that takes place when salt is thrown into the very hot kiln brought an interesting new surface to pottery. The salt volatilizes in the kiln, and fills the interior

ardy, who had neither the raw material resources nor the expertise to produce porcelain. In reaction he produced copies of the refined Chinese wares, using the materials he was familiar with. The addition of tin oxide to the lead and alkaline glazes created an opaque white base for added decoration. He also often used a white slip under the glaze to further whiten the ware, in the hope of competing with the imports. To the untrained eye, the copy and the original are very easily confused.

The same development of copies occurred in

1–30. Salt-glazed figures. English, circa 1740–1745, attributed to Aaron Wood. Courtesy of the Nelson-Atkins Museum of Art, Kansas City, Missouri. Gift of Frank P. and Harriet C. Burnap.

with fumes. The sodium gases react with the silica of the clay to form a glassy, often textured surface. Its use was initially restricted to the Germanic countries, and its often dull grey or brown color did little to increase its universal appeal. Except for small, isolated areas in England and France, its use remained very much a localized tradition until the emigration of German potters who brought the technique to the East of North America in the early nineteenth century, where it saw renewed growth.

By the end of the seventeenth century, the growth and development of all the major technical advances in pottery had occurred, and in many cases their rise and subsequent demise as fashion dictated. The only real developments left were those attempts to place our long empirical history into a scientific context. The German chemist Dr. Hermann Seger developed the scientific approach to glaze calculation with the invention of the Seger Formula in the late nineteenth century. This comparative system, generally used by industry, facilitates easy comparison between various formulae of glazes for ceramics. Dr. Seger was also responsible for the invention of ceramic cones to enable more accurate control of the firing process. The rise of industrialization, and with it, standardization, has had the unfortunate side effect of eliminating much of the personality of most of the world's pottery in the process.

The ceramic industry continues to improve its products, and the twentieth century has seen great advances in many sectors. The development of new and more stable colorants and the invention of various materials to solve the problems of space travel have given the twentieth century ceramist new materials and directions to explore. It is an exciting time.

Pigeonholing:
The Classification of Ware Types

A great deal of confusion exists in the terminology of pottery classifications. This is partly due to the recent developments of studio pottery and the resultant individual naming of various techniques, such as "Pit-fired Porcelain." This term is meant to describe a porcelain type of clay that has been used to make something which is then pit fired. Other than the fact that it is made with a white-firing clay, it really has nothing to do with porcelain. Such misnomers give rise to the ludicrous question continually asked of potters, "Is it pottery, or is it ceramics?" The word *ceramic* is derived from the Greek word *Keramos*, which means potter's clay, or burnt stuff. Over the years the word has become an all-embracing term for materials which come from the earth and are chemically altered by heat. The field of ceramics is very wide, and includes pottery, glass, vitreous enamels, refractories, clay building materials, cement and concrete, electro-ceramics, special ceramic products, and even abrasives. As one can easily see, pottery and clay objects made in plaster moulds form only a part of a huge industry, and to use the term in such a narrow way is incorrect.

Misnomers also occur due to the historical uses of terms associated with pottery types, and the tendency of archaeologists and academics of the past to give contemporary descriptive names to the newly unearthed archaic forms of pottery. We could break down the development of pottery to the usual areas of earthenware, stoneware and porcelain, separated through temperature range and body maturity, and look at these individually. However, we must realize that even these classifications are arbitrary, and are being continually criss-crossed by contemporary studio craftsmen.

As the main topic of this book is glaze and color, the classifications are minimal, intended only as basic information. They are not intended as a clay formulating guide. This aspect of ceramics is well covered in many other books, some of which will be found in the bibliography.

EARTHENWARE

Earthenware is the general name for wares normally made from clays found either on or close to the surface of the earth, and fired in the lower temperature range below 1150°C. Historically, the vast majority of the world's pottery falls into this category, including about 95 percent of the pottery produced today. Within the family of earthenware we find the following categories: pit-fired, or primitive; raku; slipware; lusterware; tin glazed ware, variously known as majolica, faience and delftware; and industrial pottery, with which I am not particularly concerned.

Pit-fired, or so-called primitive, pottery is fired in heat chambers dug out of the ground, or placed

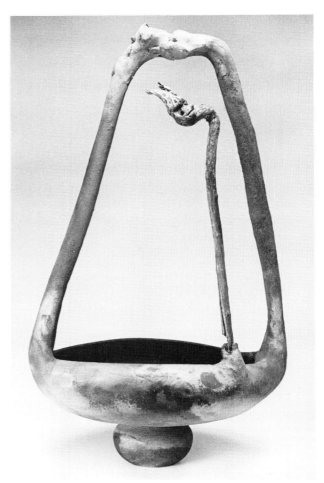

2–2. Rick Hirsch (U.S.A.). Raku. Base color achieved with underglazes airbrushed on, or terra sigillatas brushed on and slightly burnished. In post-firing, sprayed with metallic salts, i.e. cupric chloride, cupric sulfate, and ferric sulfate.

2–1. Susan Lepoidevin (Canada). "The Circus." Earthenware, coil and slab formed, burnished and smoke-fired with sawdust and steer manure.

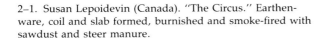

on the ground, surrounded with wood, brush, bracken, twigs, leaves or even animal dung, or sometimes fired in metal containers, lined with combustible material. The ware is often fired quickly, but sometimes undergoes a long, slow firing cycle, depending upon the individual potter. The works retain the graphic markings of the fire, and this, combined with the natural atmospheres of the fire, will determine the final result. Great variation is possible using this process, and each piece fired in this way can have wide range of both color and surface.

Raku is a firing process developed in Japan in the sixteenth century A.D., where the glazed bisque ware is put into the hot kiln and fast fired until the glaze melts, removed while still red hot, and cooled in the air. It was traditionally fired in an oxidizing atmosphere. In the last thirty years, beginning in North America, raku has been produced with a variety of post-firing reduction methods, giving an exciting range of color and surface interest to the ware.

Slipware is the name given to pottery that has been coated, while wet, half dry or bone dry, with white or colored liquid clays used in a wide variety of ways for decorative effect. Slipware pots are often covered with honey colored transparent glazes, but they can be covered with any transparent, translucent, or semi-opaque glaze that will give the desired result.

Lusterware was first developed by the potters of Islam, and is the process whereby a thin film of metal is fused to the softened surface of the glaze. Salts and carbonates of copper, silver, gold and bismuth are mixed into a paste made from fine red clays, ochre, or umber, painted on the pre-fired glaze and subsequently fired in a smoky firing to about 750°C. Another form of lusterware using resins to cause local reduction was developed for industry, and makes use of precious metals, generally gold, silver, platinum and palladium, for onglaze decoration. The fact that it was not necessary to have a smoky kiln meant that there would be little contamination of the body or glaze by carbonization, a fact of life with smoked lusters.

Tin glazed wares, majolica, faience and delftware are misnomers. Firstly, the glaze is not made of tin, but merely made opaque by the use of tin, and even then, not always so. Secondly, although different names are used, they use the same process of decorating over the unfired glaze coating with various forms of color. The work is subsequently fired and the color fuses into the glaze. The names come from the shipping centers or production centers where they were extensively made. The name majolica comes from Mallorca, an island shipping center off the coast of Spain. Faience is a French derivation of the name of the Italian city of Faenza, where a similar form of pottery was made. Delftware comes from Delft, in Holland. Things get a little confusing when we find English delft-

2–3. Walter Ostrom (Canada). Vase in the shape of a bottle, earthenware. Slip under soda blue glaze, cone 04.

ware, made using the same techniques in various centers around England. As we saw in chapter 1, the glaze actually started with the Islamic potters' need to safeguard their livelihood by making copies of the Chinese porcelain, as they did not have knowledge of or access to the necessary materials for porcelain production. Thus, by invention, the whole history of ceramic development was altered.

Another misnomer of classification occurs in Egyptian ceramics, where the early archaeologists

2–4. Marilyn Levine (U.S.A.). Small case with handle. Ceramic and mixed media. 1981.

were from France. One can imagine them exclaiming with delight, "Mon Dieu, c'est la faience!" to wares evocative of the tin-glazed earthenwares which they knew back home. They were, in fact, what we now call Egyptian paste, which was produced in quite a different way.

Clays for earthenware are usually naturally red, buff, or sandy in color. More often than not they are slightly porous after the firing, which often leads to a fairly fragile product. By the intermixing of other materials with the natural clays, clay bodies were produced to make wares which were stronger, lighter in color and therefore more easily colored, or over which colored glazes could be used to give greater brilliance.

Materials for making clay bodies fall into three categories of function: fusion or flux, color, and refractoriness. Fusion means melting together, and refers to the process of lowering the firing temperature by the addition of more glass forming materials to the clay. The selection of materials usually used for this purpose are those which are high in fluxing power, such as body frits (see chapter 6), supplemented by the addition of talc, dolomite,

whiting or pyrophyllite. Color alteration is achieved by the use of oxides, carbonates or stains, or other clays. Refractory materials are those which make the firing range higher. Materials such as sand,

2–5. Nino Caruso (Italy). "Memory Relief." Terra cotta. Color from iron oxide in the clay. Slip cast, cone 09.

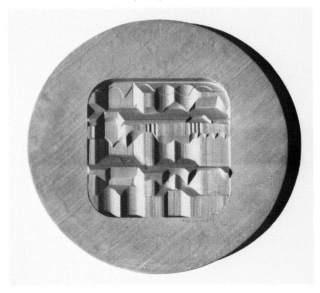

grog (crushed, previously fired clay), higher firing clays, such as fireclay or stoneware clay, or, in primitive pottery, an aggregate made from crushed rock fall into this category. These refractory materials have the effect of making the clay more porous, and less susceptible to the wear and tear of the fire, particularly those fast firings of the pit and raku processes, where great stress is placed on the ware. Variations of the materials for body development can create a very wide range of uses and effects to satisfy the desires of the potter.

STONEWARE

Stoneware is the general name applied to most wares fired between 1150 and 1300°C., with the exceptions of bone china and porcelain.

Stoneware is so named because of its resemblance to the qualities of stone. Properly fired, it is hard, durable, almost impervious to liquids, has high resistance to thermal shock, and develops a very close bond with its glazes. However, not all stonewares fit this description, as the intended function of the ware may require it to be fairly porous.

Stonewares may be classified in the following ways:

Stoneware: body and glaze integrated in a firing above 1200°C., giving low porosity.
Ovenware: body and glaze well integrated, with a porosity in the body of up to 10 percent.
Red Stoneware: very low porosity, with a firing temperature between 1100 and 1250°C.
Salt Glazed Stoneware: body and glaze well integrated, very hard, with low porosity and fired between 1200 and 1300°C.

Stoneware clays are often found as naturally occurring materials in strata below the topsoil. They may be perfectly workable as found, but it is more likely that they will require some additions to improve them for use. As with earthenware, these

2–6. John Leach (United Kingdom). Lidded jar. Stoneware, unglazed exterior, wood-fired.

additions fall into three categories of function: fusion, color and refractoriness. In stoneware, the fusion is done with materials such as feldspar and nepheline syenite, to make the body less porous, and silica is sometimes added to improve the fit of the glaze. The natural color of stoneware clays varies from buff through grey to reddish brown, due to the iron content. The color can be altered by the

2–7. Sylvia Hyman (U.S.A.). "Sporophore" series, 1981. Stoneware and porcelain. Unglazed, edged and slightly sprayed with iron oxide. Walnut base.

additions of oxides, carbonates, stains, and by kiln atmosphere. The refractoriness and working properties of the clay may be improved by additions of sand or grog. To these categories may also be added modifications to control plasticity, and thereby aid drying characteristics.

BONE CHINA

Bone china is a fabricated body made from kaolin, feldspar, and calcined animal bones for fluxing action. Calcining is the process of heating bones to release the carbon, leaving a combination of inorganic calcium and phosphorous. The first or bisque firing of bone china is generally at 1280°C., which fuses the body to translucency, followed by a glaze firing, usually below 1080°C. Bone china was first developed in the European search for the elusive secret of true porcelain, and subsequently became one of the staples of the industry.

SOFT PASTE PORCELAIN

Soft paste porcelain is similar to bone china in that it was also developed in the search for true porcelain. The basic difference lies in the fusion materials used to get the body to a state of glassification where it becomes translucent. To do this, glass forming materials such as talc (soapstone), alkalies, frits, tin and white firing clays are used. The wares are usually fired at around 1100°C.

PORCELAIN

True porcelain is a fabricated body made from white firing clays, silica, and feldspar. Depending on its constituents, it is usually fired between 1250 and 1400°C. Its properties are generally whiteness, hardness, durability, and often, but not always, translucency. When properly fired it approaches the point of total vitrification, or turning to glass. In China, where it was first developed, it is made from combinations of kaolin and petuntze, a feldspathic material having a number of trace mineral elements allowing a fine interaction of particles in the body. The contemporary studio potter usually uses a mixture containing kaolin, ball clay (a smooth plastic clay), feldspar and silica, to produce a body which is more workable, and fires at a slightly lower temperature. To this, he often adds a plasticizer, such as bentonite or macaloid, to make its working properties more appropriate for studio use.

As one can see, the usual classifications are quite arbitrary in character. In the spirit of learning and development, the studio potter often crosses boundaries in his search for an individual form of expression. In the last few years we have seen the development and use of high temperature raku, majolica, and lusterware, and low temperature stone-ware and porcelain. This all goes to show that in the world of the studio potter, where clinical

2–8. Roseline Delisle (Canada). Porcelain, thrown in one piece. Vitreous slip decoration, once-fired at cone 11.

quality control is generally neither desired or required, the individual is basically free to do just what seems necessary to bring out those particular qualities that he feels strongly about.

As long as one understands one's materials and how to make them work, the potential of ceramics is limited more by one's imagination than by material chemistry, and one can call it whatever one pleases. When we are all dead and gone, if there are any museums left, whatever remnants of late twentieth century clay culture are displayed will have the simple description *clay*.

2–9. Susan and Curtis Benzle (U.S.A.). "In the Night." Porcelain with color inlay.

2–11. Janet Mansfield (Australia). Lidded jar, salt glazed.

This has been a short discussion on what clays are and what they do. The field is immensely varied, but it all boils down to the fact that clay and glaze are subject to two basic forms of influence: internal, the materials used, and external, the processes of manufacture and firing.

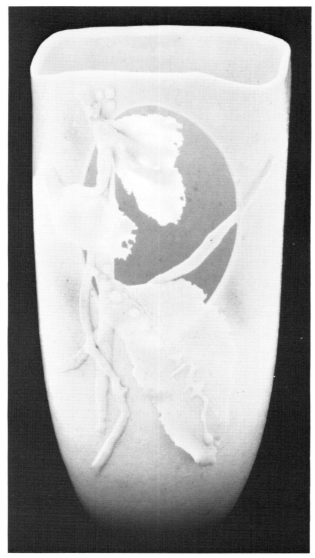

2–10. Sue Hopper (Canada). Bone china. Slip cast and altered.

3

Kilns, Temperature and Atmosphere

All pottery is fired in a kiln of some kind. A kiln is basically a pit, box, or tube, in which heat is concentrated. This may be done by using a variety of fuels, such as wood, oil, gas, coal, electricity and even animal dung. The kiln is the place where the once malleable clay material metamorphoses into a rocklike substance, retaining the form of the soft clay pieces and turning them, slightly shrunken, into permanently hardened works. The firing of the kiln requires reasonable understanding in order to complete the craftsman's work to his criteria, and for many the process imposes a considerable trauma. It is, after all, a baptism by fire, and represents the final stage of the work, a stage where the potter must work closely with the elements. The final results will tell, in no uncertain manner, if the potter is really in tune with his medium.

There are times when serendipity takes over, and the firing process is the controlling influence over the surface quality of the piece, as in pit, sawdust, and dung firings. However, for most types of firing it is the design of the kiln, its fuel, packing, speed of firing, atmospheric and temperature control, and cooling which are important factors in the final result. It is no wonder that kilns and their firing become such a phobia, and potters become paranoid. If one didn't know better from experience and from the volume of fine work readily visible in the world, one would think that kilns were tools of the devil, designed to frustrate, and turn the glorious entrant to disastrous dross at the exit from the kiln. The mere fact that the kiln has the final say is enough that one should treat it with great respect, and try to develop an intuitive relationship with it.

Almost every potter has determined by personal experience his own favorite way of firing his kiln, but conflicts often arise in the novice's mind as to the proper method or cycle for either bisque or glaze firing. There is, I'm convinced, no single right way, merely that which works for you, with maximum satisfaction and minimum heartache. As with learning to know people, developing an understanding of kilns and their idiosyncracies is a long operation. In inexperienced or unsympathetic hands, the fired result is likely to suffer. Regardless of the type of fuel used, there are some pointers which will help to speed up the learning process, and make the firing of one's kiln an enjoyable experience. All kilns vary considerably. Even mass-manufactured electric ones which one would think of as having little or no character have inexplicable quirks. If one remembers that kilns are like people, with characters of their own, one is well on the way to understanding them. To aid that understanding, the various types and some of their idiosyncracies are outlined in the following sections.

ELECTRIC KILNS

These would seem to be the easiest kilns to work with, since their control mechanisms make them similar in operation to the standard kitchen oven. The general range of switches attached to electric kilns is quite wide, but in essence they fall into two groups: the simpler ones with low, medium, and high settings, and those with more sophisticated kitchen range type infinite switches. The former are very easy to use as it is purely a matter of turning on at low for a period of time, medium for a period of time, and then high until the firing is completed. It is usually a good practice to slow down the firing towards the end of a glaze firing, and allow the fusion of the glaze materials to complete their interaction. Automatic kiln shutoff devices are often attached to electric kilns for ease of use. They can be detrimental to the quality of the final result, as the glaze doesn't get a chance to thoroughly integrate. Like guests at a party, the molecules of a glaze need to be a little soaked for the best interaction to take place. The automatic pilot tends to shut off the kiln just when the party

is beginning to get into a state of excitement, and the results usually bear this out. An interesting observation of this would be to continue the firing past the shutoff and allow the work in the kiln to soak at the desired temperature for approximately an hour. Then note the difference in glaze quality in comparison with the same glazes fired with no soak period.

KILNS USING FOSSIL FUELS

There are a number of fossil fuels in use for the firing of kilns, in the forms of gases, liquids and solids. The gases include natural gas and propane; the liquids include oil and kerosene (paraffin); the solids include coal and coke. The great majority of potters who have kilns using fossil fuels use either gas or oil. Of these two, gas, either natural or bottled, is generally the preferred fuel. This is probably due to its convenience, as well as its generally lower cost. It is clean and easy to work with, and is an efficient fuel. Oil, on the other hand, although efficient, is comparatively difficult to work with as it does not ignite readily, making the early stages of firing hazardous. It is also a dirty and smelly fuel. Kerosene, although little used, is a very efficient fuel also, and much cleaner than oil. Some people who use oil begin their firing by the use of kerosene which has easy ignition. The solid fuels of coal, coke and anthracite are not used much by studio potters, partly because of the labor required, the space required for storage, and the smoke pollution.

All fossil fuels are efficient. When buying or building a kiln, the decision as to which one may be preferable, depends on the individual's requirements and budget. Other considerations might be availability, property zoning restrictions, storage space and firing and maintenance costs.

WOOD-FIRING KILNS

Wood as a fuel for firing kilns is enjoying a great increase in use in North America. In other countries it has been in constant use for centuries. For many potters, it represents the ultimate fuel, as well as having a special mystique or cult. Wood firing is a labor intensive process, which, depending on the efficiencies of both kiln and fireman, can take a great deal of time. However, the wood-firing process is capable of imparting qualities to the ware that are unobtainable in any other way. The long licking flame caresses the ware, leaving subtle and beautiful flash markings of the fire's path. Whether the ash from the burning wood combines with the raw clay or plays its part in interacting with glazes, it gives beautiful surfaces, from the merest hint of sheen to flowing rivulets of fluxing ashes.

There are also various romantic associations with wood-firing kilns. For many, the sights, sounds, smells, and tastes have special significance. The roar and crackle of the fire and the sparks flying from the chimney give the potter that heady feeling of being in commune with nature and the gods of fire. In no other firing process does there seem to be such empathy with the ware.

Although some purists might think it crass, many potters are using either gas or oil burners to bring the kiln to a temperature of about 1000°C. and then completing the firing with wood. This probably results in significantly less accumulation of ash on the ware, but it does cut down on the sweaty labor of the process without obviously compromising the quality of the final result.

FIRING, TEMPERATURE AND ATMOSPHERE

The things that most affect the final look of a piece of work drawn from any kiln are the rate and length of firing, temperature and kiln atmosphere.

The rate and length of firing are determined by what the kiln load consists of and the method of firing being used. Basic rate and length guidelines are included at the end of this chapter, although one must remember that all kilns fire differently and any kiln takes understanding and experience before predictable use is accomplished.

Temperature controls the degree to which the glaze forming materials have entered into fusion. If underfired, the glaze surface will be abrasive and dry to the touch; if overfired, it will be excessively glassy, even to the point of boiling and running

off the walls of the work and sticking firmly to the kiln shelf.

A well formulated and fired glaze will have a quality of "rightness" difficult to put into words, but obvious to the eye and touch. The actual temperature at which a glaze is viewed to be at its best is usually a variable determined by individual taste. A glaze which may be matt at one temperature will usually be glossy when fired a little higher. The same sort of variation is likely to result from firing either slowly or quickly. The longer soaking period makes for complete fusion, whereas in fast firing the materials do not have the same chance for interaction. Temperature reflects a combination of heat and time, together referred to as heatwork. Materials for glazes individually melt at a wide range of temperatures, and it is the combination of materials that determines the degree of heatwork required to achieve the most satisfactory results. This should become clear in chapters 4–8.

Atmosphere is the third prime force exerted on the glaze materials during firing. A ceramic kiln atmosphere may be either oxidizing or reducing. It is possible, although unusual, to modulate a firing to have both atmospheres occurring during the firing process for the development of some specific colors.

An oxidation atmosphere is one in which a plentiful amount of oxygen is present in the kiln, enabling metals in clays and glazes to develop their oxide colors: greens from copper and honey colors from iron. In electric kilns the atmosphere is neutral, as there is almost always some burning of carbonates going on, at least in the early stages of firing. In firing with electricity the atmosphere can generally be stated as predominantly oxidizing, unless a reducing agent is introduced. However, for absolute oxidation the kiln should be vented with some form of air replacement system. Absolute oxidation is necessary for the proper development of some colors, such as those available from cadmium-selenium stains.

A reduction atmosphere is one where there is very little oxygen, due to the presence of an excess of carbon from the incomplete burning of carbonaceous material. The effect on the glaze materials, all of which are in oxide form to start with, is to rob them of some or all of their oxygen content and return them to their metal state. For instance, copper when oxidized is greenish, as in old copper roofs, but when reduced it is reddish, as in the metal. A modulating fire, alternating between oxidation and reduction, can give green with areas or spots of red from copper. Copper has the most obvious reaction to reducing conditions, but other materials also change their chemical state and their color in the final result. In reduced, high temperature firings, the iron pyrites in the clay give characteristic speckles to stoneware bodies. Reduction can be effected by increasing the fuel supply and thus changing the fuel to air ratio, by cutting back the available supply of oxygen through closing dampers in the kiln chimneys, by cutting back on the primary air entering at the burners, or by a combination of these methods.

REDUCTION OF ELECTRIC KILNS

Many people who work with electric kilns have a latent desire to make reduced wares, as reduction glazes often seem to have a richer and more sumptuous surface. The simpler surfaces of oxidation ware tend to make some potters view the products of the electric kiln as second rate in some way; there has, in the past, often been a strange snobbishness about the so-called inadequacies of the electric kiln. In recent years, though, many professional potters have chosen electric kilns for many reasons, such as convenience, cost, control and color availability.

An electric kiln will reduce only with a certain amount of difficulty, and usually with a significant shortening in the life of the elements. An expensive solution to this problem is a kiln equipped with silicon carbide rod elements, usually called Globars, which are not generally affected by reduction. In Japan, some electric kilns are made to fire in combination with wood to produce reducing conditions. These kilns use elements of a substantially thicker gauge than normally found in the kilns of potters of the western hemisphere, which perhaps explains why they are little affected by the reduction atmosphere.

There are always the people who, even with the drawbacks of electric fired reduction, still wish to pursue it. I personally feel that electric kilns should be used for what they do best—oxidation. However, placing combustible materials into the kiln at a suitable point in the firing cycle can bring about reduction. Various materials, such as naptha (mothballs), wood slivers, oil soaked rags, or anything that in order to complete combustion becomes oxygen hungry, may be used to produce a reducing atmosphere. The gases formed in this combustion are toxic, and if electric kilns are used in this way they must be in a well ventilated area.

When I had only the use of an electric kiln and also had the feeling of inadequacy which at the time went with it, my usual process for occasional glaze firings in reduction was to use bottled gas. The gas was introduced into the kiln by means of a flexible hose, ending with approximately 15 inches of thin copper pipe. At the time for reduction, the copper end of the pipe was fed into the spyhole of the kiln, and the gas turned slowly on. This worked like a charm until about the fifth reduction firing, when I suddenly lost 75 percent of the elements! Since that time I have used electric kilns only for oxidation, where they serve the purpose very well.

A material called silicon carbide may be added to glazes for electric firing to develop local reduction of the glaze. The material needs to be very finely ground (200 mesh), and is added in amounts from one-half to one percent of the glaze batch. Some people, when using silicon carbide in a glaze, place the glazed work in refractory boxes called "saggers" to ensure that the silicon carbide doesn't affect other glazes through fuming.

LEARNING TO LIVE WITH A DRAGON

The various aspects of firing kilns, no matter what the heat source, provide the potter with a challenge which is an important part of the total pottery cycle and one which can be creative in its own right. The process of gaining knowledge through play, as children do, is very real in learning about firing. Exploration of various cycles of heating and cooling, timing, to soak or not to soak, to smoke or not to smoke, to fume or not to fume, will all give variations to the qualities inherent in the finished wares. The knowledge of how to get the best from one's kiln comes only through experience and observation; an intuitive understanding takes time to develop. As they are such an important part of the creative process, it would be foolish to ignore the variables of firing. This would limit the potential palette of color and surface from the materials used in glaze formation. Although reducing in an electric kiln is probably not a good idea, much can be achieved by altering the firing cycles, such as long soaking at high temperatures, very slow cooling, and keeping the kiln firing during the decrease in temperature.

In fuel burning kilns the play of reduction can have a significant effect in many ways. Relighting and reducing at low temperatures during the cooling phase can drastically alter things. Oxidized low temperature earthenware with glazes containing copper can develop beautiful reds when reduced as low as 750°C. in the cooling. This makes it possible to use red clays, which might otherwise bloat from the carbon entering into the body and becoming trapped when the body fuses. This is but one of a wide range of possibilities in varying the firing process and ultimately the quality of the ware.

It should be remembered that no matter how final a ceramic object may seem, it is always possible to make alterations to the surface by additional firing or surface enrichment processes. Many ceramists make continual adjustments in the search for elusive qualities, and these are discussed in chapter 20. These adjustments may occur by the use of a variety of firing methods alone, using electricity, wood, salt, or raku; or by the addition of materials to the surface, such as overglazes, and decals. The introduction of volatile materials such as stannous chloride, barium chloride, or bismuth subnitrate into the kiln during the cooling cycle can also produce special qualities. These latter alterations need to be done with a great deal of care, as they will cause toxic fumes to be emitted from the kiln. However, the process of volatile fuming can coat the ware with random lustrous pearly effects, in a way that imparts quite different qualities than the process of using prepared resinate lusters, usually fired in an electric kiln at a low temperature.

One should treat fire with a great deal of respect, but learning how to make the most of one's kiln and its capabilities should be of paramount importance for the ceramist in the search for self-expression in his work.

Before one starts a firing, it is important to know the exact temperature at which it will finish. This can be gauged in a number of ways. Very experienced potters or kiln firemen are able to tell temperature from the color inside the kiln, visible through the spyholes, and with practice become remarkably accurate. However, most of us do not spend enough time looking at the colors of radiant heat to depend on this. We are therefore dependent on some other process. There are many temperature sampling devices available, from very sophisticated optical pyrometers, through bi-metal thermocouples attached to pyrometers, to the simplest and generally most reliable pyrometric cone, bar, or ring. Pyrometric indicators are made from the same materials as clays and glazes, and are calculated to deform and bend when reaching a specific temperature (see appendix, Orton standard cones). Cones are probably the most convenient and cheapest temperature device, and are almost foolproof as long as they are set up in the correct way. Low temperature cones are detrimentally affected by reduction, and this should be borne in mind when using them for low temperature reduction firing. Cones are made in two sizes, standard and small, and are also made by a number of companies. As a result there are slight variations in temperature calibration. Temperatures should be checked with calibration lists available from the manufacturers. The usual method of using cones is to put three into a cone pack; these serve as guide cone, firing cone, and guard cone against overfiring. Extra cones may be used to signal the start of reduction, etc. In kilns that have small spyholes, it is sometimes helpful to set the cones so that they bend in alternate directions, and set the cone pack to be viewed end on.

Another simple firing indicator is a clay ring, or draw trial, which is made of the same clay as the work in the kiln, and uses the same glazes. A number are placed just inside the spyhole of the kiln, and are fished out with a hook-ended metal rod when the temperature is nearing the required

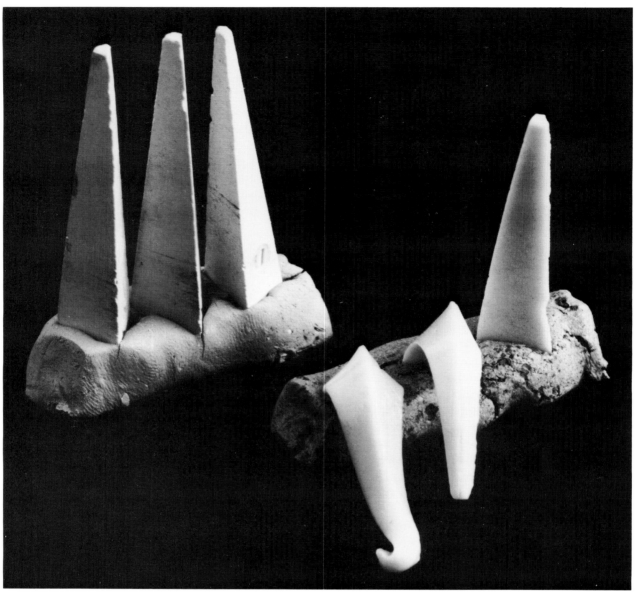

3–1. Cone packs before firing (left), and at maturity.

point. The glaze or surface can be quickly checked for maturity; when the desired result is obtained the kiln may be shut down. This system is commonly used in salt and sodium vapor glazing. It should be noted that although the draw trial is a good indicator of the degree to which a glaze has melted, in the case of a reduction firing the final color will most likely be quite different, owing to the quick cooling and re-oxidation of the glaze.

BASIC FIRING GUIDELINES

Almost every potter has his own way of firing his kiln, and each kiln is different. Nevertheless, there are some basic rules of approach common to all kilns. These rules relate to the gradual rate of firing that all clay must go through on its way to vitrification, and to certain stages of firing that must be traversed warily. Firing too quickly at these points is likely to create stress in the ware, to the point of explosion.

BISQUE FIRING

Bisque firings should proceed slowly at the start to allow physically combined water to be driven off gradually as steam. If the firing is too fast, and the work excessively thick or uneven in thickness, it is likely to blow apart as the development of steam pressure proves too much for the ware.

Complex chemical changes go on throughout the firing, and there are two points where one should proceed slowly because of them. Cristobalite forms in the clay at 200–220°C. Quartz changes its crystalline form at 573°C., resulting in a slight increase in size. If ware is packed touching the top of the kiln interior or a kiln shelf, or if pieces are packed too tightly inside one another, they may well crack when this temporary growth occurs. Kiln firings should always proceed in a uniform temperature rise through these critical points, to avoid internal stress in the ware. It is well to remember 200–250°C., the cristobalite squeeze, and 500–600°C., quartz inversion, as being potential problem areas. (It is also a good idea to take the ware slowly through these temperature ranges in cooling.) After they have been passed, the firing can proceed quite quickly towards the termination point, which may be between 950° and 1050°C.

Many potters soak the bisque kiln at its top temperature for between one and three hours, to make sure that any residual carbonaceous matter in the clay is completely burned out before shutting the kiln off. This soaking should be done with the spyholes and any other kiln ventilation open, to make certain that the carbon is completely removed from the kiln. Checking broken bisque will show whether the carbonaceous matter was burnt out: If the core is black, the soaking period should be lengthened. This will eliminate possible problems of bloating later in the glaze firing.

GLAZE FIRING

Low and high temperature glaze firings can proceed fairly quickly, remembering, of course, the problem points mentioned above. Some potters take a strange pride in the speed that they can fire their kilns. Although glaze materials will melt in fast firings, it is generally agreed that for the complete interaction of body and glaze to take place, a slower firing is preferable. For a low temperature glaze that means 6–12 hours, and for a high temperature glaze 10–24 hours. Firing times depend on the type of ware being fired. The heat rise should be smooth and even, slowing down at the end to allow soaking time, where complete interaction of materials takes place.

OXIDATION FIRING

Oxidation firing is usually done in electric kilns, but it can also be done in fuel-burning kilns, provided that the combustion of the fuel is complete, and reducing conditions are not present. The basic principles of firing electric kilns have already been discussed, and, as noted previously, the process is really quite simple. It should be remembered that the thickness of the clay has a strong bearing on the speed at which it may be fired. For work having a thickness of no more than half an inch, the following method will generally be successful. For work that is thicker, the firing should proceed more slowly; for thinner work, it may be quicker, so you may take the following as an average.

The firing usually proceeds as described under bisque firing, bearing in mind the cristobalite and quartz inversion problem points. It can be quite fast, depending on the work, and it is realistic to get to cone 04 (1060°C.) in 6–8 hours, with no detrimental effect on the ware. If the desired maturity of the glazes is around this temperature, I usually slow the firing down for approximately one hour when cone 08 (955°C.) is reached, to give the glazes time to soak. If I am aiming for a cone 6 (1222°C.) firing, the soaking period would be at approximately cone 4 (1188°C.) also for about an hour. If I am aiming at cone 9 (1280°C.), then the soak period would usually start at about cone 7 (1240°C.), also for an hour or so. In all cases, the firing would proceed at full speed until the soaking period begins. The average time for oxidation firings in my kilns are 6–8 hours for cone 04 to cone 01, 8–10 hours for cone 4 to cone 6, and 10–14 hours for cone 8 to cone 10. The kilns could easily be fired more quickly, but I prefer to keep to these firing speeds for the sake of the ware. Once one has got over the initial trauma of packing and firing the first few kilns, and generally made some mistakes in the process, the firing of oxidation kilns is really no more difficult than operating a kitchen oven. The biggest problem I've found is that it is easy to forget that one is firing. A small alarm clock or bell system when approaching the approximate time can be useful here, much like the ringing timers used on kitchen ranges.

REDUCTION FIRING

Reduction firing is generally done with a certain intuitive feeling, although there are some potters who use sophisticated carbon monoxide reading devices to accurately monitor the degree of reduction. These devices also can help a potter use fuel more economically. As an old-fashioned potter, I prefer to gauge the degree of reduction by the type and color of the flame flickering through the spyholes of the kiln, the way it has been done for centuries. When using propane fuel, a flame of 6 to 9 inches emerging from the spyhole usually signifies a good reduction in progress. Other fuels will show different lengths of flame. The color of the flame is normally orange to red, but may be quite green if there is a significant amount of copper present in the kiln. It is usually a sinuous licking flame, in comparison to the short bluish high intensity flame of an oxidizing fire.

There are basically two different approaches to reduction firing, one common to Great Britain, and the other to North America. In North America, it is common to do what is called a body reduction. This usually takes place between 850 and 1000°C., and is achieved by putting the kiln into fairly heavy reduction for all or part of this temperature rise. The result is to create extra carbon in the core of the clay, with the theory that later oxidation gives a richer toasty brown to the body of the ware. Maybe it does, but it also can cause carbon to be trapped in the pores of the clay resulting in later bloating; more seriously, it can also lower the ware's resistance to thermal shock, a great problem in the case of wares for oven use. The reason for this is the inhibition, under reducing conditions, of the formation of mullite crystals in the body. These internal crystal structures give strength and thermal shock resistance to clays used in the production of ovenware. After the body reduction, the glaze firing carries on with a low reduction level until almost the end of the firing, when it is finished with a short, 10–30 minute period of oxidation, to clear the smoke from the kiln and to develop the characteristic warm colors of the body.

The practice generally favored in Britain is to oxidize the firing until 1050–1100°C., and then put the kiln into fairly heavy reduction until shortly before the end of the firing, when it is generally re-oxidized to clear the kiln. I personally allow the reduction to continue until the kiln is shut off, because after firing oxygen will be pulled into the kiln through any spyholes and around the burners anyway, thus achieving the same results.

There are no set rules for firing kilns, merely guidelines, as rules seem to be made to be broken. Dogmatic attitudes towards the process of firing are common, and within any small group of ceramists many seemingly conflicting approaches will probably be found. From my experience, it is better to learn a sound firing method initially, and vary it as one learns the control and understanding necessary to make the most of what the kiln has to share.

If it offers any consolation, even potters with a great deal of expertise and experience do have the odd disastrous firing. This can happen through over-familiarity or forgetfulness, but maybe it is the powers above telling us to beware of playing with devilish objects. This is probably the reason why in a great number of cultures of the world, small effigy gods are made which sit on the kiln to protect its load and appease the gods of fire! A wise precaution!

PART TWO

The Development of Glaze

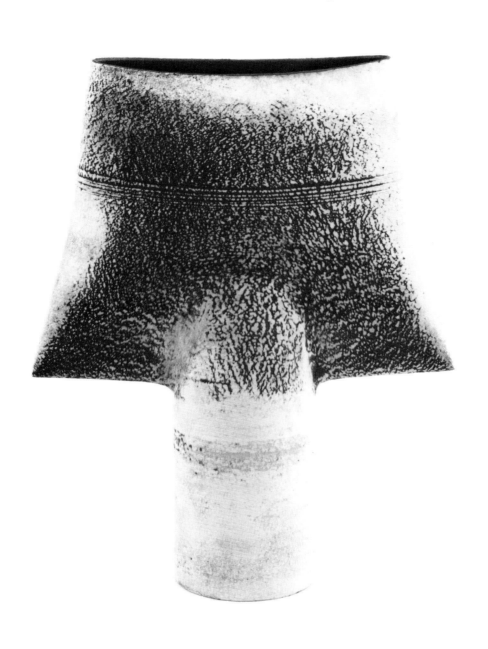

4

Record-Keeping and Testing Procedures

Every business needs to have some bookkeeping, and the business of glaze development is really no different. Records are for one's own benefit and should be kept as simply as possible.

RECORDING GLAZE DEVELOPMENT

It is amazing how many students and full-time clay workers go about making glazes with a fairly lengthy and time-consuming process, only to forget to write down clearly just what they have done. It seems to be quite normal to work with scraps of paper and the odd hieroglyphic on the back or base of the test tile or test pot. I know from bitter experience that the finest glaze that one ever develops is, of course, the one where the scrap of paper gets lost, or the heiroglyphics get obliterated by an accident of firing, if any record has been made at all. Somehow, that one gem which might have been a crowning glory is lost forever. I am sure that this has happened to every potter at some time, but it doesn't have to. It is very easy to start in the glaze-making process with good working habits.

Good working habits begin with a few basic principles:

1 Keep an accurate notebook
2 Develop a serial numbering system
3 Work as neatly as possible
4 Make sure that you write down everything in your notebook
5 Take basic health precautions when handling materials

1 Keeping an accurate notebook is very important, and may be set up in many ways. It is best to get a hardbacked book, as these have a greater longevity in the wear and tear of studio life. The book can be sectioned for glaze development at various temperatures. It can also be vertically lined for tabulation of procedures followed, as in the accompanying illustration. Starting with this or a similar format, it is easy to keep records.

Notebook entry

Glaze or material test	Cone or temp.	Serial no.	Result; observation

2 Developing a serial numbering system is quite simple, and if you use a combination of letters and numbers, duly recorded, it is easy to follow. For example, the process for serial numbering the section of glaze development explained later in chapter 10, called "Flux Variations," was as follows. The basic entry is MFV, which stands for Matt Flux Variations. This is followed by a number which represents the particular flux being used in this series. The fourth flux, for example, would appear as MFV4. This gives us all we need to record the basic glaze. To this we add colorants (see chapter 15), which are given a lower case letter (a, b, c, etc.), and a number (1–6) which tells us what percentage of color, from 0.625 to 10 percent, is in the glaze. We end up with a number, both on the test and recorded in the book, along the lines of this: MFV4a4. Put simply this means Matt Flux Variation, with dolomite as the flux, and colored with 5 percent iron oxide, but denoted by six serial letters of numbers, instead of by a lengthy description.* If testing is being done in both oxidation and reduction, it is helpful to append an O or an R as well, as the differences in the same glazes from the two atmospheres is often very marked.

Numbering of tiles or other test pieces should be done on a section that will remain unglazed, using either a black underglaze pencil or painting with a mixture of equal parts of iron and manganese, mixed with a little gum and water. The gum lessens the likelihood of smudging the numbers. There is a list of various gums in chapter 12.

* The serial numbering system used for the glaze tests in this book appears in the appendix, page 202.

4–1. Typical glaze test tile.

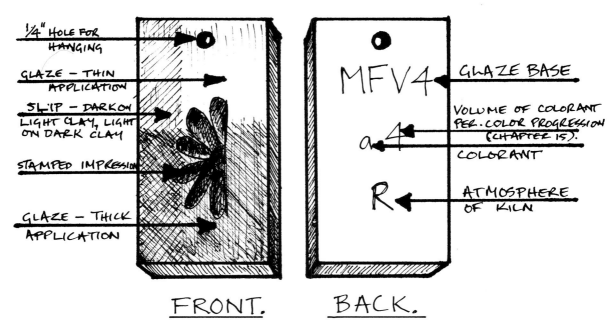

¼" HOLE FOR HANGING

GLAZE – THIN APPLICATION

SLIP – DARK ON LIGHT CLAY, LIGHT ON DARK CLAY

STAMPED IMPRESSION

GLAZE – THICK APPLICATION

FRONT.

MFV4

GLAZE BASE

VOLUME OF COLORANT PER. COLOR PROGRESSION (CHAPTER 15).

COLORANT

ATMOSPHERE OF KILN

BACK.

Some gums, such as gum arabic, should be mixed with alcohol, but other powdered gums may be mixed with hot water and allowed to soak overnight. This mixture can be kept in a jar, and thinned with water when needed.

3 Neat and efficient working habits are essential to gain the most from one's efforts. From accurate measuring and weighing of materials, through serial numbering, to the recording of observations and results, care and a certain amount of patience pay off with great dividends. The old fishing story of "the one that got away" need not become a reality if disciplined work habits are started from the beginning.

4 Make sure that you write down everything in the notebook, even variations in firing, as over a period of time one tends to forget some important detail. If it is on paper, and the paper isn't lost, recall comes more easily.

5 Take care of your health by basic protection from materials which can be toxic, carcinogenic, or silicotic. It is a wise precaution to use dust masks during the mixing of glazes, to prevent the breathing of airborne dust particles. For some materials, such as wood ash and barium, rubber gloves are also helpful to prevent problems. Washing hands after using materials is also a good practice, and one should never eat or smoke in areas which may have dust contamination, or chew fingernails when glazing or mixing glazes. The concerns with basic health protection have become a hot issue of the last few years, and are quite sensible. However,

4–2. Test pieces made from thrown ring, cut into sections. Slip on half of each section.

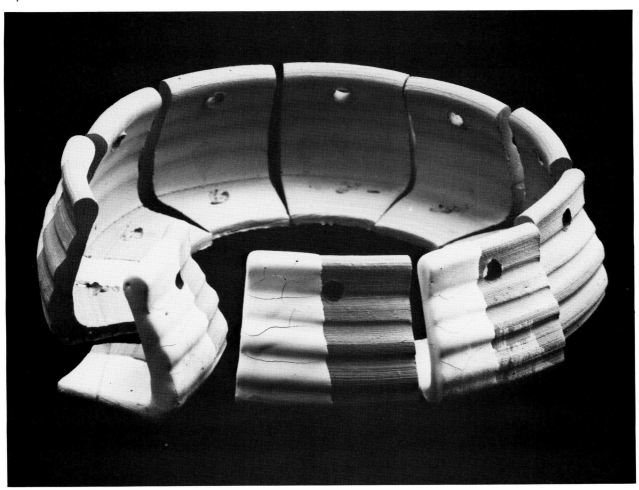

there is still the fact that although health hazards are fairly prevalent in the ceramic industry, the majority of potters live to a good old age, and whatever carried them off in the past was seldom attributable to the materials used in the work.

MAKING GLAZE TESTS

Glaze and material testing can be done in a variety of ways, using tiles, small bowls or crucibles, extruded test forms, sections of thrown forms, or even clay squeezed between the fingers, as in figures 4.2, 4.3 and 4.4. The most important features to include are some alteration of surface, either throwing ridges or stamped, impressed patterns, and enough flat space on the unglazed portion to

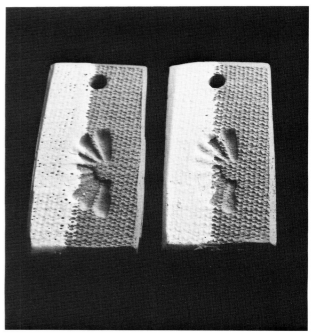

4–4. Tiles used for testing in this book.

4–3. Test pieces made from pinched lumps of clay. Slip on half of each.

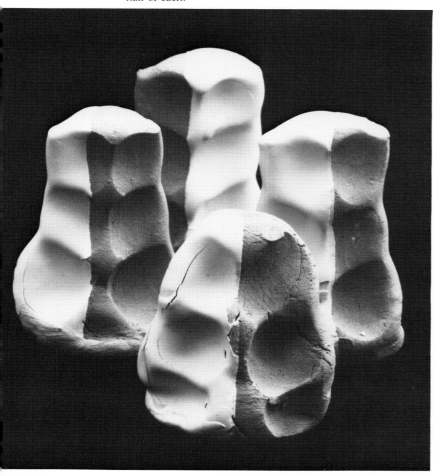

write or paint the serial numbers. The alteration of the surface gives some idea of how the glaze will behave on a textured background, or will behave on thin edges as the glaze generally runs slightly. Because of the tendency of glazes to flow, many people prefer to do testing on sections of thrown forms, or some other vertical test surface. When testing new glazes or doing material fusion tests, it is a wise precaution to make sure that the kiln shelves are well protected, with a kiln wash (equal parts kaolin and flint, with added water to make a creamy mixture) or powdered flint, to diminish the likelihood of ruined shelves. If tests are being done on small bowls or similar objects, a saucer or slice of insulating brick can be placed underneath to eliminate damage from running glazes.

It is generally preferable to do glaze tests on clays which are as white as possible, so that the true colors of the glazes will show. I usually put a stripe of medium iron slip down one side of the tile, to give indication of the behavior of the glaze over a dark clay. On dark clays, I usually put on a stripe of white slip for the reverse reason. It is also useful to make an impression in the clay, to indicate the quality of the glaze when pooled. The mixtures are tested on bisque-fired clay, except where the tests are for the development of glazes for work that will be fired only once.

The quantity of powdered materials required are measured out using a variety of ways. Pinches and handfuls, spoonfuls and kitchen measuring cups, and very sophisticated electronic scales used in chemistry laboratories are methods used. Perhaps the most convenient method is to be found somewhere in the middle of this range, in the form of a triple-beam balance scale using grams as the unit of measurement. This makes it much easier to calculate percentages. However one does the weighing out, it should be done as accurately as possible, for consistent results. A small error in compounding a test batch of glaze mixture can easily become a giant one if the glaze later gets made up or mixed into a large volume. A few grams out in the test could mean a kilogram out in a large batch of glaze.

In this book, all glaze guidelines are intended to be made up as "parts by weight" mixtures. The materials should be weighed out first. Then they can be mixed with water until the mixture is of a creamy, brushable consistency. The usual ratio of dry mixture to water is 4:3 for most glazes. When glazes are being made up in larger volumes, a convenient measure of dry mix to water is with kilograms and liters, where 1 kilogram (Kg) equals 1 liter (l). Therefore, 4 Kg of dry mixture can be added to 3 l of water for approximately the right consistency. This approximation can then be adjusted by the addition or removal of a small amount of water.

Once an optimum thickness for a given glaze is established, its specific gravity can be recorded with a hydrometer (see chapter 20).

The mixtures are painted on the tiles with a variation of thickness from one end to the other, to give an indication of the behavior of the glaze with differing thickness. These variations can produce remarkably different results from the same glaze, and a glaze test should yield a good deal of information.

Glaze tests that are initially promising should be retested on pots, as they often then seem to change character. These changes can be due to various things: thickness, firing time, temperature and atmosphere variables, and even the more complete interaction of materials when used in bulk glaze. Before covering all of your favorite pieces with inadequately tested glazes, it is advisable to spend a little more time with the groundwork. Glazes, like people, need to be lived with before they reveal their full potential. Good first impressions don't always produce the best friends!

It should be remembered when one is doing the work of glaze development, and probably heartily sick of weighing out little bowls of powders, that a few days or weeks of careful testing can be enough to set one up with a lifetime of glazes, developed for one's own personal requirements. The important part of the process is not just the arrival at a good recipe or formula, but the search that led you there.

5

Basic Raw Materials in Ceramics

In order for the ceramist to better understand his working materials, it is helpful to have a little knowledge of the earth and its origins, since all of the raw materials that we use come from that source. After all, the clays and minerals have already experienced the processes of heating and mineral alteration to a far greater degree than they will be exposed to in our kilns. We can learn a great deal from observation of their structure and their coloration.

GEOLOGICAL BEGINNINGS

Scientists and mathematicians tell us that the earth was formed by the gradual accumulation of heated gases, spinning in space and gathering into a nearly spherical object. After the passing of eons of time, condensation developed on the surface of the spinning sphere, causing the mass to cool and contract. This contraction created a hardened crust, leaving the interior hot and partly molten. The earth may be thought of as resembling a round loaf of bread, fresh from the oven, where the inside is hot and soft, and the outside is hard, crusty and deeply textured. The outside crust was formed and perforated by violent volcanic action. Hot gases forced the disgorgement of superheated flows of lava and rock. This process is still continuing, although at a reduced rate, with the occasional eruptions which take place from active volcanoes the world over. The rocks formed and ejected through internal ignition are called igneous rocks. During their cooling, large numbers of different minerals coalesced into a variety of crystalline structures. The crystals differed in size and density, depending on the rate of cooling. The slower the cooling, the larger the crystal.

Through the effects of weathering by rain, frost, sun and wind, as well as through the intrusive action of plants sending roots into the most improbable places, the rocks have gradually broken down and decomposed. The more soluble minerals, such as sodium and potassium, have been leached out by the rain and washed down rivers, eventually to the sea, giving it its characteristic salty taste. Less soluble, yet comparatively fragile materials such as sand, clay and calcium have also been moved by alluvial action and have formed layers of sediment. Under compression these have been gradually altered into another form of rock, which we call sedimentary. These pressures have formed sandstone, shale, and limestone from the previously mentioned materials.

A third form of rock develops from the previous types, through further forms of alteration, superheating, acidic action, and increased pressures. This form of rock is known as metamorphic. Shale and limestone, under conditions of metamorphosis, become slate and marble. The following chart shows some of the more common of the basic forms.

Igneous	Sedimentary	Metamorphic
Porphyry	Conglomerate	Gneiss
Granite	Coal	Schist
Pegmatite	Shale	Slate
Syenite	Limestone	Marble
Gabbro	Sandstone	Quartzite

The composition of rocks is made up from a large number of different minerals. Minerals are made up of various chemicals, and regardless of the rock types from which they come, their chemical constituents remain the same. For example, calcium from any source rock, whether it be igneous, sedimentary, or metamorphic, will always be calcium. When used in a clay body or glaze as calcium oxide, it reacts in the same way, forming calcium silicates. The chemical constituents can also be known as either acid or alkaline. It is these chemical constituents which make up the necessary ele-ments for the formation of clay, glaze and color for the ceramist, and give us an unlimited opportunity to develop the ceramic surface.

The avid glaze maker will probably use materials found in their natural state at some time, and many people spend a lifetime in such pursuits. It is a heady experience to play at being God and make a rock turn to glass, and with additions of other rocks transmute it into yet another form of rock. Like the alchemist of old, the ceramist is constantly forming and altering new materials in the course of his work. Minerals formed in nature can be removed from their natural form and developed into obscure new mutations. If one thinks about glazes in this way it becomes obvious that glaze development is essentially accelerated microcosmic geology.

The diverse forms of rocks and their elemental or chemical constituents dictate how they can be used for glaze development. Some materials may be used simply by grinding them down to a fine powder. Other materials may go through various methods of purification and precipitation to give the ceramist refined materials.

An interesting correlation to the developments of ceramic history exists here, but in reverse. The materials that we use for the more recently developed high temperature glazes come from the oldest forms of rock. The older, lower temperature glazes use materials that are much more recent in geological formation. The crystals of some soluble alkaline materials, such as sodium and potassium, are continually forming at ambient temperatures around the edges of salt lakes. It was these highly fusible materials which gave us the earliest forms of glaze and glass, as found in Egypt about 4500 years ago.

When a glaze is being fired, it goes through a series of physical changes common to all glazes, no matter what the temperature of maturity is. First, the water leaves by evaporation, or as steam. As the firing progresses, the components of the glaze will gradually start to sinter and intermix, with the lower fusing materials melting first. Gradually they interact with the others until the melt is complete. This process is called eutectic development and is explained in more detail in chapter 7. During this fusion, the glaze will go through a violent stage of bubbling and boiling, until it settles down to a smooth liquified glass. The easiest time to watch this fascinating reaction is during a raku firing, where one can view the complete process in a very short time. Even glazes that are matt when they emerge from the kiln will appear shiny and glassy at the maturing temperature of the glaze. This applies to true matt glazes, and not those where a matt, dry surface is developed through either immature glaze, or an excess of non-fusible material which remains undissolved in the glaze. In true matt glazes, the glass that has been formed will devitrify, forming a coating of miniature crystals, often invisible to the naked eye. The miniature crystals do not reflect light uniformly or coherently, making the surface appear flat, or matt.

Any glaze, fired at any temperature, is a combination of three components: **Fluxes, alumina** (or bonding agents) and **glassformers.** I call this **the FAG Principle,** FAG being an acronym for the three component groups. It could equally well be taken as meaning **F**or **A**ny **G**laze. The relationship between the amounts of oxides in the three groups, as well as the fusion and eutectic points of the individual materials, determines the type of glaze and its firing range. One can also think of the three components in anthropomorphic terms. The glassformers, such as silica, form the bones of the glaze. The fluxes, which are used to make the glassformer melt at a required temperature and also to give the glaze its special surface and color developing characteristics, forms the blood and skin. The third, alumina or clay, forms the bonding agent which holds the glaze onto the form being glazed; it is the muscle. Without all three interacting properly, the glaze will be amorphous, and the skin blemished. Beyond the three basic components are two optional ones, colorants and opacifiers, which could be thought of as cosmetics, a possible improvement of the skin, but not strictly necessary. Many individual materials used in ceramics contain all three basic components, and will easily fuse to a glass given a high enough temperature. Obvious examples of these would be Albany clay, from the United States, and powdered nepheline syenite or other feldspar materials. Many such materials will produce good usable glazes at stoneware temperatures with little or no adjustment.

In publications that deal with molecular equations, the basic components will be listed in three columns, as in the following illustration:

$$RO, R_2O \quad R_2O_3 \quad RO_2$$

The first column contains the majority of the fluxes, and is known as the radical oxide column, where the materials' chemical symbol ends with "O." The second column, containing the clays, is known as the amphoteric column, where the materials' chemical symbol ends with "$_2O_3$." The third column is the glassformer column, where the materials' chemical symbol ends with "O_2." There are various ways of calculating glazes by mathematical methods, with molecular formulae, limit formulae and typical or ultimate percentage analysis. None of them tell us the complete story, however, as the subtle trace elements or colorants, which, for the artist, are perhaps the most important part, seldom show up in analysis. The formulae used for the materials are usually the theoretical composition. Most feldspar suppliers, for instance, provide a "typical formula" as the composition of a naturally occurring material which is certain to vary from one part of the mine to another. Therefore, the scientific method of calculation is in fact only as accurate as the analysis.

No matter how one creates a glaze, the key to understanding the phenomena of glaze development lies with understanding the individual materials involved, their expected behavior under variations of temperature and atmosphere, and their interaction with each other. As one develops knowledge of these materials, one is also likely to develop intuition as to their potential interaction. Intuition leads to the type of understanding which allows and encourages individual growth.

The major part of this chapter consists of a list of the most commonly used ceramic materials, and will assist in understanding their behavior. There are two words which occur regularly in the materials list, **soluble** and **toxic.** Solubility refers to the process whereby a material will enter into a solution when mixed with a liquid, as salt or sugar do in water. Soluble materials used in ceramics are usually fritted, or heated to a point where the chemical change alters the physical properties, so that they become insoluble in water. If they were not fritted, these materials could enter the pores of the clay body and could well cause various problems in the glaze firing. Materials for glazes must be in a state of suspension, so that when a glaze is applied to a ceramic piece, the mixture of materials develops a thin coat on the surface. Upon fusion, this coating will bond itself to the form through the amphoteric (alumina) or bonding agent of the glaze, in what is called an interface layer. The closer the fusion point of the glaze is to the vitrification point of the body, the greater the degree of interface mixing. It can develop in low temperature wares, particularly when a body frit or flux is added to the clay. In porcelain, it is virtually impossible to tell where the body ends and the glaze begins.

Toxicity refers first to the poisonous state of the raw material, which obviously represents a hazard to the person using it. Basic safety precautions are needed in the studio to minimize the potential dangers of these materials. Wearing a suitable mask during mixing or spraying operations should help eliminate the problems for the potter. Toxicity also refers to the potential hazard from improperly formulated glazes using lead compounds, or lead glazes containing cadmium-selenium, copper, and other heavy metal colorants. A heavy metal glaze containing lead is capable of being leached out of the glaze by food or drink acids, such as vinegar, wine or fruit juices. It can then go into solution with the liquid juice or food to produce a mild poison, which can be immediately lethal for children, and cumulatively poisonous for all.

The materials listed in this book are coded with one or more of the letters **F,A,G,C,O,** representing their function within the glaze:

F = Flux
A = Alumina (refractory, amphoteric or bonding agent)
G = Glassformer
C = Colorant
O = Opacifier

There are times when materials can fulfill various functions. The most obvious of these are listed with more than one letter, in order of the impor-

tance of their function. These letters are written in **bold** type, and are placed directly after the material name for ease of reference.

Where a material is coded with the letters **F, A, G,** this will indicate that the material contains all the necessary ingredients to form a balanced glaze. It does not, however, tell at what temperature the material might fuse to become a glaze. This has to be learned by experience, or can be calculated using reference tables.

CLAYS

Since clay is the most important material that the potter uses in his work, and also because there is a wide variety of clay types, clays are listed first. Other materials follow in alphabetical order.

CLAY (A,G) Al_2O_3 $2SiO_2$ $2H_2O$. All clay comes from decomposed feldspathic rock. The clay's characteristics, and how far it has been removed from its original source or mother rock, will determine its potential usefulness in the ceramic industry. Clay can be divided into two major types, primary and secondary. Primary clays are those which are found at or close to their source. They are of large particle size and are relatively pure. Kaolin, or china clay, is in this category.

KAOLIN is the purest form of clay, with a relatively coarse grain structure and, usually, low plasticity. Kaolin (china clay) is used in the manufacture of white clays, particularly porcelain, and bone china. It is also used to provide the alumina content in glazes, as Kaolin has little contamination from iron. Although the purest forms of kaolin are found at their source, there are relatively pure forms found as secondary clays in some parts of the world. Kaolins are used extensively in the ceramic industry, as well as many other industries including the paper industry, as a coating for fine quality paper.

Secondary, or sedimentary, clays are those which have been removed from their original source by the action of water, wind and weathering. In the process, they have been ground finer by abrasion, and their plasticity has been increased. They have absorbed impurities, primarily through contamination with iron, as well as with various forms of carbonaceous matter from organic sources, such as plant and animal life. Some names given to secondary clays are ball clays, fireclays, sagger clays, stoneware clays, earthenware clays, adobe, flint clay, shale, bentonite, terra cotta, high alumina clay and gumbo.

BALL CLAYS are much the opposite of kaolin in their properties. They are higher in iron content, more fusible, more plastic, and finer in particle size. Ball clays and kaolins are really complementary in character, and are often combined in clay bodies to adjust the mixture to a workable consistency. They are also used to provide the alumina in glazes, but will usually add some iron, thus darkening the glaze slightly. Ball clays are found all over the world.

FIRECLAYS are not as well defined as either ball clay or kaolin. The term "fireclay" refers to the refractoriness or resistance to heat, and clays which may vary widely in other properties may be called fireclays if they are refractory. These clays are relatively pure and free from iron, although they may have small chunks of iron shale. Because of their refractory qualities, they are greatly used for kiln and furnace building. Fireclays may be used for formulating clay bodies for high firing. They are also mixed with lowfire terra cotta clay and used for large sculptural work, where the lowfire material melts and bonds the refractory particles.

SAGGER CLAYS are, in many respects, similar to fireclays, often being found between coal seams, and firing to a light buff color. They are frequently used as an addition to stoneware, terra cotta and earthenware bodies. The name comes from the word sagger, which is a refractory box into which glazed wares are sometimes put to protect them from the direct flame of the kiln. In some areas of North America, notably Kentucky, clays called sagger clays are almost as smooth as ball clay, whereas in England sagger clays are always very coarse.

STONEWARE CLAYS are clays which mature or become vitreous between cones 5 and 11. They fire from light grey or buff through dark grey to brown. They vary widely in plasticity and firing range, and there is no sharp distinction between what might be called a fireclay, sagger clay, or stoneware clay. The classification really hinges on the possible use

in ceramics, rather than the actual chemical or physical nature, or geological origin. For instance, one clay might be successfully used both as a fireclay for making bricks and as a stoneware for making high-fired stoneware pottery. Many clays are suitable for making stoneware pottery without further additions. Such clays may have just the right plasticity for wheel work, as well as having desirable drying and firing properties. These naturally occurring clays may fire to very pleasing colors and textures, and may respond well to salt glazing and slip glazing, as well as the usual high-fired glazing.

EARTHENWARE CLAYS, or common red clays, are the most abundant clays found in nature. They contain iron and other mineral impurities in sufficient quantity to cause the clay to become tight and hard fired at temperatures ranging from cone 08 to 2. In the raw state, such clays may be red, brown, greenish, grey or blue, as a result of both the iron and the decomposed organic matter in the clay. When fired, the color may vary from pink to tan, orange, red, brown or black, depending on the clay and firing conditions. Most of the world's pottery has been (and still is) made of earthenware clay, and it is also a major constituent in bodies used for bricks, tiles, roofing and drainage tiles, and other heavy clay products.

Common red clays may be highly plastic, even too plastic to be used by themselves. On the other hand, they may be quite non-plastic, because of the presence of sand or other rocky fragments. The potter will generally look for a smooth, plastic earthenware clay, which he can adjust to his own satisfaction with the addition of some sand or other non-plastic material. The brickmaker or terra cotta sculptor will look for a clay which is naturally coarse, and which contains considerable sand or other non-plastic material, so that his bricks or sculptures do not shrink, crack or warp excessively. Vast quantities of common red clay outcrop on the earth's surface. Much of it is unusable for ceramic purposes because it contains soluble calcium salts in the form of selenite, and soluble akaline salts such as potassium and sodium salts. There are immense reserves of usable clay, however.

Many red clays are used to form dark iron-rich glazes at cones 6–10, where fusion is caused

See Appendix, page 203, for serial numbers of glaze and color tests.

1	2	3	4	5	6
7	8	9	10	11	12
13	14	15	16	17	18
19	20	21	22	23	24

Glaze test 2:   Color variations from *cobalt* in various glaze bases.

Glaze test 1:   Color variations from *iron* in various glaze bases.

Glaze test 4: Color variations from *manganese* in various glaze bases.

Glaze test 3: Color variations from *copper* in various glaze bases.

See Appendix, page 203, for serial numbers of glaze and color tests.

1	2	3	4	5	6
7	8	9	10	11	12
13	14	15	16	17	18
19	20	21	22	23	24

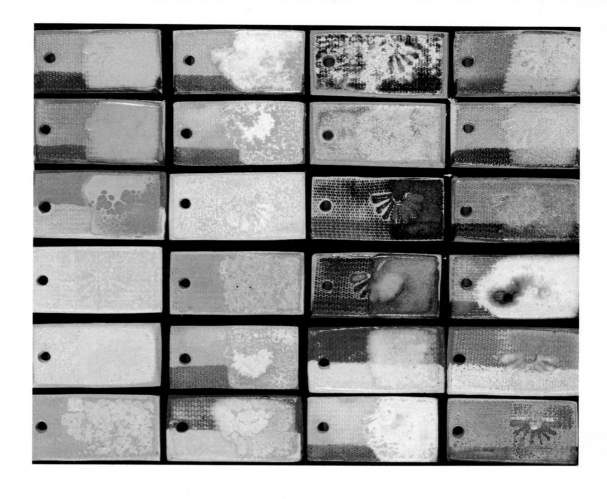

Glaze test 6: Color variations from *rutile* in various glaze bases.

Glaze test 5: Color variations from *nickel* in various glaze bases.

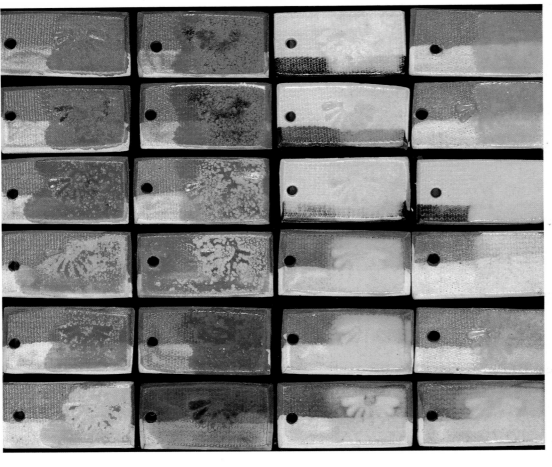

Glaze test 8: Color variations from *uranium* (top two rows) and Blythe Yellow Glaze Stain (bottom rows) in various glaze bases.

Glaze test 7: Color variations from *chromium* in various glaze bases.

See Appendix, page 203, for serial numbers of glaze and color tests.

1	2	3	4	5	6
7	8	9	10	11	12
13	14	15	16	17	18
19	20	21	22	23	24

Glaze test 10: Color variations from cross-blends of *nickel, manganese and cobalt* in various glaze bases.

Glaze test 9: Color variations from *copper and tin,* and *copper and titanium* in various glaze bases.

Glaze test 12: Color variations from cross-blends of *rutile, tin, manganese, cobalt and chromium* in various glaze bases.

Glaze test 11: Color variations from cross-blends of *rutile, iron, cobalt and manganese* in various glaze bases.

See Appendix, page 203, for serial numbers of glaze and color tests.

1	2	3	4	5	6
7	8	9	10	11	12
13	14	15	16	17	18
19	20	21	22	23	24

by the amount of iron in conjunction with other fluxing materials. Such clays are often found in nature by river or creek beds, or in estuary areas, such as Albany clay, which is mined near Albany, New York. These clays may be easily used for once-fire glazes, slips, or as a basic constituent in other glazes.

ADOBE CLAY is a surface clay which is suitable for making adobe or sundried bricks. It has limited plasticity, and generally contains a high percentage of sand.

FLINT CLAY is a refractory clay which has been compacted into a hard, dense, rock-like mass.

SHALE is a metamorphic rock, formed by pressures from sedimentary clay. It has little plasticity, unless it is finely pulverized and allowed to temper for a long period. Shale may be used as an addition to, or as the principal ingredient of, bricks and other heavy clay products.

BENTONITE is a colloidal clay of volcanic origin. Although its chemical composition is like clay, its physical properties are very different. Bentonite cannot be used by itself because of its tendency to swell when wet, turning to a gel, and also because of its stickiness and extremely high shrinkage. Bentonite is used to lend plasticity to clay bodies. A small addition of 1–2 percent will bring about a marked increase in plasticity. It is also used in glazes, to keep them in suspension. Approximately 1–2 percent may be added to the dry glaze mix, before adding any water.

TERRA COTTA is a low-grade fireclay, usually pink to dark red in color, which may be used in the production of large sculptural pieces. It has an open grain structure, which permits rapid and even drying.

HIGH ALUMINA CLAYS, such as bauxite or diaspore, contain a high percentage of alumina. These clays are highly refractory and are used as the raw material for the metal aluminum. In ceramics, they have a wide range of uses, from refractories to glaze development.

GUMBO is a surface or soil clay which is very plastic and sticky, and which contains a considerable amount of organic matter. It is not generally used in ceramic work, but it could be pressed into service to give results similar—though not identical—to Albany slip clay.

GROG is a previously fired clay which has been ground to various degrees of fineness. It is used as an addition to clay bodies to counteract shrinking, warping and cracking, and to give them texture.

OTHER GLAZE MATERIALS

ALBANY CLAY (F,A,G,C). See Clay.

ALBITE (F,A,G). See Feldspar.

ALKALI. Properly should mean only the hydroxides and carbonates of sodium, potassium and lithium, but is generally used to include all alkaline metals and earths. From an Arabic word referring to the ashes of desert plants, an early source of sodium and potassium for glazes in the Middle East.

ALKALINE EARTHS. The oxides of calcium, barium and strontium, with magnesium frequently included.

ALKALINE METALS. The oxides of sodium, potassium and lithium.

ALKALINE GLAZE. A term usually used to describe earthenware glazes which have been fluxed with alkaline materials, having a particular response to certain coloring oxides; for example, turquoise from copper and purple brown from manganese in oxidation atmospheres.

ALUMINA HYDRATE (A). $Al_2(OH)_6$. Occasionally used as a source of alumina for glazes (see Kaolin). It is especially used in the formulation of color stains to create pink colors with chromium, or coral with iron. It is commonly used as a refractory kiln wash, or for wads in the setting of ware for saltglaze firing.

ALUMINA, CALCINED (A). Al_2O_3. Alumina hydrate which has been brought to red heat to drive off chemically combined water.

AMBLYGONITE (F). $2LiF\ Al_2O_3\ P_2O_6$. A source of lithium and phosphorous, high in alumina. An interesting material which can form a fine glaze on its own between cone 6 and 8, but is not commonly used.

ANORTHITE (F,A,G). See Feldspar.

ANTIMONIATE OF LEAD (C). $Pb_3(SbO_4)_2$. **TOXIC.** Colorant—see chapter 14.

ANTIMONY OXIDE. (C,G,O). Sb_3O_4. **TOXIC.** A material used in low temperature glazes (10–20 percent) to produce a weak white. In the presence of lead and iron it has a tendency to give a yellow color.

ARSENIOUS OXIDE. See Glassformers.

BALL CLAY. See Clay.

BARIUM CARBONATE (F). $BaCO_3$. **TOXIC.** A secondary flux in stoneware glazes, most frequently used to produce a satin matt surface. With boron it makes a free flowing glaze, producing a smooth and glossy finish. As an alkaline material, it strongly affects some colors. Small amounts (1–2 percent) are used in earthenware bodies to prevent scumming from soluble salts.

BARIUM CHLORIDE (F). $BaCl$. **TOXIC, SOLUBLE.** A material used to develop iridescent surfaces by fuming at a low temperature, subsequent to the glaze firing.

BAUXITE. A non-plastic, clay-like material and naturally occurring source of alumina.

BENTONITE. See Clay.

BISMUTH SUBNITRATE (F). $BiONO_3$ H_2O. **TOXIC, SOLUBLE.** A material used in the development of low temperature pearly luster for use over fired glaze.

BONE ASH, CALCIUM PHOSPHATE (F). $3CaO$ P_2O_3. **TOXIC.** A secondary flux in glazes. The essential ingredient in the production of bone china, giving it its characteristic translucency. A source of phosphorous, helping in the production of interesting red-brown colors from iron.

BORAX (F,G). Na_2O $2B_2O_3$ $10H_2O$. **SOLUBLE.** Sodium tetraborate. A natural combination of glassmaker (B) and flux (Na), producing bright alkaline colors with oxides. As it is soluble, it is usually used in fritted form (see Frits—chapter 6). It may be used

as a supplement to salt (sodium chloride) for salt glaze, producing a lower firing, glassy glaze through volatilization. With 47.2 percent water content, borax is unstable and the water slowly diminishes during storage.

BORAX—DEHYDRATED (F,G). Na_2O $2B_2O_3$. **SOLUBLE.** Anhydrous or fused borax.

BORAX FRIT. See Frits—chapter 6.

BORIC ACID, BORACIC ACID (F,G). H_3BO_3. **SOLUBLE.** A source of boron used in the preparation of boro-silicate frits.

BORO-CALCITE (F,G). $2CaO$ $3B_2O_3$ $5H_2O$. Calcium borate, a powerful flux in low temperature glazes. It is similar to colemanite, and is a secondary flux at high temperatures. It is insoluble and can be thought of as a natural frit.

CADMIUM OXIDE. See Colorants—chapter 14.

CALCINED CLAY. Clay which has been heated to remove chemically combined water. It is used in situations where the shrinkage of the clay content of a glaze could cause such problems as crawling.

CALCIUM BORATE. See Boro-calcite.

CALCIUM CARBONATE (F). $CaCO_3$. Whiting, chalk, paris white, cliffstone, limestone, lime. The usual source of calcium carbonate in North America is limestone. The main source of calcium for glazes and the most frequently used flux in high temperature glazes. It produces a hard, durable glass. An excess of calcium produces a microcrystalline, flux-matt glaze.

CALCIUM CHLORIDE. $CaCl_2$ $6H_2O$. **SOLUBLE.** A flocculant used in slips and glazes in the amount of 0.05 percent of the dry weight.

CALCIUM FLUORIDE. See Fluorspar.

CALCIUM MAGNESIUM CARBONATE. See Dolomite.

CALCIUM METASILICATE. See Wollastonite.

CALCIUM OXIDE. See Calcium carbonate.

CALCIUM PHOSPHATE. See Bone ash.

CALCIUM ZIRCONIUM SILICATE. See Opacifiers—chapter 17.

CERIUM OXIDE (F,O). CeO. **TOXIC.** A rare flux, which at low temperatures can be used as a substitute for tin as an opacifier. At high temperatures, it can combine fluxing and opacifying action. It gives yellow colors in conjunction with titanium.

CHALK. See Calcium carbonate.

CHINA CLAY. See Clay.

CHINA STONE. See Cornwall stone.

CHROMIUM OXIDE (C). Cr_2O_3. **TOXIC.** Colorant—see chapter 14.

COBALT CARBONATE (C). $CoCO_3$. **TOXIC.** Colorant—see chapter 14.

COBALT OXIDE (C). CoO. **TOXIC.** Colorant—see chapter 14.

COLEMANITE (F). 2CaO 3B_2O_3 5H_2O. A natural hydrated calcium borate. An insoluble form of boron, with a powerful fluxing action. Colemanite, calcium borate and gerstley borate have, in the past, been regarded as interchangeable materials. Colemanite is mined naturally, and over the years has changed in available quality. Much of the natural colemanite now seems to cause crawling, spitting and sputtering of glazes. Most ceramists in North America use gerstley borate, a similar material containing some sodium, in its place.

COPPERAS (C). $FeSO_4$ 7H_2O. **SOLUBLE.** Colorant—see chapter 14, Iron.

COPPER CARBONATE (C). $CuCo_3$. **TOXIC.** Colorant—see chapter 14.

COPPER OXIDE, CUPRIC OXIDE (C). CuO. **TOXIC.** Colorant—see chapter 14.

COPPER SULFATE (C). $CuSO_4$ 5H_2O. **TOXIC, SOLUBLE.** Colorant—see chapter 14.

CORNWALL STONE, CORNISH STONE. See Feldspar.

CRISTOBALITE. See Silica.

CROCUS MARTIS (C). Fe_2O_3. Colorant—see chapter 14, Iron.

CRYOLITE (F). Na_3AlF_6. Sodium aluminum fluoride. A secondary flux material and natural source of insoluble sodium, which produces characteristic alkaline colors. Fluorine decomposes at high tem-

peratures and may cause bubbling of the glaze through the release of gases.

CUPRIC OXIDE. See Copper oxide.

DIATOMACEOUS EARTH (A). Diatomaceous silica, diatomite, kieselguhr. A material with a very high silica content derived from the skeletons of diatoms (microscopic organisms). Used for making low temperature insulating bricks.

DOLOMITE (F). $CaCO_3$ $MgCO_3$. Calcium magnesium carbonate. A high temperature flux with a combination of calcium and magnesium. It strongly affects certain colors, notably cobalt and iron.

EPSOM SALTS. See Magnesium sulfate.

FELDSPAR, and related alumino–silicates. Feldspar, or felspar, is an alumino–silicate mineral, as clay is, but it has a proportionally higher content of fluxes. At stoneware temperatures, feldspar fuses to form glass by itself, and needs only minor additions to produce an infinite variety of useful and beautiful glazes. For this reason, it is the most important single glaze material for the ceramist working at high temperatures. Feldspar is the most common of minerals, and is mined in many parts of the world. There are several different kinds of feldspars and many variations within each kind. Feldspars are given general theoretical formulae which do not take into account the trace elements which may also be present, the variations in materials from different parts of the same mine, or the difference between feldspars from different sources. Potash and soda feldspars are commonly listed with general formulae. Individual analyses are sometimes available from the suppliers, but they are still general in nature. There are several other alumino-silicates widely used by ceramists that fulfill the same function in glazes as feldspar. These are cornwall stone, carolina stone, nepheline syenite, petalite, spodumene and lepidolite. Although they behave in similar ways to feldspar, it is inaccurate to call them feldspars, because the term "feldspar" indicates a certain crystal form, with which not all these materials comply.

NOTE: In this book, where material mixtures are listed using feldspar, the type of feldspar used is the common variety of potash feldspar, unless otherwise stated. Different feldspars will show some variation from one another when used in the same proportions in glazes. Some variations will be quite noticeable, some not.

FELDSPAR—POTASH (F,A,G). $K_2O\ Al_2O_3\ 6SiO_2$. An orthoclase or microcline feldspar. This is the most common form and is the type generally used in glaze recipes, unless another type is specified. Potash feldspars also contain some sodium.

FELDSPAR—SODA (F,A,G). $Na_2O\ Al_2O_3\ 6SiO_2$. An albite feldspar. Soda feldspar, which is less common than potash feldspar, is very similar in general performance. The difference lies in the relative proportions of sodium and potassium.

FELDSPAR—LIME (F,A,G). $CaO\ Al_2O_3\ 2SiO_2$. A rare anorthite feldspar. It can be used in the same way as other feldspars, in that it is interchangeable in the way it makes things melt, but its scarcity makes it expensive.

CORNWALL STONE (F,A,G). Also known as cornish stone, china stone, and hard purple stone. It is a feldspathoid material mined in the west of England, and is traditionally the cheap substitute for imported feldspar for the British ceramic industry. Cornwall stone is a more complex material than either potash or soda feldspar and contains a number of trace elements. These are calcium, magnesium, fluorine, iron and titanium, in addition to sodium, potassium, alumina and silica. Because of its complexity it is not usually given a generalized formula.

CAROLINA STONE (F,A,G). Carolina stone is similar to cornwall stone and mined in the U.S.A. as a substitute for cornwall stone.

NEPHELINE SYENITE (F,A,G). $K_2O\ 3Na_2O\ 4Al_2O_3\ 8SiO_2$. Nepheline syenite is mined in Canada, and is the American ceramic industry alternate to feldspar. It has a very active fluxing power, producing bright clear glazes. The high sodium content may cause crazing to occur. It is slightly soluble, as are many feldspars, and sometimes causes deflocculation in slips and clays in which it is used. This is especially noticeable in the preparation of casting slips and filter-pressed clay bodies.

PETALITE (F,A,G). $LiO_2\ Al_2O_3\ 8SiO_2$. This feldspar-like material contains lithium, and produces color responses similar to nepheline syenite, but is less likely to cause crazing. The lithium minerals produce fired silicates with low thermal expansion, and are used in the formulation of flameproof clay bodies. This characteristic may cause difficulty in glaze fit, and be responsible for the fault known as shivering.

SPODUMENE (F,A,G). $Li_2O\ Al_2O_3\ 3SiO_2$. A lithium alumino-silicate, similar in behavior to petalite. Also used in flameproof bodies.

LEPIDOLITE (F,A,G). $(LiNaK)_2\ (FOH)_2\ Al_2O_3\ 3SiO_2$. A complex alumino silicate with alkaline fluxes. It contains fluorine, a volatile material which can cause blistering at high temperatures.

FERRIC CHROMATE (C). $Fe_2O_3\ Cr_2O_3$ **TOXIC.** Colorant— see chapter 14.

FERROSO—FERRIC OXIDE (C). Fe_3O_4. Colorant—see chapter 14).

FERROUS OXIDE (C). FeO. Colorant—see chapter 14.

FERROUS SULFATE (C). $FeSO_4\ 7H_2O$. **SOLUBLE.** Colorant—see chapter 14.

FERROUS TITANATE (C). $FeO\ TiO_2$. Colorant—see chapter 14.

FIRECLAY. See Clay.

FLINT—SILICA (G). SiO. A black, grey or brown variety of quartz. The common source of silica, as glassmaker in both glazes and clay bodies. See Silica.

FLUORSPAR (F). CaF. A source of calcium and fluorine. Fluorine atoms replace oxygen in the silicate chain, causing fluid melts at low temperatures. Some of the fluorspar will decompose and the resulting gases can cause blistering of the glaze. Fluorspar can help in the development of unusual blues from cobalt and copper.

FRENCH CHALK. See Talc.

FRIT. See chapter 6.

GALENA. See Lead sulfide.

GERMANIA. See Glassformers.

GERSTLEY BORATE (F,G). $2CaO$ Na_2O $3B_2O_3$ $7H_2O$. Calcium—sodium—borate, used as a replacement for colemanite, and mined in California.

GLASSFORMER. The oxides of the elements that will form the non-crystalline, super-cooled liquid which we call glass. Almost without exception, glass and glazes use silica (SiO_2) as the glassformer. In some glazes, particularly at low temperatures, boron oxide (B_2O_3) is used as a supplementary glassformer. Phosphorous pentoxide (P_2O_5) is also used as a supplementary glassformer, usually in the form of bone ash. It is said to encourage iridescent, opalescent glass, and is also used as a supplementary glassformer in bone china bodies. The other glassformers are antimony oxide, arsenious oxide, and the oxide of germania. In glaze calculation, all of the glassformers should be included with silica in establishing glaze analyses.

GROG. See Clay.

GYPSUM. See Plaster of paris.

ILMENITE (C). FeO TiO_2. Colorant—see chapter 14.

IRON MATERIALS. Colorants—see chapter 14.

KAOLIN. See Clay.

LEAD CARBONATE (F). $2PbCO_3$ $Pb(OH)_2$. **TOXIC.** White lead.

LEAD CHROMATE (C). $PbCrO_4$. **TOXIC.** Colorant— see chapter 14.

LEAD OXIDE (F). Pb_3O_4. **TOXIC.** Red lead.

LEAD OXIDE (F). PbO. **TOXIC.** Yellow lead, litharge.

LEAD SULFIDE—GALENA (F). PbS. **TOXIC.** The source of lead used for glazing in Medieval times. Glazing was achieved by dusting the damp ware with powdered galena, or with a simple glaze made up with approximately one part of galena and three parts of red clay. Galena glazes are often scummed with a whitish powder due to sulphuration.

Lead is a very active flux in glazes up to 1100°C. The lead compounds are extremely toxic, and for this reason, lead is usually used in a fritted form (see chapter 6). In the calculation of lead glazes, *extreme care* must be taken, or a potentially poisonous glaze may result. Such a glaze may dissolve part of its lead content into acid liquids, such as fruit juices, and cause lead poisoning. Such glazes are called high solubility glazes. Low solubility glazes, which fall within current government regulations on lead solubility, are perfectly safe for use. However, the care with which such glazes must be calculated and controlled, combined with public suspicion of all lead containing glazes, has made the production of domestic wares using lead glazes almost impossible for the studio potter.

There are two separate aspects of toxicity from lead: raw lead compounds, and high solubility glazes. The first is dangerous only to the person who works with the unfired materials. The second is dangerous to anyone who may use the fired glaze with mild food acids.

It is just as possible to produce a non-toxic glaze from toxic lead materials as it is to produce a toxic glaze from non-toxic materials, such as low solubility lead frits. A toxic glaze can develop from improper glaze formulation, or by the addition of certain colorants, such as copper, chromium, or potassium dichromate, to the fritted glaze. Potentially toxic glazes may be employed in non-functional ceramics, such as sculpture and architectural work. Lead glazes may be needed here for the development of specific colors, which cannot be achieved in any other way.

Why is lead used when it seems to be fraught with so many problems? There are three basic reasons. First, its ease of fusion; second, its brilliance and durability when properly formulated into a glaze; and third, its responsiveness to the development of certain colors (see chapters 10, 14 and 16). Lead glazes can be tested for lead release. This should be carried out in a laboratory recommended by government health regulatory bodies.

LEPIDOLITE (F,A,G). See Feldspar.

LOCAL REDUCTION. See Silicon carbide.

LIME, LIMESTONE. See Calcium.

LITHARGE. See Lead oxide.

LITHIUM CARBONATE (F). $LiCO_3$. An active alkaline flux with similar color responses as sodium and potassium. With lithium, greater amounts of alumina, silica, and calcium can be used in alkaline glazes for the retention of typical alkaline colors. It can be used in place of lead in mid-range glazes, where volatilization of lead might be a problem. When used as a substitute for sodium and potassium, it reduces glaze expansion and promotes crystallization.

MAGNESITE (calcined) (F). $MgO\ MgCO_3$. A flux.

MAGNESIUM CARBONATE (F). $MgCO_3$. A high temperature flux which produces a smooth, buttery, matt surface. Higher quantities may produce a dry appearance. It strongly affects certain colorants, particularly cobalt. See also Dolomite.

MAGNESIUM SILICATE. See Talc.

MAGNESIUM SULFATE (F). $MgSO_4\ 7H_2O$. SOLUBLE. Epsom salts. A flocculant used in glazes and slips to aid in keeping them in suspension. Suggested addition to the dry weight: 0.2–1 percent.

MANGANESE CARBONATE (C). $MnCO_3$. TOXIC. Colorant—see chapter 14.

MANGANESE DIOXIDE (C). MnO_2. TOXIC. Colorant—see chapter 14.

MOLYBDENUM OXIDE (F,C). MoO_3. TOXIC. An unusual flux. See also colorants, chapter 14.

NAPLES YELLOW. See Antimoniate of lead.

NEPHELINE SYENITE (F,A,G). See Feldspar.

NICKEL OXIDE (C). NiO. TOXIC. Colorant—see chapter 14.

NITER. See Potassium nitrate.

OCHRE (C,A,G). The name given to various earthy materials consisting of hydrated ferric oxide (Fe_2O_3), plus clay and sand. The iron content of ochre is variable and rarely more than 50 percent.

OPACIFIERS. See chapter 17.

ORTHOCLASE See Feldspar.

PARIS WHITE. See Calcium carbonate.

PEARL ASH. See Potassium carbonate.

PETALITE (F,A,G). See Feldspar.

PHOSPHOROUS PENTOXIDE. See Bone ash, Glassformers.

PLASTER OF PARIS (F). $CaSO_4\ \frac{1}{2}H_2O$. Calcined gypsum, a source of calcium.

PLASTIC VITROX (F,A,G). A complex mineral mined in California that is a source of potassium, alumina and silica. It resembles both potash feldspar and cornwall stone in composition.

POTASSIUM ALUMINO—SILICATE. See Feldspar.

POTASSIUM BICHROMATE (C). $K_2Cr_2O_7$. EXTREMELY TOXIC, SOLUBLE.

POTASSIUM CARBONATE (F). K_2CO_3. SOLUBLE. Pearl ash, potash. A highly soluble form of potassium, usually used in a fritted form.

POTASSIUM PERMANGANATE (C). $KMnO_4$. TOXIC, SOLUBLE. Soluble source of manganese—see chapter 14.

PRASEODYMIUM OXIDE (C). Pr_2O_3. TOXIC. Colorant—see chapter 14.

PYROPHYLLITE (A,G). $Al_2O_3\ 4SiO_2\ H_2O$. A hydrous alumino—silicate material used to replace some or all of the flint and feldspar in industrial tile clays. It brings about a decrease in thermal expansion.

QUARTZ (G). SiO. A source of silica for glazes and clay bodies. See Silica.

RED LEAD See Lead.

RUTILE (C). TiO_2. Colorant—see chapter 14.

SALT. See Sodium chloride.

SALTPETER. See Sodium nitrate.

SAND, SILICA SAND (G). SiO_2. Pure sand is crystalline quartz. It is used as an addition to clay bodies to promote an open texture and reduce shrinkage and warping. When used in clays it should be of a grain size less than 50 mesh. It is also used as a ware shelf separator, and to support some bone china and porcelain forms, as a placing sand, in high temperature bisque firing. Only pure sand is considered as SiO_2. Sand is frequently found mixed with clay or, on beaches, with calcium from ground shells.

SILICA (G). SiO_2. Silicon, next to oxygen, is the most abundant element found in nature. Its oxide, silica, is found in crystalline forms as quartz, tridymite and cristobalite; in cryptocrystalline forms such as flint, chert and chalcedony; in hydrated forms such as opal; and in organic forms such as wood ash and diatomaceous earth. As a ceramic material, it is used in both its pure forms, flint and quartz, and as alumino-silicates, clay and feldspar. Silica is the glassformer upon which all ceramics and glass-making depend.

SILICON CARBIDE (G). SiC. An electrical fusion of sand and coke, best known as Carborundum. Silicon carbide is used in the manufacture of high-grade refractories for kiln shelves and other kiln parts. Finely ground silicon carbide, 200 mesh, can be mixed into a glaze to effect local reduction, as in copper red glazes in electric kilns (an addition of 0.5–2 percent). More than a small percentage addition, or silicon carbide which is larger in grain size than 200 mesh, may cause pitting or bubbling of glazes. In a medium grind, 50–100 mesh, silicon carbide can be used to form "crater" or "volcanic" glazes.

SODA ASH. See Sodium carbonate.

SODIUM ALUMINUM FLUORIDE. See Cryolite.

SODIUM ALUMINUM SILICATE. See Feldspar.

SODIUM BORATE. See Borax.

SODIUM CARBONATE, SODA ASH (F). $NaCO_3$. **SOLUBLE.** The common source of sodium for glazes. It is soluble and is usually used in the fritted form. It is also used in casting slips, as a deflocculant, in combination with sodium silicate. Soda ash is used as a vapor glaze material, similar to salt, both to lower the temperature range needed and to eliminate the harmful effects which are likely to occur from released chlorine gas. See Sodium chloride.

SODIUM CHLORIDE, COMMON SALT (F). NaCl. **SOLUBLE.** The best known ceramic use is in salt glazing. Unglazed pots are fired to a low stoneware temperature and then salt is thrown into the kiln chamber or firebox. The salt dissociates and forms sodium silicate glass on the surface of the ware. The chlorine, combined with moisture, is given off as hydrochloric acid (HCl) and goes up the chimney as a cloud of toxic acid gas. This gas is very poisonous, and can act as a defoliant on nearby plants.

SODIUM DI-URANATE (C). $Na_2O \cdot UO_3$. **TOXIC, RADIOACTIVE.** Colorant—see chapter 14.

SODIUM NITRATE, SALTPETER (F). $NaNO_3$. **SOLUBLE.** A source of sodium which is soluble and usually fritted. See Frits—chapter 6.

SODIUM SILICATE, WATERGLASS (F). $Na_2O \cdot xSiO_2$. A deflocculant, used alone or in combination with sodium carbonate, to change the electric particle charges so that they repel rather than attract or flock; hence this material is called an electrolyte. It reduces the amount of water needed to make a clay liquid, for casting or decorative purposes.

SPAR. See Feldspar.

SPODUMENE (F,A,G). $Li_2O \cdot Al_2O_3 \cdot 4SiO_2$. See Feldspar.

STANNIC OXIDE, TIN OXIDE (O). SnO_2. Opacifier—see chapter 17.

STANNOUS CHLORIDE (C). $SnCl_2$. **TOXIC, SOLUBLE.** A metallic salt used for fuming to achieve iridescence.

STRONTIUM CARBONATE (F). $SrCO_3$. A rare alkaline earth, used as a flux. It is similar in behavior to both calcium and barium, and may be used as both a body flux and a glaze flux. It has similar color responses to those expected from barium, and is non-toxic. This would suggest that it should be a convenient, if expensive, substitute in situations where toxicity is likely to cause problems.

TALC, MAGNESIUM SILICATE (F,G). $3MgO \cdot 4SiO_2 \cdot H_2O$. Steatite, soapstone, French chalk. A secondary flux in glazes, having a strong effect on certain colorants, notably cobalt and nickel. It is also used as a body flux, particularly at low temperatures. It inhibits crazing, and helps develop a smooth, buttery surface in high temperature glazes.

TIN OXIDE, STANNIC OXIDE. Opacifier—see chapter 17.

TITANIUM DIOXIDE (O). TiO_2. Opacifier—see chapter 17.

ULTROX. Opacifier—see chapter 17.

UMBER. A form of ochre with a significant manganese content.

URANIUM OXIDE (C). U_3O_8. TOXIC, RADIOACTIVE. Colorant—see chapter 14.

VANADIUM PENTOXIDE (C). V_2O_5. TOXIC. Colorant—see chapter 14.

VOLCANIC ASH (F,A,G,C). A naturally occurring material used either as a high temperature glaze on its own, or as an ingredient in glazes of a wide temperature range. Like wood ash and granite, volcanic ash contains many trace elements, and is a naturally fritted alumino-silicate. It can be used as a substitute for wood ash in many situations, particularly in glaze bases as suggested for wood ash in chapter 11.

WHITE LEAD. See Lead.

WHITING. See Calcium carbonate.

WOLLASTONITE, CALCIUM METASILICATE (F,G). $CaSiO_2$. A natural calcium silicate, which can be used as a replacement for whiting and flint, to reduce both firing shrinkage and thermal shock resistance in bodies and glazes.

WOOD ASH. See chapter 11.

ZINC OXIDE (F,O). ZnO TOXIC. Zinc is a useful flux from mid to high temperatures. It is very active, producing smooth, trouble-free glazes when used in small amounts. When used as a principal flux in amounts over 25 percent, it may cause crawling, pitting and pinholing (see chapter 12—Faults and Defects). Large amounts are sometimes used to produce mattness, opacity and dry surfaces. Zinc is used as a principal flux in the development of crystalline glazes and has a strong effect on certain colorants. Those faults usually associated with zinc may be improved by calcining up to half of the material to be used.

ZIRCONIUM OXIDE (O). ZrO_2. Not usually used on its own as an opacifier, but used in the formation of zirconium opacifiers, in a fritted form. It is also used in as an ingredient in many stains.

ZIRCONIUM SILICATE (O,G). $ZrSiO_2$. Zirconium silicates are used in glazes to give hard, opaque, white surfaces, in amounts up to 15 percent. They are often used in conjunction with tin and/or zinc as opacifiers (see chapter 17). They are also used in the preparation of stains in conjunction with vanadium, praseodymium and iron, for a range of yellow, coral and blue colors.

The above has been a reference list of the most common materials used in ceramics, and some unusual ones as well. Over a period of time, the glazemaker should develop a good understanding of a significant number of them. Through their continued use, he will evolve an intuitive relationship with them, and, like a good cook, will add with equanimity a pinch of this and a shake of that to improve the quality.

TESTING AND USING
INDIVIDUAL GLAZE
INGREDIENTS

The simplest way to learn about the behavior of raw materials under the influence of heat is to test very small quantities of those glaze materials that are easily available. This can be done by placing small amounts of dry materials on clay tiles, in small cups, or in crucibles, and firing them to the temperatures at which one normally fires pottery.

The firing temperatures selected for materials testing are, of course, an individual choice, related to the needs of the potter and to the flexibility of the firing range of the available kiln. If one's kiln is electric, with a top temperature of cone 6, there obviously would be little point in testing cone 10 glazes designed for reduction. However, if one has a reduction kiln, there would be a much wider range of development potential with the testing programs outlined throughout this book.

For the sake of convenience, and to add to the learning process, it is generally helpful to fire

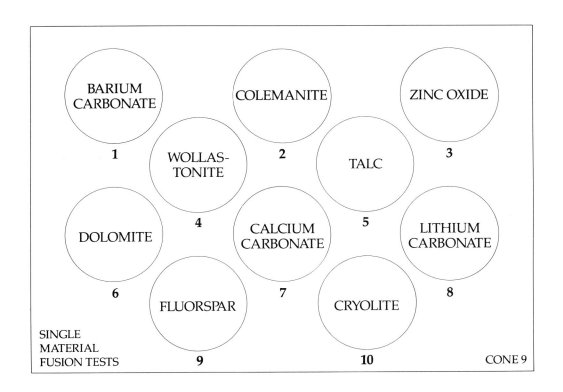

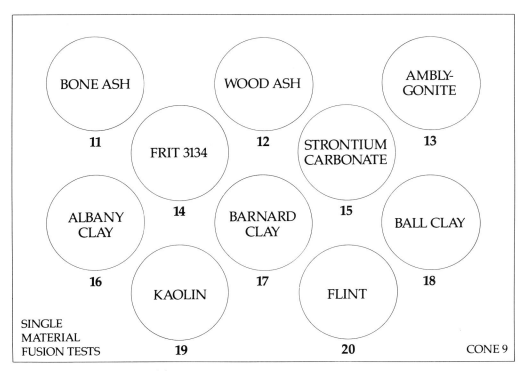

5–1. Layout of single material fusion tests.

the tests within the temperature ranges of cones 04–1, cones 3–6, and cones 8–10. It will be quickly observed that whereas few materials flux or melt at the lower temperatures, most of them will fuse to something approaching glass or glaze at the higher temperatures. Such observations form the important first step in developing a real understanding of material behavior, which will lead to good control of materials for glazemaking.

Everything has a melting point. There are charts and tables which give the melting points of minerals and chemicals available in many books on chemistry and minerals. Many materials used by ceramists are complex mixtures, such as feldspars, wood and volcanic ashes, etc., incorporating the **FAG** Principle in their makeup. These materials need to be tested to determine their fusion point. The most convenient way is to prepare slabs of clay, approximately six inches by four inches, one-half-inch thick, with depressions approximately one

5–2. Single material fusion tests after firing.

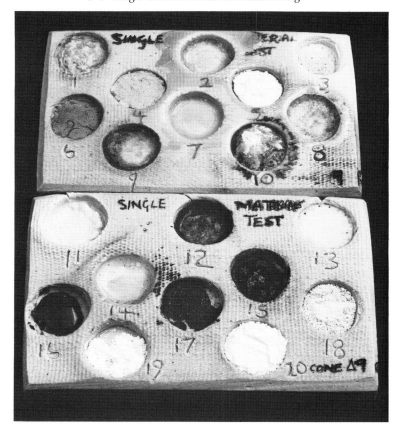

inch in diameter, and a quarter-inch deep, set out as shown in figures 5.1 and 5.2.

The numbers should be scratched into the clay slab, not just painted on, as it will be found that some materials will fume and obliterate painted information. A half-teaspoonful of dry material placed in the depression is all that is needed for initial single material testing. Placing the materials to be tested in a depression eliminates the problem of some of the more fusible materials running over the kiln shelves. The fired test remains as a good basic reference, and will become part of a library of melting patterns of a wide variety of materials.

Almost any material can be tested in this way, even a compound that might not initially seem to offer much potential. My personal credo has always been *Try it and see!* Products such as soap powders, water softeners, photographic chemicals, spray paints, crushed egg shells, local clays and many others offer interesting potential. Some of these materials may be extremely volatile, and only small amounts should be used in initial testing. However, one never knows when one might be stuck somewhere, where the only retail outlet is a grocery store, and the opportunity to purchase refined ceramic materials is nil. It is quite amazing just how much can be done in the creative production of glazes with standard grocery items, particularly when mixed with local clay.

It will be observed that at cone 9 many of the feldspars form an unctuous glass. They can be seen to better advantage if small mounds of the material are created by pressing it into a half-inch chemistry lab crucible (see figure 5.3). This is then inverted onto a tile, and the base tapped until the crucible releases the material, in the same way as children use buckets for making sand castles. Test serial numbers should either be scratched into the clay or previously be written on the back of the tiles with a pigment as described in chapter 4. Learning the "try it and see" approach leads to understanding the empirical method of glaze development, and helps to develop a healthy, inquisitive attitude.

There is often a reticence on the part of the student to see the point of these testing procedures. However, just as a child follows a process of mobilization through first crawling, then standing, walking and later running, so we should also

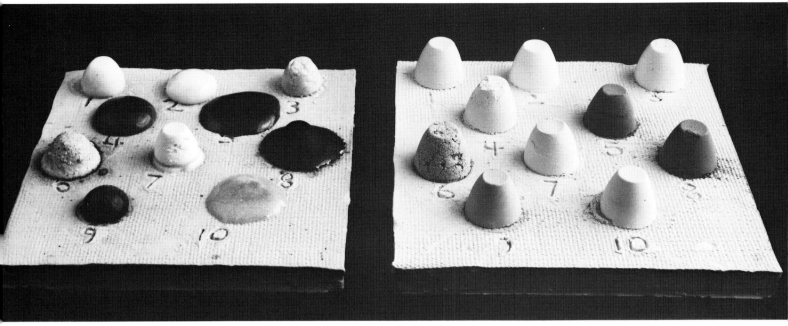

5–3. Feldspar fusion tests before (right) and after (left) firing.

follow the same pattern of growth. No child can go from lying flat on his back to running without the intermediate steps; the novice glaze maker should not expect perfect performance without first experiencing the faltering steps of learning.

The failures and seemingly useless glazes which often materialize during glaze testing should be assessed from other viewpoints which might be more advantageous for later development. All ceramic surfaces have a potential for use, and one person's throwout might be just what another has searched for, to express an idea, or to clothe a form.

Frits

Frits are materials prepared by the ceramic industry for a wide range of products that employ a clay, glass or glaze base. They can be used as an additive to clay bodies to strengthen them, improve the glaze fit, limit problems of glaze defects and lower the vitrification point. Their main use is in glazes, where carefully compounded frits can simplify the glaze preparation for industrial situations. They also promote quicker melting than would occur with the raw materials in the glaze batch. They are the basic material used in the coating of vitreous enamels for appliances such as cooking stoves, and refrigerators, and for a wide variety of other products, where the special qualities of a fused glass surface are deemed desirable.

According to Webster's dictionary, frit is "glass variously compounded that is quenched and ground as a basis for glazes and enamels." Frit has nothing to do with the making of flat glass, glass containers or glass lenses, and is not a step in the making of glass objects. It is not made from the crushing of glass products. Crushed glass is called cullet. Frit, although it sometimes has the appearance of crushed glass, is entirely different in its formulation, processing and end use.

FRITTING MATERIALS FOR CERAMIC USE

Fritting of materials for ceramic use is done for a number of reasons. Many of the chemicals used in the preparation of ceramic glazes, particularly for low temperatures, have undesirable characteristics, such as solubility and toxicity. If they are fused together, the resulting glassy composition eliminates most of the problem aspects of the raw materials.

Frits are made in a simple five-step process. The materials for the frit batch are selected from borax, silica, soda ash, feldspar, boron and so on down a long list of raw materials, according to the desired formula. This mixture is then thoroughly blended and is heated to a temperature in the range of 1200°C., at which point the glass composition becomes molten. The molten glass is then made to flow continuously into water, or through water-cooled rollers, to cool it quickly. Thermal shock shatters the glass; when shattered in water, the frit may resemble coarse salt. When quenched through rollers it looks like small flakes of a broken sheet of very thin glass. The resulting material is then finely ground for its many future uses.

The compositions, or formulas, can vary to an almost limitless degree. The chemicals and minerals selected, the quantities of each, the blending, the smelting rate, and the smelting atmosphere all contribute to the final properties of the frit. But despite the nearly infinite variety of available frits, for ease of reference they are categorized as either lead frits or leadless frits.

The serial numbering of frits made for industrial use by a number of companies all over the world ensures quality control over the fritted material. Thus a frit manufactured by Pemco, Ferro, O'Hommel, or Podmore, and carrying a code or serial number, should have the same chemical composition as the same number frit made by the same company anywhere in the world. See appendix, page 201, for a list of commonly used frit compositions, and comparable frits by Ferro, Pemco, and O'Hommel.

It becomes obvious, when one knows how frits are compounded and the stringency of the quality controls observed during manufacture, that frits can be a real boon to the ceramist who wishes to be sure of his glaze results. They are particularly useful for the person who wishes to work in the lower temperature ranges where few materials melt readily, and those that do, such as borax, boron, and lead, have various properties which cause them to be difficult or dangerous to use.

FRITS IN BODIES AND GLAZES

As stated earlier, frits may be used in both bodies and glazes. Commonly used frits for bodies are Ferro 3110 or Pemco P1505, although many other leadless frits can be used. In earthenware glazes, frits can be used as the primary material, where only the addition of a small amount of clay is needed to bond the raw glaze to the body. They can also be thought of as one material which can be used in the group of materials that cause fluxing action in the formation of glaze at any temperature. They can be used, at low temperatures, in much the same way as feldspar materials are used at high temperatures, or they can be used in combination with one another for specific effect. Thus the potential employment of frits as a glaze material is very wide, and in fact has seen less application than would be expected of such useful materials. Probably the cost of the frits may have something to do with their limited use, but there are often times where slight excesses in cost are more than justified by the results obtained.

Because of the enormous variety of frit formulations to choose from, and the variety of materials they contain, it becomes quite difficult to make choices. However, if one thinks of them as single materials and tests them in the same way as any other single materials already mentioned, their potential use will soon become evident. The only difficulty in this approach occurs when one creates a glaze containing frits only to discover later that certain needed colors are inhibited by materials contained within the frit. On the other hand, some colors are very much enhanced by the right selection of fritted material. These color affecting conditions will be covered in chapters 14 and 16.

It is, of course, possible to develop one's own frits, but it is not a process recommended for the studio potter for a number of reasons. In the first place, the act of pouring molten glass from a crucible into cold water can be dangerous; secondly, toxic dusts or fumes may be given off in the compounding and melting of the materials; and thirdly, frits need to be made in fairly large batches to be a viable proposition. The process is too costly for general use, and industry provides, at reasonable cost, a huge variety for almost any eventuality in the development of ceramic glazes.

7

Eutectics and Glaze Development
with Two Materials

EUTECTIC MATERIAL COMBINATIONS

Glaze development, at any temperature, is totally bound up with a rather obscure and seemingly illogical scientific phenomenon called *eutectics*.

An eutectic is the lowest common melting point of two or more materials, which individually have melting points sometimes considerably higher than that of their mixture. For example, silica melts at 1710°C. and lead oxide melts at 880°C. Logically one would expect a mixture of equal parts of silica and lead to melt at the halfway point of 1295°C., whereas they in fact melt at about 800°C. This temperature is lower than the melting points of both materials, but by no means the lowest eutectic point at which a combination of silica and lead will melt. This point would be reached at approximately

510°C., with a mixture of 90 percent lead and 10 percent silica. Other materials behave in similar fashion in conjunction with silica, causing it to melt at a variety of temperatures. These materials are mainly known as the fluxes, and will be discussed at length in chapter 10. It is an over-simplification to say that the flux attacks and melts the silica, because in reality they react with each other. And it is not only the fluxes which create eutectics with silica; clay materials, or amphoterics, also react in this way, because they also contain fluxing materials in their makeup.

As a glaze is heated, the simplest eutectic combinations will melt first. Once fluid, they will soak into the surrounding material and find other oxides or combinations with which to produce more complex eutectics. This process continues until the whole mass is molten. If it is stopped before the end point, it will be found that some parts have completely melted producing a glass, but within this glass are specks of unmelted material. The overall effect may be a desirable opaque glaze, but the maturity point, where all the eutectic combinations have occurred, would be a transparent and possibly colored glass.

The process of chemical change is basic to the development of glaze, and in the majority of glazes various eutectics are developed during the firing cycle. The theory of eutectics is very complex; for the ceramist it is not essential to understand every detail, but one should be aware that eutectic combinations cause the melting of materials at various percentages and temperatures. One must accept that this is the underlying control mechanism for the temperature at which a glaze matures.

Perhaps the best place to witness the development of some eutectic reactions is in the simple line blend method of glaze development, using two materials. The selection of materials is important,

and should contain a flux and either a glassformer or an amphoteric which contains a glassformer (according to the **FAG** principle—see chapter 5, page 46). This selection will allow eutectics to be formed at a workable temperature. In most cases, but certainly not all, a mixture of two materials will develop in fusion as they move towards the middle of the line blend, as will be shown in the following section. The point of most fusion will be the eutectic.

TWO-MATERIAL TESTING BY THE LINE BLEND METHOD

The line blend is the simplest method for mixing a complete variation of two materials. It is done by increasing the amount of one material while decreasing the amount of the other. It is usually done by increasing or decreasing at 10 percent intervals; the sum of the two materials should always add up to 100, as in the following table:

Test #	1	2	3	4	5	6	7	8	9	10	11
Material A (%)	100	90	80	70	60	50	40	30	20	10	0
Material B (%)	0	10	20	30	40	50	60	70	80	90	100
Total	100	100	100	100	100	100	100	100	100	100	100

7–1. Line blend of two materials. Top line is whiting (left) and nepheline syenite, bottom line is nepheline syenite (left) and wood ash.

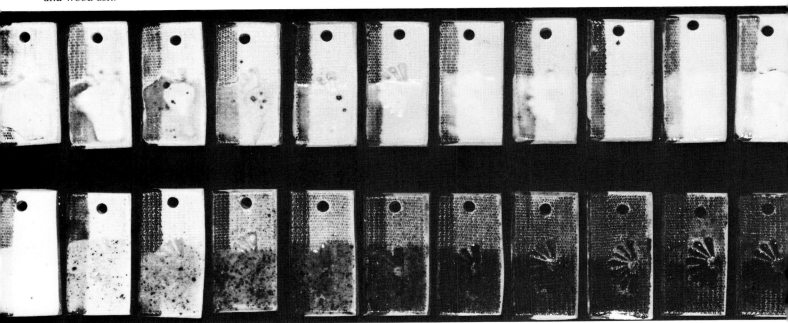

There will be times when the most interesting mixtures could benefit from a smaller interval variation, usually after testing at 10 percent intervals.

This will be found in the area between 80/20 and 20/80, and can be done simply as follows:

Test #	1	2	3	4	5	6	7	8	9	10	11	12	13
Material A (%)	80	75	70	65	60	55	50	45	40	35	30	25	20
Material B (%)	20	25	30	35	40	45	50	55	60	65	70	75	80
Total	100	100	100	100	100	100	100	100	100	100	100	100	100

7–2. Imre Schrammel (Hungary). Heavily textured chamotte stoneware relief. Unglazed, 1200°C.

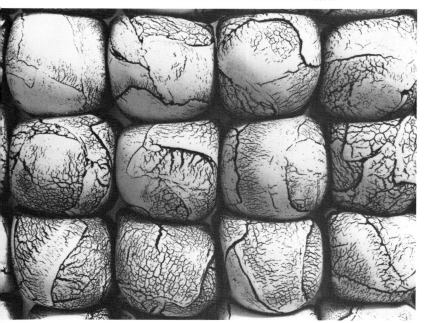

7–3. Ulla Viotti (Sweden). Detail of relief. White stoneware, painted with cobalt oxide, which is then rubbed off with steel wool. Once-fired in electric oxidation at cone 9.

In fact, after the initial understanding of how materials fuse together is achieved, from 100–0 and 0–100, it will be noticed that the section between the 80/20 and the 20/80 variation is probably the area where most usable fusions and glazes develop. Many very beautiful glazes, in all temperature ranges, are simply a matter of combining two materials.

The following list of suggested dual materials for line blend testing will give some idea of where to start in the process. It is divided into *lowfire*, from cone 04–1, *midfire*, from cone 3–6 and *highfire*, from cone 8–11. Where frits are used they should be thought of as one material.

Lowfire Line Blends Cone 04–1

1 Gerstley borate and any clay
2 Gerstley borate and any feldspar
3 Any frit and any clay
4 Any frit and any feldspar
5 Lead and clay (any form of lead—use with care!)
6 Lead and feldspar
7 Any frit and any flux (see materials list, chapter 5)
8 Any frit and flint
9 Borax and any clay
10 Borax and any feldspar
11 Boric acid and clay
12 Boric acid and feldspar
13 Any frit and any other frit
14 Gerstley borate and any frit

In most cases, a mixture of materials which has only just started to fuse at the lowfire temperature will enter a more complete fusion at a slightly higher temperature, and so many of those mixes suggested above could also be used for the midfire area.

Midfire Line Blends Cone 3–6

1 Frit and any clay
2 Frit and wood ash (see also chapter 11, wood ash)
3 Gerstley borate and wood ash)
4 Gerstley borate and any frit
5 Gerstley borate and any feldspar
6 Gerstley borate and red clay
7 Gerstley borate and any other flux
8 Frit and any flux

7–4. Sarah Honeyman (United Kingdom). "Rocking Hare," derived from an Edward Lear limerick, 7 in. high. Porcelain, colored with body stains. Once-fired at cone 7–8. Later fired with overglaze enamels for color details.

9 Wood ash and any flux
10 Wood ash and red clay, or Albany clay

Once again, mixtures where incomplete fusion has taken place at a lower temperature will develop into a more fusible mix at the higher range.

Highfire Line Blends Cone 8–10

1 Wood ash and any clay
2 Wood ash and any feldspar
3 Wood ash and any flux
4 Whiting and any clay

5 Whiting and any feldspar

6 Wollastonite and any feldspar

7 Wollastonite and any clay

8 Cornwall stone and wood ash

9 Any feldspar and any flux

10 Any feldspar and any clay

11 Nepheline syenite and Albany clay, or red clay

12 Cornwall stone and kaolin

13 Porcelain clay body and wollastonite

14 Porcelain body and wood ash

The above lists could have been much longer and more specific as to which frits, which feldspars and which fluxes to use for best results. However, I feel that this would possibly lead to the imposition of limitations, which could inhibit the learning process.

Within the above suggested highfire tests may be found a number of simple and beautiful glazes that are quite similar to some of the earliest and best Chinese glazes of the Han, Tang and Sung dynasties.

8

Triaxial Blends

Triaxial blending of materials is an old process, mainly used for the intermixing of three existing glazes to create a new, fourth glaze. In the same way, the line blend discussed in the previous chapter was also generally used to mix two glazes together. No matter how one uses them, both the line blend and the triaxial are very useful devices for the mixing of raw materials, glazes or colorants.

The triaxial is simply a grid based on the form of a triangle, which in turn has been divided to form smaller triangles. Each point where two lines meet, or intersect, represents a combination of materials, and is given a serial number. Depending on the desired complexity one can use a triangle cut into 10, 15, 21, 28, 36, 45, 55, or 66, or even more points of intersection. However, I have found the 21 point and 66 point triaxial format to be the most useful, the former for either generalized mixing or glaze intermixing, and the latter for the more complex development of new glazes.

Triaxials are easy to understand, since every junction or intersection on the triangle refers to a variation in the quantities of material being used, and in all cases it should add up to 100 percent. This is done to make it easier to add percentages of colorants or opacifiers, if the glaze is to be made colored or opaque.

THE 21-POINT TRIAXIAL GRID

Figure 8–1 shows a 21 point triaxial. Each of the three corners is given a letter, A, B, or C, and each corner is shown to contain 100 percent of whatever material is used in that corner. The line A–B, down the left of the triangle, represents diminishing amounts of material A. The line B–C, at

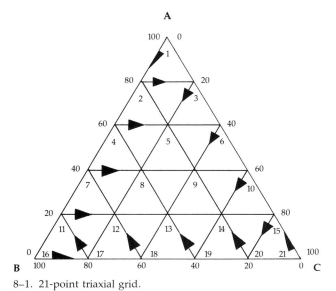

A

8-1. 21-point triaxial grid.

material C is read on the other diagonal lines, parallel to line A–B. It sounds complicated, but it isn't.

Table 8–1 gives the percentages which should be in the material mixture at any given point on the 21-point triaxial.

The 21-point triaxial is also a very useful tool in understanding the process of altering a known glaze. The known glaze is weighed out beforehand, thoroughly dry-mixed, and used as point A on the triaxial. Point B uses silica (flint), and point C uses a clay. The glaze will usually be noticeably affected by the silica, giving a brighter glossy glaze, whereas the added clay content will make it more matt, often dull and cloudy. This is only true up to a certain point, where an excess of either silica or clay will cause mattness. It is useful, however, in learning about eutectic reactions. If one thinks of the glaze being used at point A as a single material, it makes it easier to understand the reactions which occur. It is quite simple to work out the amount of basic ingredients at any point on the triaxial. Since mattness from both excess silica and clay will usually develop by line 11–15, it is probably more useful to make Point A = 100 (known glaze), and point B = 50 (silica), and C = 50 (clay), with a subsequent alteration in the mathematics. In this way a more useful series of reactions is likely to take place.

the base of the triangle, represents diminishing amounts of material B. The line C–A represents diminishing amounts of material C. To read the figure properly, the volume of material A is read on the horizontal lines; the material B is read on the diagonal lines, parallel to line C–A; and the

Table 8-1. 21-Point Triaxial Mixtures

The bold number in top left corner of each box refers to the junction point on the grid in figure 8–1.

1		2		3		4		5		6	
	A 100		A 80		A 80		A 60		A 60		A 60
	B 0		B 20		B 0		B 40		B 20		B 0
	C 0		C 0		C 20		C 0		C 20		C 40
	100		100		100		100		100		100
7		8		9		10		11		12	
	A 40		A 40		A 40		A 40		A 20		A 20
	B 60		B 40		B 20		B 0		B 80		B 60
	C 0		C 20		C 40		C 60		C 0		C 20
	100		100		100		100		100		100
13		14		15		16		17		18	
	A 20		A 20		A 20		A 0		A 0		A 0
	B 40		B 20		B 0		B 100		B 80		B 60
	C 40		C 60		C 80		C 0		C 20		C 40
	100		100		100		100		100		100
19		20		21							
	A 0		A 0		A 0						
	B 40		B 20		B 0						
	C 60		C 80		C 100						
	100		100		100						

8–2. 21-point triaxial blend test.

Table 8-2. 66-Point Triaxial Mixtures—Variation 1

The bold number in the top left corner of each box refers to the crossing or junction points of the 66-point triaxial in figure 8–3.

1 A 100	**2** A 90 B 10	**3** A 90 C 10	**4** A 80 B 20	**5** A 80 B 10 C 10	**6** A 80 C 20	**7** A 70 B 30	**8** A 70 B 20 C 10	**9** A 70 B 20 C 10	**10** A 70 C 30	**11** A 60 B 40
12 A 60 B 30 C 10	**13** A 60 B 20 C 20	**14** A 60 B 10 C 30	**15** A 60 C 40	**16** A 60 C 40	**17** A 50 B 50	**18** A 50 B 40 C 10	**19** A 50 B 30 C 20	**20** A 50 B 20 C 30	**21** A 50 B 10 C 40	**22** A 40 B 60
23 A 40 B 50 C 10	**24** A 40 B 40 C 20	**25** A 40 B 30 C 30	**26** A 40 B 20 C 40	**27** A 40 B 20 C 40	**28** A 40 B 10 C 50	**29** A 30 B 70	**30** A 30 B 70	**31** A 30 B 60 C 10	**32** A 30 B 40 C 30	**33** A 30 B 30 C 40
34 A 30 B 20 C 50	**35** A 30 B 10 C 60	**36** A 30 C 70	**37** A 20 B 80	**38** A 20 B 80	**39** A 20 B 70 C 10	**40** A 20 B 60 C 20	**41** A 20 B 50 C 30	**42** A 20 B 40 C 40	**43** A 20 B 20 C 60	**44** A 20 B 10 C 70
45 A 20 C 80	**46** A 10 B 90	**47** A 10 B 90	**48** A 10 B 80 C 10	**49** A 10 B 70 C 20	**50** A 10 B 60 C 30	**51** A 10 B 50 C 40	**52** A 10 B 40 C 50	**53** A 10 B 30 C 60	**54** A 10 B 10 C 80	**55** A 10 C 90
56 B 100	**57** B 90 C 10	**58** B 80 C 20	**59** B 80 C 20	**60** B 40 C 30	**61** B 60 C 40	**62** B 50 C 50	**63** B 40 C 60	**64** B 30 C 70	**65** B 10 C 90	**66** C 100

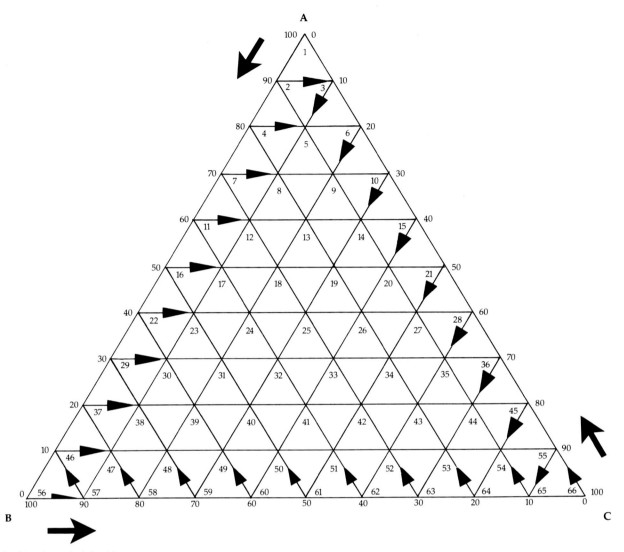

8–3. 66-point triaxial grid.

THE 66-POINT TRIAXIAL GRID

The 66 point triaxial is merely an enlargement of the previous one, where the mixture of materials becomes a little more complex, and thus one can expect a much wider range of results from any test series which uses it. The triaxial in figure 8–3 shows the intersecting points at which each new mixture is made, and is read in exactly the same way as the previous one. The mathematical chart (Table 8–2) relating to the 66 point triaxial gives the mixtures to be found at any one point. It is called Variation 1. The number in the upper left corner of each box refers to the number of the intersection point at

which that particular mixture comes on the triaxial. Variation 2 (Table 8–3) gives the mathematics for a more complex triaxial.

One can also use more than one material in each corner, to further increase the potential of the mixtures. Variation 2 gives the mathematics for using five materials, where the B corner has equal amounts of materials B1 and B2, and the C corner has equal amounts of materials C1 and C2. I have found that by leaving material A as a single material, better results are achieved. These guidelines can be used in an infinite variety of ways, and it is up to the individual to make the decisions as to which materials to select for the corners. However,

Table 8-3. 66-Point Triaxial Mixtures—Variation 2

The bold number in top left corner of each box refers to the crossing or junction points of the 66-point triaxial in figure 8–3.

1	2	3	4	5	6	7
A. 100	A. 90 B1. 5 B2. 5	A. 90 C1. 5 C2. 5	A. 80 B1. 10 B2. 10	A. 80 B1. 5 B2. 5 C1. 5 C2. 5	A. 80 C1. 10 C2. 10	A. 70 B1. 15 B2. 15
8	**9**	**10**	**11**	**12**	**13**	**14**
A. 70 B1. 10 B2. 10 C1. 5 C2. 5	A. 70 B1. 5 B2. 5 C1. 10 C2. 10	A. 70 C1. 15 C2. 15	A. 60 B1. 20 B2. 20	A. 60 B1. 15 B2. 15 C1. 5 C2. 5	A. 60 B1. 10 B2. 10 C1. 10 C2. 10	A. 60 B1. 5 B2. 5 C1. 15 C2. 15
15	**16**	**17**	**18**	**19**	**20**	**21**
A. 60 C1. 20 C2. 20	A. 50 B1. 25 B2. 25	A. 50 B1. 20 B2. 20 C1. 5 C2. 5	A. 50 B1. 15 B2. 15 C1. 10 C2. 10	A. 50 B1. 10 B2. 10 C1. 15 C2. 15	A. 50 B1. 5 B2. 5 C1. 20 C2. 20	A. 50 C1. 25 C2. 25
22	**23**	**24**	**25**	**26**	**27**	**28**
A. 40 B1. 30 B2. 30	A. 40 B1. 25 B2. 25 C1. 5 C2. 5	A. 40 B1. 20 B2. 20 C1. 10 C2. 10	A. 40 B1. 15 B2. 15 C1. 15 C2. 15	A. 40 B1. 10 B2. 10 C1. 20 C2. 20	A. 40 B1. 5 B2. 5 C1.25 C2. 25	A. 40 C1. 30 C2. 30
29	**30**	**31**	**32**	**33**	**34**	**35**
A. 30 B1. 35 B2. 35	A. 30 B1. 30 B2. 30 C1. 5 C2. 5	A. 30 B1. 25 B2. 25 C1. 10 C2. 10	A. 30 B1. 20 B2. 20 C1. 15 C2. 15	A. 30 B1. 15 B2. 15 C1. 20 C2. 20	A. 30 B1. 10 B2. 10 C1. 25 C2. 25	A. 30 B1. 5 B2. 5 C1. 30 C2 30
36	**37**	**38**	**39**	**40**	**41**	**42**
A. 30 C1. 35 C2. 35	A. 20 B1. 40 B2. 40	A. 20 B1. 35 B2. 35 C1. 5 C2. 5	A. 20 B1. 30 B2. 30 C1. 10 C2. 10	A. 20 B1. 25 B2. 25 C1. 15 C2. 15	A. 20 B1. 20 B2. 20 C1. 20 C2. 20	A. 20 B1. 15 B2. 15 C1. 25 C2. 25
43	**44**	**45**	**46**	**47**	**48**	**49**
A. 20 B1. 10 B2. 10 C1. 30 C2. 30	A. 20 B1. 5 B2. 5 C1. 35 C2. 35	A. 20 C1. 40 C2. 40	A. 10 B1. 45 B2. 45	A. 10 B1. 40 B2. 40 C1. 5 C2. 5	A. 10 B1. 35 B2. 35 C1. 10 C2. 10	A. 10 B1. 30 B2. 30 C1. 15 C2. 15
50	**51**	**52**	**53**	**54**	**55**	**56**
A. 10 B1. 25 B2. 25 C1. 20 C2. 20	A. 10 B1. 20 B2. 20 C1. 25 C2. 25	A. 10 B1. 15 B2. 15 C1. 30 C2. 30	A. 10 B1. 10 B2. 10 C1. 35 C2. 35	A. 10 B1. 5 B2. 5 C1. 40 C2. 40	A. 10 C1. 45 C2. 45	B1. 50 B2. 50
57	**58**	**59**	**60**	**61**	**62**	**63**
B1. 45 B2. 45 C1. 5 C2. 5	B1. 40 B2. 40 C1. 10 C2. 10	B1. 35 B2. 35 C1. 15 C2. 15	B1. 30 B2. 30 C1. 20 C2. 20	B1. 25 B2. 25 C1. 25 C2. 25	B1. 20 B2. 20 C1. 30 C2. 30	B1. 15 B2. 15 C1. 35 C2. 35
64	**65**	**66**				
B1. 10 B2. 10 C1. 40 C2. 40	B1. 5 B2. 5 C1. 45 C2. 45	C1. 50 C2. 50				

if one stays within the **FAG** Principle framework (chapter 5) there shouldn't be any real problem. As with the previous chapter, a number of possible avenues for fruitful development are provided, but a great deal of the fun and excitement of glaze making comes from the individual decision on which materials to use where.

General recommendations for materials to use are as follows:

Lowfire	Variation 1	Variation 2
Cone 04–1	A = Any frit B = Any other frit C = Any clay	A = Any frit B1 = Any other frit B2 = Any flux C1 = Gerstley borate C2 = Any clay

Midfire	Variation 1	Variation 2
Cone 3–6	A = Nepheline syenite B = Any frit C = Any clay	A = Any feldspar B1 = Any frit B2 = Any clay C1 = Any flux C2 = Flint

Highfire	Variation 1	Variation 2
Cone 8–10	A = Any feldspar B = Any clay C = Any flux	A = Any feldspar B1 = Any clay B2 = Any flux C1 = Any other flux C2 = Flint

Because of the obviously greater interaction of materials, Variation 2 will generally give the more interesting results. However, a great number of really fine glazes contain only three materials, and using the above guidelines for experimentation should lead to a wide range of glazes from each triaxial.

The following list gives a few possible starting points.

Lowfire Triaxial Blends Cone 04–1

1 Any frit, any other frit, any clay
2 Any frit, gerstley borate, any clay
3 Any frit, any other frit, any feldspar
4 Gerstley borate, any feldspar, any frit
5 Any frit, any other frit, wollastonite
6 Frit, any other frit, dolomite, gerstley borate, clay
7 Frit, any other frit, barium, gerstley borate, clay

8 Frit, gerstley borate, dolomite, clay, feldspar
9 Frit, feldspar, clay, wollastonite, frit
10 Gerstley borate, clay, wollastonite, frit, feldspar

Midfire Triaxial Blends Cone 3–6

1 Nepheline syenite, any frit, any clay
2 Any frit, Albany clay, nepheline syenite
3 Any feldspar, any flux, any frit
4 Any frit, any feldspar, wollastonite
5 Any frit, any feldspar, gerstley borate
6 Feldspar, frit, clay, gerstley borate, flint
7 Feldspar, gerstley borate, clay, barium, flint
8 Nepheline syenite, frit, clay, dolomite, flint
9 Cornwall stone, frit, clay, zinc, flint
10 Feldspar, zinc, clay, frit, flint

Highfire Triaxial Blends Cone 8–10

1 Any feldspar, any clay, wood ash
2 Cornwall stone, red clay, wood ash
3 Dolomite, red clay, barium
4 Cornwall stone, wollastonite, wood ash
5 Spodumene, wood ash, any clay
6 Nepheline syenite, clay, wollastonite, barium, flint
7 Cornwall stone, gerstley borate, clay, dolomite, flint
8 Feldspar, whiting, clay, zinc, flint
9 Feldspar, lithium, clay, whiting, flint
10 Lepidolite, feldspar, clay, wollastonite, flint

The first five groups in each list are for Variation 1, and the second five groups are for Variation 2. In each case the materials are A, B and C, or A, B1, B2, C1, C2, in order, as listed.

If you are using this book as a step-by-step approach to learning about materials and the development of glaze, and have done testing of individual materials, it may occur to you that the nature of glaze development is similar to the process of playing a game of chess. One makes observations, followed by decisions. Many different decisions are possible, and one never knows which alternative might have proved more productive. All moves will lead somewhere, some to a blind alley, some to the elusive king. The more one plays, observes, and makes decisions, the easier it becomes to get to the king. The more games one loses, the more incentive to improve one's game.

9

Quadraxial Blends

A blending method that leads to more complex mixtures than the triaxial grid is called the quadraxial. Instead of working on a triangle basis, a square grid is formed from two line blends at right angles to each other. As with the triaxial, it is, in fact, much simpler than it looks when written. It can also be of varying sizes, but I have found the most use and flexibility from those with either 36 or 121 junctions or intersections on the grid.

THE 36-POINT QUADRAXIAL GRID

The 36-point quadraxial (figure 9–1) works like this. Corner A has 50 percent of material A. Going down the line A–B, material A decreases by 10 percent for each horizontal line to the right. Corner B has 50 percent of material B. Going across the line B–C, material B decreases by 10 percent for each vertical line up. Corner C has 50 percent of material C. Going up the line C–D, material C decreases by 10 percent for each horizontal line to the left. Corner D has 50 percent of material D. Going across the line D–A, material D decreases by 10 percent for each vertical line down. At any junction on the grid, which represents a combination of materials, the total of the materials must add up to 100. The simple mathematics of the 36 point quadraxial grid are given in Table 9–1. Where only two or three materials are shown, the remaining materials are taken to be zero.

As with the triaxial grid in chapter 8, there are a number of suggested mixtures for testing listed later in this chapter, but by now you could make

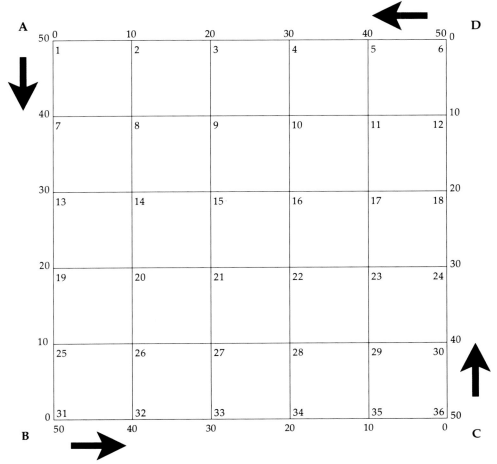

9–1. 36-point quadraxial grid.

an educated guess as to which materials would have the greatest potential.

THE 121-POINT QUADRAXIAL GRID

A larger and much more complete quadraxial is shown in figure 9–3, which works on exactly the same principles as the previous one, but gives a much wider view of what the materials are all doing in the glaze matrix. Depending on the selection of the materials A, B, C and D, it is quite possible to get 121 usable glazes from one quadraxial. Again, depending on the material selection, the glazes developed can cover the complete range of ceramic surfaces: shiny, satin or vellum matt, matt, and dry. They may be clear, translucent, or opaque.

Once again there are two variations, the first(Table 9–2) using single materials in the corners, and the second (Table 9–3) using multiple materials that give a much more complex mix and usually produce the best glazes. The mathematics for the two variations follow the grid chart.

GENERAL RECOMMENDATIONS

There is a definite pattern to these selections or guidelines. General recommendations for materials to use in quadraxial blends are as follows, selected according to the **FAG** Principle (see chapter 5).

	Cone 04–1	
Lowfire	**Variation 1**	**Variation 2**
	A = Any frit	A = Any frit
	B = Any flux	B1 = Gerstley borate
	C = Any frit	B2 = Any clay
	D = Any clay	C1 = Any flux
		C2 = Any other frit
		D1 = Same frit as A
		D2 = Flint

Table 9-1. 36-Point Quadraxial Mixtures

The bold number in the top left corner of each box refers to the junction point of A, B, C, D in figure 9–1.

1	2	3	4	5	6
A 50 B 50 _____ 100	A 50 B 40 D 10 _____ 100	A 50 B 30 D 20 _____ 100	A 50 B 20 D 30 _____ 100	A 50 B 10 D 40 _____ 100	A 50 D 50 _____ 100
7 A 40 B 50 C 10 _____ 100	**8** A 40 B 40 C 10 D 10 _____ 100	**9** A 40 B 30 C 10 D 20 _____ 100	**10** A 40 B 20 C 10 D 30 _____ 100	**11** A 40 B 10 C 10 D 40 _____ 100	**12** A 40 C 10 D 50 _____ 100
13 A 30 B 50 C 20 _____ 100	**14** A 30 B 40 C 20 D 10 _____ 100	**15** A 30 B 30 C 20 D 20 _____ 100	**16** A 30 B 20 C 20 D 30 _____ 100	**17** A 30 B 10 C 20 D 40 _____ 100	**18** A 30 C 20 D 50 _____ 100
19 A 20 B 50 C 30 _____ 100	**20** A 20 B 40 C 30 D 10 _____ 100	**21** A 20 B 30 C 30 D 20 _____ 100	**22** A 20 B 20 C 30 D 30 _____ 100	**23** A 20 B 10 C 30 D 40 _____ 100	**24** A 20 C 30 D 50 _____ 100
25 A 10 B 50 C 40 _____ 100	**26** A 10 B 40 C 40 D 10 _____ 100	**27** A 10 B 30 C 40 D 20 _____ 100	**28** A 10 B 20 C 40 D 30 _____ 100	**29** A 10 B 10 C 40 D 40 _____ 100	**30** A 10 C 40 D 50 _____ 100
31 B 50 C 50 _____ 100	**32** B 40 C 50 D 10 _____ 100	**33** B 30 C 50 D 20 _____ 100	**34** B 20 C 50 D 30 _____ 100	**35** B 10 C 50 D 40 _____ 100	**36** C 50 D 50 _____ 100

	Cone 3–6			Cone 8–10	
Midfire	**Variation 1**	**Variation 2**	**Highfire**	**Variation 1**	**Variation 2**
	A = Any frit	A = Any frit		A = Any feldspar	A = Any feldspar
	B = Any clay	B1 = Any clay		B = Any clay	B1 = Same feldspar
	C = Any flux	B2 = Any flux		C = Any flux	as A
	D = Flint	C1 = Any other frit		D = Flint	B2 = Any flux
		C2 = Flint			C1 = Any other
		D1 = Any other			feldspar
		flux			C2 = Any clay
		D2 = Same frit as			D1 = Any other
		C1			flux
					D2 = Flint

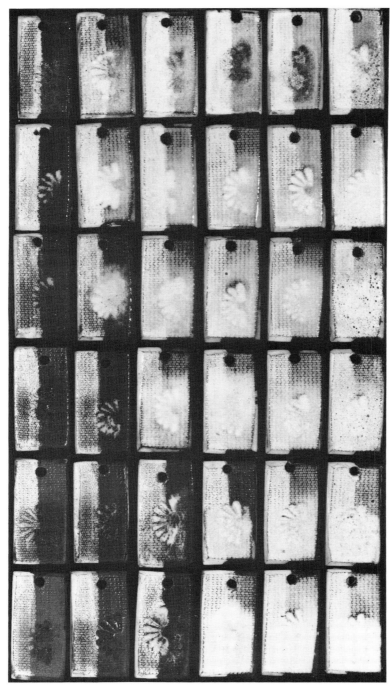

9–2. 36-point quadraxial blend test.

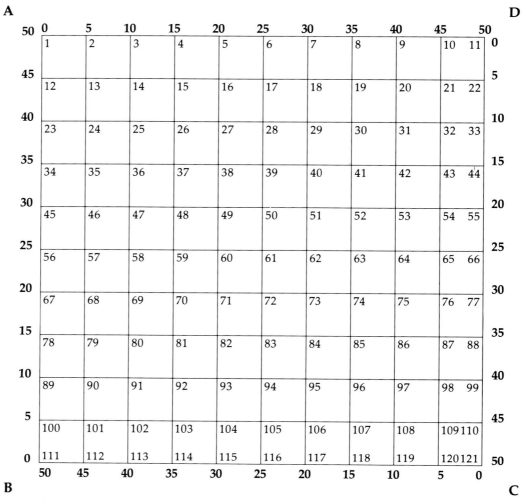

9–3. 121-point quadraxial grid.

Of the many quadraxials that have been tested, some of those that have given particularly satisfactory results are listed below. Gerstley borate may be used as a replacement where colemanite is listed, as the latter sometimes causes problems to occur.

Lowfire Cone 04–1

1 A = Frit, B = Colemanite, C = Frit, D = Clay
2 A = Frit, B = Fluorspar, C = Frit, D = Clay
3 A = Frit, B = Red lead, C = Frit, D = Albany clay
4 A = Frit, B1 = Colemanite, B2 = Ball clay, C1 = Fluorspar, C2 = Other frit, D1 = Frit, D2 = Flint

5 A = Frit, B1 = Colemanite, B2 = Kaolin, C1 = Cryolite, C2 = Other frit, D1 = Frit, D2 = Flint
6 A = Frit, B1 = Colemanite, B2 = Albany clay, C1 = Lithium, C2 = Other frit, D1 = Frit, D2 = Flint

Midfire Cone 3–6

1 A = Frit, B = Albany clay, C = Colemanite, D = Flint
2 A = Frit, B = Kaolin, C = Amblygonite, D = Flint
3 A = Frit, B = Ball clay, C = Colemanite, D = Flint

Table 9–2. 121-Point Quadraxial Mixtures—Variation 1

The bold number at top left corner of each box refers to the junction point of the four elements, A, B, C, D in figure 9–3.

1	2	3	4	5	6	7
A50 B50	A50 B45 D 5	A50 B40 D10	A50 B35 D15	A50 B30 D20	A50 B25 D25	A50 B20 D30
8	**9**	**10**	**11**	**12**	**13**	**14**
A50 B15 D35	A50 B10 D40	A50 B 5 D45	A50 D50	A45 B50 C 5	A45 B45 C 5 D 5	A45 B40 C 5 D10
15	**16**	**17**	**18**	**19**	**20**	**21**
A45 B35 C 5 D15	A45 B30 C 5 D20	A45 B25 C 5 D25	A45 B20 C 5 D30	A45 B15 C 5 D35	A45 B10 C 5 D40	A45 B 5 C 5 D45
22	**23**	**24**	**25**	**26**	**27**	**28**
A45 C 5 D50	A40 B50 C10	A40 B45 C10 D 5	A40 B40 C10 D10	A40 B35 C10 D15	A40 B30 C10 D20	A40 B25 C10 D25
29	**30**	**31**	**32**	**33**	**34**	**35**
A40 B20 C10 D30	A40 B15 C10 D35	A40 B10 C10 D40	A40 B 5 C10 D45	A40 C10 D50	A35 B50 C15	A35 B45 C15 D 5
36	**37**	**38**	**39**	**40**	**41**	**42**
A35 B40 C15 D10	A35 B35 C15 D15	A35 B30 C15 D20	A35 B25 C15 D25	A35 B20 C15 D30	A35 B15 C15 D35	A35 B10 C15 D40
43	**44**	**45**	**46**	**47**	**48**	**49**
A35 B 5 C15 D45	A35 C15 D50	A30 B50 C20	A30 B45 C20 D 5	A30 B40 C20 D10	A30 B35 C20 D15	A30 B30 C20 D20
50	**51**	**52**	**53**	**54**	**55**	**56**
A30 B25 C20 D25	A30 B20 C20 D30	A30 B15 C20 D35	A30 B10 C20 D40	A30 B 5 C20 D45	A30 C20 D50	A25 B50 C25
57	**58**	**59**	**60**	**61**	**62**	**63**
A25 B45 C25 D 5	A25 B40 C25 D10	A25 B35 C25 D15	A25 B30 C25 D20	A25 B25 C25 D25	A25 B20 C25 D30	A25 B15 C25 D35
64	**65**	**66**	**67**	**68**	**69**	**70**
A25 B10 C25 D40	A25 B 5 C25 D45	A25 C25 D50	A20 B50 C30	A20 B45 C30 D 5	A20 B40 C30 D10	A20 B35 C30 D15

Table 9–2. Variation 1, *continued*

71	72	74	75	76	77	73
A20 B30 C30 D20	A20 B25 C30 D25	A20 B20 C30 D30	A20 B15 C30 D35	A20 B10 C30 D40	A20 B 5 C30 D45	A20 C30 D50
78	**79**	**80**	**81**	**82**	**83**	**84**
A15 B50 C35	A15 B45 C35 D 5	A15 B40 C35 D10	A15 B35 C35 D15	A15 B30 C35 D20	A15 B25 C35 D25	A15 B20 C35 D30
85	**86**	**87**	**88**	**89**	**90**	**91**
A15 B15 C35 D35	A15 B10 C35 D40	A15 B 5 C35 D45	A15 C35 D50	A10 B50 C40	A10 B45 C40 D 5	A10 B40 C40 D10
92	**93**	**94**	**95**	**96**	**97**	**98**
A10 B35 C40 D15	A10 B30 C40 D20	A10 B25 C40 D25	A10 B20 C40 D30	A10 B15 C40 D35	A10 B10 C40 D40	A10 B 5 C40 D45
99	**100**	**101**	**102**	**103**	**104**	**105**
A10 C40 D50	A 5 B50 C45	A 5 B45 C45 D 5	A 5 B40 C45 D10	A 5 B35 C45 D15	A 5 B30 C45 D20	A 5 B25 C45 D25
106	**107**	**108**	**109**	**110**	**111**	**112**
A 5 B20 C45 D30	A 5 B15 C45 D35	A 5 B10 C45 D40	A 5 B 5 C45 D45	A 5 C45 D50	 B50 C50	 B45 C50 D 5
113	**114**	**115**	**116**	**117**	**118**	**119**
B40 C50 D10	B35 C50 D15	B30 C50 D20	B25 C50 D25	B20 C50 D30	B15 C50 D35	B10 C50 D40
120	**121**					
B 5 C50 D45	 C50 D50					

4 A = Frit, B1 = Ball clay, B2 = Whiting, C1 = Any frit, C2 = Flint, D1 = Lithium, D2 = Same frit as C1.

5 A = Frit, B1 = Albany clay, B2 = Barium, C1 = Any frit, C2 = Flint, D1 = Zinc, D2 = Same frit as C1.

6 A = Frit, B1 = Kaolin, B2 = Colemanite, C1 = Any frit, C2 = Flint, D1 = Talc, D2 = Same frit as C1

Highfire Cone 8–10

1 A = Custer feldspar, B = Kaolin, C = Whiting, D = Flint

2 A = Cornwall stone, B = Red clay, C = Colemanite, D = Flint

3 A = Feldspar, B = Barium, C = Red clay, D = Dolomite

4 A = Nepheline syenite, B1 = Kaolin, B2 = Dolomite, C1 = Ball clay, C2 = Colemanite, D = Silica

5 A = Feldspar, B1 = Another feldspar, B2 = Talc, C1 = Red clay, C2 = Wollastonite, D1 = Whiting, D2 = Flint

6 A = Cornwall stone, B1 = Cornwall stone, B2 = Colemanite, C1 = Feldspar, C2 = Local or Albany clay, D1 = Dolomite, D2 = Flint

Table 9–3. 121-Point Quadraxial Mixtures—Variation 2

The bold number at top left of each box refers to the junction point of A, B, C, D in figure 9–5.

1	**2**	**3**	**4**	**5**	**6**	**7**
A 50	A 50	A 50	A 50	A 50	A 50	A 50
B1 25	B1 22.5	B1 20	B1 17.5	B1 15	B1 12.5	B1 10
B2 25	B2 22.5	B2 20	B2 17.5	B2 15	B2 12.5	B2 10
C1	C1	C1	C1	C1	C1	C1
C2	C2	C2	C2	C2	C2	C2
D1	D1 2.5	D1 5	D1 7.5	D1 10	D1 12.5	D1 15
D2	D2 2.5	D2 5	D2 7.5	D2 10	D2 12.5	D2 15

8	**9**	**10**	**11**	**12**	**13**	**14**
A 50	A 50	A 50	A 50	A 45	A 45	A 45
B1 7.5	B1 5	B1 2.5	B1	B1 25	B1 22.5	B1 20
B2 7.5	B2 5	B2 2.5	B2	B2 25	B2 22.5	B2 20
C1	C1	C1	C1	C1 2.5	C1 2.5	C1 2.5
C2	C2	C2	C2	C2 2.5	C2 2.5	C2 2.5
D1 17.5	D1 20	D1 22.5	D1 25	D1	D1 2.5	D1 5
D2 17.5	D2 20	D2 22.5	D2 25	D2	D2 2.5	D2 5

15	**16**	**17**	**18**	**19**	**20**	**21**
A 45	A 45	A 45	A 45	A 45	A 45	A 45
B1 17.5	B1 15	B1 12.5	B1 10	B1 7.5	B1 5	B1 2.5
B2 17.5	B2 15	B2 12.5	B2 10	B2 7.5	B2 5	B2 2.5
C1 2.5	C1 2.5	C1 2.5	C1 2.5	C1 2.5	C1 2.5	C1 2.5
C2 2.5	C2 2.5	C2 2.5	C2 2.5	C2 2.5	C2 2.5	C2 2.5
D1 7.5	D1 10	D1 12.5	D1 15	D1 17.5	D1 20	D1 22.5
D2 7.5	D2 10	D2 12.5	D2 15	D2 17.5	D2 20	D2 22.5

22	**23**	**24**	**25**	**26**	**27**	**28**
A 45	A 40	A 40	A 40	A 40	A 40	A 40
B1	B1 25	B1 22.5	B1 20	B1 17.5	B1 15	B1 12.5
B2	B2 25	B2 22.5	B2 20	B2 17.5	B2 15	B2 12.5
C1 2.5	C1 5	C1 5	C1 5	C1 5	C1 5	C1 5
C2 2.5	C2 5	C2 5	C2 5	C2 5	C2 5	C2 5
D1 25	D1	D1 2.5	D1 5	D1 7.5	D1 10	D1 12.5
D2 25	D2	D2 2.5	D2 5	D2 7.5	D2 10	D2 12.5

29	**30**	**31**	**32**	**33**	**34**	**35**
A 40	A 40	A 40	A 40	A 40	A 35	A 35
B1 10	B1 7.5	B1 5	B1 2.5	B1	B1 25	B1 22.5
B2 10	B2 7.5	B2 5	B2 2.5	B2	B2 25	B2 22.5
C1 5	C1 5	C1 5	C1 5	C1 5	C1 7.5	C1 7.5
C2 5	C2 5	C2 5	C2 5	C2 5	C2 7.5	C2 7.5
D1 15	D1 17.5	D1 20	D1 22.5	D1 25	D1	D1 2.5
D2 15	D2 17.5	D2 20	D2 22.5	D2 25	D2	D2 2.5

36	**37**	**38**	**39**	**40**	**41**	**42**
A 35	A 35	A 35	A 35	A 35	A 35	A 35
B1 20	B1 17.5	B1 15	B1 12.5	B1 10	B1 7.5	B1 5
B2 20	B2 17.5	B2 15	B2 12.5	B2 10	B2 7.5	B2 5
C1 7.5	C1 7.5	C1 7.5	C1 7.5	C1 7.5	C1 7.5	C1 7.5
C2 7.5	C2 7.5	C2 7.5	C2 7.5	C2 7.5	C2 7.5	C2 7.5
D1 5	D1 7.5	D1 10	D1 12.5	D1 15	D1 17.5	D1 20
D2 5	D2 7.5	D2 10	D2 12.5	D2 15	D2 17.5	D2 20

The more experience one gets in working with the materials used to make up glazes, the easier glaze-making becomes. The intuitive aspects of individual exploration and the growth of a personal understanding begin to allow creativity and freedom in the use of materials. It offsets inhibiting effects of mathematics, technology and science.

Until this point in this book, I have not been too concerned with the development of color in glaze. However, I should make it clear that in the selection of materials to be put into any glaze, there is more to think about than just how the glaze

Table 9–3. Variation 2, *continued*

	43	44	45	46	47	48	49
A	35	35	30	30	30	30	30
B1	2.5		25	22.5	20	17.5	15
B2	2.5		25	22.5	20	17.5	15
C1	7.5	7.5	10	10	10	10	10
C2	7.5	7.5	10	10	10	10	10
D1	22.5	25		2.5	5	7.5	10
D2	22.5	25		2.5	5	7.5	10

	50	51	52	53	54	55	56
A	30	30	30	30	30	30	25
B1	12.5	10	7.5	5	2.5		25
B2	12.5	10	7.5	5	2.5		25
C1	10	10	10	10	10	10	12.5
C2	10	10	10	10	10	10	12.5
D1	12.5	15	17.5	20	22.5	25	
D2	12.5	15	17.5	20	22.5	25	

	57	58	59	60	61	62	63
A	25	25	25	25	25	25	25
B1	22.5	20	17.5	15	12.5	10	7.5
B2	22.5	20	17.5	15	12.5	10	7.5
C1	12.5	12.5	12.5	12.5	12.5	12.5	12.5
C2	12.5	12.5	12.5	12.5	12.5	12.5	12.5
D1	2.5	5	7.5	10	12.5	15	17.5
D2	2.5	5	7.5	10	12.5	15	17.5

	64	65	66	67	68	69	70
A	25	25	25	20	20	20	20
B1	5	2.5		25	22.5	20	17.5
B2	5	2.5		25	22.5	20	17.5
C1	12.5	12.5	12.5	15	15	15	15
C2	12.5	12.5	12.5	15	15	15	15
D1	20	22.5	25		2.5	5	7.5
D2	20	22.5	25		2.5	5	7.5

	71	72	73	74	75	76	77
A	20	20	20	20	20	20	20
B1	15	12.5	10	7.5	5	2.5	
B2	15	12.5	10	7.5	5	2.5	
C1	15	15	15	15	15	15	15
C2	15	15	15	15	15	15	15
D1	10	12.5	15	17.5	20	22.5	25
D2	10	12.5	15	17.5	20	22.5	25

	78	79	80	81	82	83	84
A	15	15	15	15	15	15	15
B1	25	22.5	20	17.5	15	12.5	10
B2	25	22.5	20	17.5	15	12.5	10
C1	17.5	17.5	17.5	17.5	17.5	17.5	17.5
C2	17.5	17.5	17.5	17.5	17.5	17.5	17.5
D1		2.5	5	7.5	10	12.5	15
D2		2.5	5	7.5	10	12.5	15

fluxes, and whether the glaze is shiny, satin or vellum matt, matt, or dry, in surface. The materials that go into a glaze (mainly the fluxes) also control the way that colorants behave, and the way that the wide range of surface potential develops which makes up the ceramic spectrum.

The ceramist who makes up his own glazes is not so lucky as the painter who mainly works with materials from a tube. The painter mixes his materials to his visual satisfaction, and except for a slight tonal change between wet and dry paint, the color he mixes is the color he wants and the

Table 9–3. Variation 2, *continued*

85	86	87	88	89	90	91
A 15 B1 7.5 B2 7.5 C1 17.5 C2 17.5 D1 17.5 D2 17.5	A 15 B1 5 B2 5 C1 17.5 C2 17.5 D1 20 D2 20	A 15 B1 2.5 B2 2.5 C1 17.5 C2 17.5 D1 22.5 D2 22.5	A 15 B1 B2 C1 17.5 C2 17.5 D1 25 D2 25	A 10 B1 25 B2 25 C1 20 C2 20 D1 D2	A 10 B1 22.5 B2 22.5 C1 20 C2 20 D1 2.5 D2 2.5	A 10 B1 20 B2 20 C1 20 C2 20 D1 5 D2 5

92	93	94	95	96	97	98
A 10 B1 17.5 B2 17.5 C1 20 C2 20 D1 7.5 D2 7.5	A 10 B1 15 B2 15 C1 20 C2 20 D1 10 D2 10	A 10 B1 12.5 B2 12.5 C1 20 C2 20 D1 12.5 D2 12.5	A 10 B1 10 B2 10 C1 20 C2 20 D1 15 D2 15	A 10 B1 7.5 B2 7.5 C1 20 C2 20 D1 17.5 D2 17.5	A 10 B1 5 B2 5 C1 20 C2 20 D1 20 D2 20	A 10 B1 2.5 B2 2.5 C1 20 C2 20 D1 22.5 D2 22.5

99	100	101	102	103	104	105
A 10 B1 B2 C1 20 C2 20 D1 25 D2 25	A 5 B1 25 B2 25 C1 22.5 C2 22.5 D1 D2	A 5 B1 22.5 B2 22.5 C1 22.5 C2 22.5 D1 2.5 D2 2.5	A 5 B1 20 B2 20 C1 22.5 C2 22.5 D1 5 D2 5	A 5 B1 17.5 B2 17.5 C1 22.5 C2 22.5 D1 7.5 D2 7.5	A 5 B1 15 B2 15 C1 22.5 C2 22.5 D1 10 D2 10	A 5 B1 12.5 B2 12.5 C1 22.5 C2 22.5 D1 12.5 D2 12.5

106	107	108	109	110	111	112
A 5 B1 10 B2 10 C1 22.5 C2 22.5 D1 15 D2 15	A 5 B1 7.5 B2 7.5 C1 22.5 C2 22.5 D1 17.5 D2 17.5	A 5 B1 5 B2 5 C1 22.5 C2 22.5 D1 20 D2 20	A 5 B1 2.5 B2 2.5 C1 22.5 C2 22.5 D1 22.5 D2 22.5	A 5 B1 B2 C1 22.5 C2 22.5 D1 25 D2 25	A – B1 25 B2 25 C1 25 C2 25 D1 D2	A – B1 22.5 B2 22.5 C1 25 C2 25 D1 2.5 D2 2.5

113	114	115	116	117	118	119
A – B1 20 B2 20 C1 25 C2 25 D1 5 D2 5	A – B1 17.5 B2 17.5 C1 25 C2 25 D1 7.5 D2 7.5	A – B1 15 B2 15 C1 25 C2 25 D1 10 D2 10	A – B1 12.5 B2 12.5 C1 25 C2 25 D1 12.5 D2 12.5	A – B1 10 B2 10 C1 25 C2 25 D1 15 D2 15	A – B1 7.5 B2 7.5 C1 25 C2 25 D1 17.5 D2 17.5	A – B1 5 B2 5 C1 25 C2 25 D1 20 D2 20

120	121					
A – B1 2.5 B2 2.5 C1 25 C2 25 D1 22.5 D2 22.5	A – B1 B2 C1 25 C2 25 D1 25 D2 25					

color he gets. Not only does the ceramist generally make his own "canvas" to paint on, he also has a host of other phenomena to contend with in the development of his color. It would be so easy if the ceramist could just squeeze out a color. Temperamental kilns, different atmospheres and temperature ranges, and the wide variety of available materials can all create their share of problems.

The next chapter starts to deal with the question of the effect that various fluxes will have in the alteration and control of the color potential of a given glaze.

10

Fluxes, Flux Variations, Flux Saturations

Within the makeup of any glaze, there are some materials that have a profound effect on the development of color. Although the additions of white or light clays and silica do have some effect on color, they generally fall into a neutral, inhibiting, or negative effect, whereas the variations of color potential brought about by the different fluxes are of an enhancing or positive nature. The major "color-affecting" fluxes are alkaline or alkaline earths, lead, boron, magnesia, zinc, barium, and strontium.

ALKALINE OR ALKALINE EARTHS

Alkaline glazes have a high percentage of one or more of the compounds of sodium, lithium and potassium. They are generally glossy, glassy, fluid, brilliant and clear. Due to excessive expansion and contraction, they frequently craze and are difficult to fit to a clay body. It is possible to make a matt alkaline glaze, but other adjustments generally have to be made that will dull some of the brilliance of the color. Lithium crazes less than sodium or potassium and, in small amounts, allows a less fluid glaze, while still giving intense colors. Low levels of alumina in the glaze are also necessary for the best colors. Most alkaline glazes also contain a mixture of other fluxes (lead and boron, for example) in order to produce a more functional glaze.

In glaze batches, alkaline glazes are likely to be high in the following materials:

Sodium	Lithium	Potassium
Nepheline syenite	Lithium carbonate	Potash feldspar
Soda feldspar	Spodumene	Potash
Alkaline frits	Lepidolite	Pearl ash
Borax	Petalite	Niter (saltpeter)
Soda ash	Some alkaline frits	Most wood
Cryolite		ashes
Sodium nitrate		Alkaline frits
Sodium silicate		

LEAD

Lead may be used as the only flux in a very low fired glaze (as low as cone 022). It is a strong flux, and is used the world over for earthenware glazes. It produces smooth, bright, glossy, blemish-free glazes. It has a fairly low coefficient of expansion, and is relatively easy to fit to clay bodies. It can be used in glazes varying from matt to shiny, and from clear to opaque. It has a very strong and pleasant effect on most colorants, allowing pure color to develop.

Lead should not be used in reduction at any temperature, as it converts to toxic lead oxide. It will also cause the glaze to bubble and blister. Similarly, lead should not be used, for either oxidation or reduction, in glazes to be fired above cone 6. At temperatures above cone 6, lead will become volatile and leave the glaze as a gas.

Lead frits are compounded industrially as mono-silicates and bi-silicates. Lead mono-silicates are soluble, and therefore liable to be toxic. Lead bi-silicates are usually insoluble and usually safe, provided that one does not add any other heavy metal colorants to them (see chapter 14).

Transparent lead glazes have a tendency to be yellowish, so additions of alkalines or boron should be added for a perfectly clear glaze. Colors in lead glazes usually have a soft warm look. Transparent lead glazes over red clay look deep red brown.

In glaze batches, lead oxide is usually provided by high lead frits, white lead (carbonate), red lead and lead silicates.

BORON

Boron can be the main flux in a glaze and is similar to lead and the alkalines in its power. It is a strong flux from the lowest to the highest temperatures, although it may give a weak, somewhat soluble glaze. In leadless glazes with high boron, it is recommended that three or more fluxes be used to give glazes durability, if they are to be used for domestic ware. Boron frequently produces a milky blue opalescence. It may also cause a streaked, cloudy quality and mottled effects with colorants. It has less expansion than the alkalines, and is often used in conjunction with lead, to produce hard, smooth, glossy, transparent dinnerware glazes. In reduction, boron gives a slight greenish color to the base, but can still produce brilliant colors.

In glaze batches, boron is usually supplied by colemanite, gerstley borate, boron frits, boric acid and borax.

MAGNESIA

Magnesia in glazes has a strong effect on color and texture, even when used in comparatively small amounts. In lowfire glazes the magnesium acts as a refractory and may make the glaze cloudy, with sugary matt textures. In highfire, smooth buttery glazes may result. Magnesia in glaze batches may be provided by talc (steatite or soapstone), dolomite and magnesium carbonate.

ZINC

Zinc is always used with other fluxes in a glaze, but often its percentage is quite high. In small amounts, zinc acts as a flux and was used to replace lead oxide in Bristol glazes in England, to prevent lead poisoning. In large amounts, zinc can cause mattness. It has good properties of expansion, hardness and durability. It also acts as an opacifier in both oxidation and reduction. Zinc affects some colors in peculiar ways. It turns chromium brown, cobalt grey-blue and iron muddy yellow. Calcined zinc should be added to high zinc glazes to prevent crawling and peeling of glaze due to high wet-dry shrinkage of raw zinc oxide. Zinc adds whiteness to the base glaze, and has the effect of turning colors into opacified pastel-like colors. Zinc in glaze batches is provided by zinc oxide.

BARIUM

Barium acts as a strong flux, usually producing soft, silky, or frosty matts. When used in large amounts, it sometimes causes the glaze to run. When boron is present in the glaze, the barium forms a glassy surface. Barium with lead in lowfire glazes can produce smooth matts. Very high amounts of barium in highfire glazes usually produces smooth dry matts (see Flux Saturations later in this chapter). Barium often gives a base glaze a more noticeable bluish grey color in reduction, due to the way that it pulls iron from the body. Barium produces very brilliant colors in both oxidation and reduction. The only practical source of barium is barium carbonate.

STRONTIUM

Strontium and barium have a similar effect in the glaze, and on the development of color. Strontium may be used in larger amounts than barium, at lower temperatures, and is an active flux from cone 04 to cone 12. It is a non-toxic material and may be used in place of barium where toxicity of materials is a potential problem, although it is considerably more expensive. It is also used as a body flux for a wide temperature range. Strontium is supplied by strontium carbonate.

FLUX VARIATIONS

The specific effect that fluxing materials have on colorants will be discussed at length in chapter 14. Although their potential effect on color is very important, for the time being I am more concerned with how they react as fluxing materials in the glaze melt. This can be demonstrated quite easily in what I call the Flux Variations Method, a process of developing glazes at the higher temperature ranges, where several basic ingredients remain constant and only the flux content is allowed to vary.

This next series of glaze developments was produced by averaging out the contents of 50 stoneware glazes from various books and publications and separating the major color-affecting fluxes from the recipe. The general average of these glazes produced a mixture comprising the following cone 9 base:

Feldspar	35%
Kaolin	12%
Ball clay	17%
Whiting	12%
Flint	7%
Total	83%

The average of the color-affecting fluxes filled the remaining 17 percent, making a total of 100 percent. In this method, as long as the basic unit is kept at 83 percent, the remaining 17 percent can be made up of any single flux, or any mixture of fluxes, provided that they total 17 percent. This allows simple alterations to a basic glaze, and a wide potential range of both color and texture. It also makes it possible to easily add some of the materials that are normally used in small amounts for their special effects, such as cryolite, fluorspar and bone ash.

The initial testing was done primarily for matt glazes, in both oxidation and reduction, and proved so successful that it was further developed for shiny glazes and for glazes at cone 6. This was done by slight alteration of the first average, by removing the kaolin and adding its volume (12 percent) to the flint, for the shiny variation. This change altered the balance of the glaze by increasing the glassformer. For the cone 6 variation, an additional 5 percent of the clay was removed, and its volume added to the whiting, thus decreasing alumina and increasing flux. The chart below shows these comparisons.

Material	Matt Variation Cones 8–10	Shiny Variation Cones 8–10	Variation for Cone 6 Shiny to Matt
Feldspar	35	35	35
Kaolin	12	—	—
Ball clay	17	17	12
Whiting	12	12	17
Flint	7	19	19
Total	83	83	83

To make the glaze up to 100 parts, add any flux or mixture of fluxes to a total of 17, depending on the desired color and texture qualities. This is sometimes best decided on after testing!

The following list gives some of the fluxes and mixtures of fluxes which have been used in this process of glaze development.

1 17% Zinc
2 17% Barium
3 17% Colemanite or gerstley borate
4 17% Dolomite
5 17% Talc
6 17% Wood ash
7 17% Lithium carbonate
8 17% Any frit; several have been used
9 17% Zircopax
10 17% Soda ash
11 17% Volcanic ash
12 17% Bone ash
13 10% Colemanite or gerstley borate, 7% barium
14 12% Colemanite, 5% bone ash
15 7% Colemanite, 5% cryolite, 5% fluorspar
16 7% Talc, 5% bone ash, 5% any frit
17 10% Wood ash, 7% lithium
18 7% Barium, 5% colemanite, 5% fluorspar
19 5% Colemanite, 7% cryolite, 5% amblygonite
20 10% Wollastonite, 7% barium
21 5% Lithium, 5% barium, 7% zinc
22 7% Barium, 7% zinc, 3% lithium
23 5% Fluorspar, 10% barium, 2% lithium
24 10% Frit, 5% cryolite, 2% lithium
25 7% Colemanite, 7% barium, 3% lithium

I could go on with this list, ad infinitum. However, one of the most satisfying things about this process of developing glazes is that although one is working within an almost foolproof framework, the most important decisions as to which materials to use are left to the individual. I have my personal favorites, and use them regularly. Perhaps you will find yours.

FLUX SATURATION GLAZES

Many spectacular glaze effects and colors may be achieved by glazes made with unusually high amounts of some fluxes, particularly at the higher temperature ranges. In many books concerning the subject of glaze development, one often finds materials listed in *limit formulae*. These limits refer to the normal limitations of volume or percentages for given materials in the glaze. Flux saturation glazes use fluxing materials well beyond the normal limit. They will, of course, need testing thoroughly. Reference should be made in this chapter, and in chapters 14 and 16, to the color affecting aspects of the fluxes. As I mentioned earlier, some single materials will fuse to a usable glaze surface, but these materials are few. Mixtures of two materials are likely to prove more useful and, in fact, many glazes are made in this way. A basic **FAG** material (see chapter 5) mixed with high percentages of fluxes should be a good starting point for further development.

The major flux groups are covered earlier in this chapter. Materials from these groups may be mixed with feldspars, and possibly a small amount of kaolin and/or flint, to produce glazes with rich color potential. Because of the low to non-existent clay content in most of these glazes, it may be necessary to add up to 3 percent bentonite or some other suspender (see chapter 12) to keep them in suspension. The following list gives some bases for flux saturation glazes, intended for cone 8–10.

1 Nepheline syenite 50%, barium carbonate 50%
2 Soda feldspar 50%, barium carbonate 50%
3 Soda feldspar 45%, barium carbonate 45%, kaolin 10%
4 Nepheline syenite 60%, barium 30%, lithium 5%, flint 5%
5 Soda feldspar 50%, barium 30%, kaolin 10%, flint 10%
6 Feldspar 35%, barium 40%, zinc 15%, kaolin 5%, flint 5%
7 Feldspar 60%, dolomite 20%, talc 10%, kaolin 10%
8 Spodumene 50%, talc 30%, kaolin 10%, flint 10%
9 Amblygonite 90%, feldspar 10%
10 Soda spar 40%, dolomite 30%, kaolin 20%, flint 10%
11 Feldspar 40%, whiting 40%, kaolin 20%
12 Whiting 50%, feldspar 30%, kaolin 20%

13 Soda feldspar 50%, whiting 35%, kaolin 15%

14 Soda feldspar 45%, zinc 30%, flint 25%

15 Feldspar 50%, zinc 30%, flint 10%, whiting 10%

The above bases which contain barium in high volume are particularly good for the development of brilliant turquoise from copper, yellows from iron, bright blue from cobalt and occasionally dark purple and bright pinkish reds from nickel. Those containing dolomite or talc are particularly good for the development of purple, mauve and lilac from cobalt, yellow browns from iron, grey to orange from copper and lime to olive green from nickel.

Those containing whiting are good with a wide range of colorants, and those containing zinc, barium or combinations of both are likely to form crystalline glazes, particularly with additions of rutile or nickel.

Many other variables are possible, such as the line blends shown in chapter 7, as well as simple half and half mixtures of a great many materials. The above bases are just starting points for further exciting exploration. One note of caution before firing glazes such as these: it is wise to make certain that the kiln shelves are well protected, as there may be some running.

11

Wood Ash and Glazes for Once-Firing

Wood ash or, more correctly, ash from organic vegetation, has been used as an ingredient for the development of glazes for at least two thousand years. Glazes utilizing wood ash are firmly rooted in the ceramic traditions of the orient, and have been described in many publications dealing with oriental glazes.

Organic ashes come from the burnt remains of trees, bushes, grasses, and even vegetables. Since their cellular structure gets its mineral sustenance from the soil, it is logical to assume that the residue or ash from the burnt matter contains those minerals also. Different plants absorb different amounts of minerals, and even ashes from the same type of plant taken from different sites, or at different times of the year, will vary considerably in their chemical content. With these variables in mind, organic ash is likely to contain mineral oxides in following amounts:

Silica	30–70%
Alumina	10–30%
Calcium	up to 30%
Potassium	up to 15%
Phosphorous	up to 13%
Magnesia	up to 10%
Iron	up to 5%

There would almost certainly be various trace elements of other mineral oxides present. These mineral oxides are all materials fundamental to glazes, and can be easily seen to fit into the **FAG** principle. In fact, all organic ashes will turn to glaze at a temperature between cone 6 and cone 10.

Perhaps the simplest form of ash glaze, other than the natural deposits of ash that occur in a wood-fired kiln, is created by spraying pots with wood ash, or painting a pot with glue and rolling it in sieved ash, shaking off the excess and firing to cone 9. At this temperature the ash will easily melt and the result, to the non-purist, is almost indistinguishable from pottery fired in a wood-firing kiln. I remember visiting a well-known pottery in Japan renowned for its wood-fired pots, and seeing a woman swathed in indigo cloth spraying wood ash in a fairly thick coating onto the pots. The pots, I subsequently found out, were going to be fired in an electric kiln!

MAKING WOOD ASH GLAZES

There are very simple ways of making glazes by the use of wood ash alone, or ash can be a major or minor ingredient in a recipe. While ash will melt readily at higher temperatures, at lowfire it can only be used as a minor material to give special qualities in conjunction with low temperature fluxes. Many people have spent a great deal of time studying ash glazes in the processes of collection, burning, analyzing, washing and using. Depending on one's personal reasons for the making of ash glazes, whether for research, refinement, general use, or to develop a surface similar to that of wood-fired ware, one may be either very careful or very lax in the collecting and processing. But there are a number of steps which should be followed to make ash a usable glaze ingredient.

1. COLLECTING THE RAW MATERIAL FOR BURNING

Material should be collected in a large volume to ensure that there is enough residual ash to be of use. It takes quite a lot of combustible material to get enough residual ash for even a fairly modest amount of prepared ash. If you want to be able to duplicate your results, make a note of the type of material, site, and date of collection.

11–1. David Shaner (U.S.A.). Vase, 12 in. high. Wood-fired stoneware. No glaze except fly ash.

11–2. Shigaraki. Japanese production soup or noodle bowl. Stoneware, glazed with fly ash only. Collection of the author.

2. BURNING THE RAW MATERIAL

The material should be burnt on a dry, clear, windless day, on an area such as a cement slab or cement blocks where there will be as little contamination as possible from other sources. Material burnt in iron grates or garbage bins is likely to become contaminated with, and subsequently colored by, iron scale from the rust invariably present. Light the fire and allow it to burn completely, raking unburnt material to the center of the fire, so that as much turns to fine grey ash as possible. Collect the fine ash as soon as it is cool. If it looks as though it might rain before the ash is collected, the ash should be covered by something non-combustible, as rain will leach some of the minerals from the ash.

3. SEIVING THE DRY COLLECTED ASH

In order to remove the charcoal and other heavy, partially burnt material from the ash, it is best to first screen it through an ordinary garden sieve of approximately half-inch mesh. After this it can be screened through a kitchen flour sieve, until only a fairly fine powder remains. A dust mask and eye protection should be worn when dry sieving ash; it is a caustic material which can easily damage eyes and lung tissue.

11–3. Ruth Gowdy McKinley (Canada). Teapot, porcelain cone 10. Glazed with rutile colored barium matt glaze. Wood-fired, ash markings and crystalline formation from fly ash. Collection of the author.

4. WASHING THE ASH

There are two differing views on whether ash should be washed or not. When it is washed, various soluble alkaline materials are removed in solution with the washing water, and many feel that one is throwing away precious trace ingredients and fluxes. The reasons for removing these materials are, one, that they might enter the pores of the clay body and create various problems when they melt, and two, that they are caustic. However, this is a personal choice generally best made from the experience of doing it both ways. Personally, I prefer to use unwashed ash, with the soluble materials intact.

Whether washing ash or using unwashed ash, it is important to wear rubber gloves. Ash materials can easily cause skin problems from even short contact. When I was new to making ash glazes, I worked at sieving a large amount of ash, in water, with no protection. After an hour or so, my hands started to itch, and a little while later blood started to seep from the pores on the back of my hands. The net result was an inability to work for three weeks while they healed. So precautions are important!

The usual process of washing ash is to put it into a plastic container and cover with water. After a day, remove floating particles and discard them. Let the ash soak for a week, then replace the water, and soak for another week. Repeat this process until the water is clear and has lost any soapy feeling. By this time there should be little or no soluble caustic materials left, so there should be no risk from them.

5. DRYING THE ASH

After washing is complete, the water is siphoned off and the remaining sludge dried out, using bisque-fired bowls or plaster drying bowls. When dry, it is sieved through a 60 or 80 mesh screen and stored for use.

USING ASH AS A GLAZE
INGREDIENT

The process of washing, drying and sieving is generally that followed by people who are being very careful in the preparation of the ash they use. However, it is not strictly necessary if the ash is not going to be washed for the removal of soluble alkalies. In this case, the collected ash, from whatever source, can be merely sieved through a 30 mesh screen and used directly. Ash used in this way will probably be somewhat gritty, but it usually smooths out in the firing and creates different textures from ash which is finely prepared. It is important to remember to wear rubber gloves when using glazes containing unwashed ash.

It should be remembered that because ash is a highly variable material, enough should be collected at one time for a reasonable future supply. It can be frustrating when one has developed a really fine glaze and the source of the ash disappears. For several years, I used a glaze which I made with equal parts ball clay and ash from the fireplace of a local pub, consisting mainly of the ash from the sawdust used to soak up the spilled beer and whatever other sundry material was swept up. I moved away from that location, and never did find another comparable supply. The beautiful

pale, grey-green glaze, with yellow-green fluid markings, was never the same again.

Since ash is a complex material, which, on its own, is capable of producing very interesting effects, it follows that simple additions of other materials, to add to the melting or to add color and texture, may be all that is needed for the prodution of subtle and interesting glazes.

It is quite simple to develop glazes using ash as a major ingredient by the line blend, triaxial and quadraxial methods as outlined in chapters 7, 8, and 9, and in the Flux Saturations section of chapter 10. Because of its infinite variation, ash is always an exciting material to use and responds to glaze coloration in interesting ways. Here are a few possible mixtures for ash glazes, which will give a wide variety of surfaces and color potential at the higher temperature ranges.

Ash Glaze Development Cones 8–10

1. Ash and any clay—line blend
2. Ash and feldspar—line blend
3. Ash and nepheline syenite—line blend
4. Ash and cornwall stone—line blend
5. Ash, feldspar and clay—triaxial
6. Ash, feldspar and whiting—triaxial
7. Ash, feldspar and dolomite—triaxial
8. Ash, feldspar and barium—triaxial
9. Ash, 2 parts; feldspar, 2 parts; clay, 1 part
10. Ash, 2 parts; feldspar, 2 parts; whiting, 1 part
11. Ash, 2 parts; feldspar, 2 parts; dolomite, 1 part
12. Ash, 2 parts; feldspar, 2 parts; barium, 1 part

For glazes in the lowfire range the use of ash is more limited, due to its lack of fusion at the lower temperatures. However, it can be used with great success in glazes where there is a good deal of other fluxing material, and can provide a very interesting subject for study and use. Here are a few suggestions for glazes developed with ash at lowfire.

Ash Glaze Development Cone 04–1

1. Ash and any frit—line blend
2. Ash and colemanite or gerstley borate—line blend

11–4. John Leach (United Kingdom). Wood-fired store jars, glazed inside. Outside glazed only with fly ash from the firing.

3 Ash and borax—line blend
4 Ash and lead—line blend
5 Ash, frit and gerstley borate—triaxial
6 Ash, frit and red clay—triaxial
7 Ash, gerstley borate and lead—triaxial
8 Ash, 1 part; frit, 2 parts; colemanite, 1 part
9 Ash, 1 part; frit, 2 parts; red clay, 1 part
10 Ash, 1 part; frit, 2 parts; any flux, 1 part

Much of the quality of ash glazes lies in their rather individual and changeable nature, fluid

11–5. Robin Hopper (Canada). "Krater." porcelain, 13 in. high. Once-fired with slip glaze made from porcelain clay, barium and lithium. Sprayed with rutile and copper.

quality, and intriguing effects on color and surface, mainly from the all-important trace elements, particularly phosphorous. Exciting surface effects can also be developed using the natural fusion, at high temperatures, of organic materials applied directly to the surface of the clay. Techniques of wrapping pots in brine-soaked straw have long been used by the Bizen potters of Japan. The combination of salt and ash leaves calligraphic markings on the clay. Most organic materials will leave enough ash to fuse and make flashings of color and glaze. They do not need to be soaked in salt to fuse. Similar fuming effects can be obtained by placing pieces of bone on the unglazed ware, and firing to cone 8–10. The bones will shrink considerably, usually leaving tracings and fumings from their calcination.

GLAZES FOR ONCE-FIRING

Glazes for "once-firing," or "raw-glazing" as it is sometimes called, can provide the ceramist with certain economical advantages in both fuel costs and in the time spent in handling the wares. Most important, it can be done without detrimental effect to either the aesthetic or functional quality of the ware.

There are two reasons why once-firing is not all that common. One is that the work has not previously been bisque fired; thus, certain difficulties in the handling process become evident. The other is that in order to be sure that the glaze adheres satifactorily to the body, and will shrink at the same rate as the body, the glaze will normally require a fairly large amount of clay in it. Although the high clay content undoubtedly has the effect of limiting some of the glaze pallette, once-fired glazes may be colored in all the usual ways.

There are many who prefer the once-firing process because of its immediacy. The work may be fresh in maker's mind, so that a more spontaneous result develops. For others, many surface decoration techniques, such as carving, sgraffito, some slipware techniques and glaze trailing, seem to work particularly well with it. Once-firing glazes are also good in conjunction with the vapor glazing processes of salt and sodium firing.

11–6. Hans Coper (United Kingdom). Envelope form, stoneware, 9 in. high. Once-fired with multiple application of
white slip glaze, and manganese rubbed into the textured
surface. Fired in electric kiln at approximately cone 8. Collection of the author.

What makes a good starting point for once-firing glazes? Basically, any glaze that has a clay content of 20 percent or more will probably work quite well as a once-firing glaze. Many naturally occurring clays, such as Albany clay and surface clays found close to streams and rivers, can be used with little or no additions as once-firing clays at high temperatures. Many of the glaze bases suggested throughout this book that contain a fairly high percentage of clay work well when used in single firing.

Problems arise with the handling of the object when wet, and with the clay of the object itself, which may not be particularly amenable to absorbing fairly large amounts of water. It will be necessary to find a clay which has enough green strength to neither crack nor distort when it is coated with glaze. Some clays are best glazed when bone dry, and others when the ware is in a leather-hard condition. The only way to find the solution to all these questions is by trial and error.

The best pointers to the successful development of once-fired glazes, for use at any temperature, are:

1 Use a clay body which has not been opened with more than 10 percent grog and preferably contains at least 20 percent of ball clay.
2 Use a glaze base which contains at least 20 percent clay.
3 Mix the glazes with as little water as possible, even to the point of adding a small amount of deflocculant such as sodium silicate (1 percent maximum of the overall weight or 0.2 percent of the clay content—more may cause a gel to develop).
4 Do not apply too thickly. The glaze might flake off, leaving bald patches on the work and glaze on the kiln shelf.

12

Alterations, Glaze Properties,
Faults and Defects

Exceptional cooks alter recipes to suit their needs and taste. Exceptional ceramists do likewise, in the pursuit of a special, elusive quality. You may want to modify a glaze recipe to simplify the mixture, change the firing temperature, alter the fluxes, change the glaze surface quality, improve glaze fit, or to substitute materials when those suggested in a recipe are not available.

Glazes can be altered in a number of ways and for a variety of reasons. However, it should be remembered that when one alters a glaze, there is almost certainly going to be some change in the way that the glaze will respond to color development and in the way that it will flow on a vertical surface. Faults and defects may occur in the process of altering, requiring new solutions. There are many generalities in this chapter, because for each new glaze alteration, there is inevitably a new set of questions. For each new question, there can be several answers. As you will have seen by now, there are no absolute solutions, and every alteration demands exploration.

GLAZE ALTERATIONS

Some of the most common and reliable methods for altering glazes are covered below.

SIMPLIFYING THE MIXTURE

When a glaze is developed through calculation methods, it will often have numbers following the decimal point, as in the following commonly used High Alumina Matt glaze from *Clay and Glazes for the Potter*, by Daniel Rhodes.

Feldspar	48.9
China clay	25.1
Dolomite	22.4
Whiting	3.5
	99.9

This glaze can be easily simplified to either of the following, with little discernible difference in quality, but with much easier measuring.

Alteration 1

Feldspar	50
China clay	25
Dolomite	20
Whiting	5
	100

Alteration 2

Feldspar	50
China clay	25
Dolomite	25
	100

Many ceramists around the world are using either of the above slight modifications of the original, and the principle used here works for all glazes which I have worked with. I have altered standard recipes in this way for many years and have had no problems in the process. I simply remove all decimal points and round off to the nearest whole number, or nearest multiple of five; for example, china clay went from 25.1 to 25, and dolomite from 22.4 to either 20 or 25, purely to aid in simple addition. The rationale behind these changes in the above glaze relate to the chemical constituents of whiting and dolomite. Both materials are calcium, although dolomite also contains approximately 50 percent magnesium. Making minor alterations in these two fluxes has little effect on the melt of the glaze. There might be a small effect on the color potential, particularly with cobalt, when the glaze is made up without whiting, but there is negligible effect on other qualities.

The concept of this form of glaze alteration is more important than the actual recipe given above, because many other fluxes could be interchanged with the dolomite and calcium, with obviously different results. It could be a very good exercise, rather like the section on flux variations in chapter 10, to maintain the feldspar at 50 percent, the kaolin at 25 percent, and make up the balance by the addition of any flux or combination of fluxes. Limitless variations are possible, and it all becomes part of the creative play process of individual glaze development.

CHANGING THE FIRING TEMPERATURE

To raise the firing temperature, add refractory materials such as kaolin or ball clay. This can be easily done in percentage increments of 5, 10, 15 and so on until the glaze is altered enough to fire at the desired temperature. Alterations like this will undoubtedly affect the color potential of the glaze to some extent.

Lowering the firing range in glazes is generally done by removing some of the refractory materials, increasing silica or fluxes, or using more active fluxes which will fuse at a lower temperature. In some circumstances, it is possible to increase the volume of some of the fluxes. However, the erratic behavior of many fluxing agents causes a reversal in melting characteristics at a given point, after which any greater addition of the same flux will usually cause the glaze to fuse less. The reason lies with the development of eutectics within the glaze, and their seemingly illogical behavior (see chapter 7). These variations make the simplistic approach to glaze alteration unpredictable in these cases. One of the most useful active fluxes for this form of alteration, and one which works at almost any temperature, is colemanite, or its near cousin, gerstley borate. These materials have an extremely wide temperature range. For highfire glazes, the substitution of nepheline syenite for other forms of feldspathic material will generally lower the firing range by a cone or two. Midfire glazes can be lowered by substituting frits or colemanite for feldspathic materials.

ALTERING THE FLUXES

As demonstrated in chapter 10, altering the fluxes is one way of developing the color potential of a given glaze, and it is one where much research needs to be done. I have found that interchanging the color-affecting fluxes up to 20 percent can radically alter the color potential of the glaze, as well as its surface quality. Some of the more potent materials such as cryolite, fluorspar and lithium are best used in only small amounts up to 5 percent, where they will have a profound effect.

CHANGING THE GLAZE SURFACE QUALITY

Making a glaze more matt requires the same procedures as increasing the firing temperature. By adding refractory materials, such as kaolin, the glaze is made temperature sensitive, as it is in effect being slightly underfired. It is probably better to use one of the fluxes which produce mattness in glazes. These are calcium, magnesium and barium. If the glaze contains calcium, increase the calcium to form a "lime matt." A "lime matt" is likely to develop in a high temperature glaze when the calcium content is over 20–25 percent, depending upon which other fluxes are in the glaze. Calcium can also be used in lowfire glazes as a matting agent, as it is refractory at low temperatures. Glazes which are matted by the use of magnesium may develop a smooth buttery surface, while glazes matted with barium will usually form frosty surfaces. If there is boron present in the glaze, barium may not work as a matting agent; a reaction can take place between the two that increases the gloss.

Making the glaze more shiny can be achieved in the same way as lowering the firing range. Decrease the refractory materials, calcium, magnesium and barium, and/or increase the other fluxes.

IMPROVING THE GLAZE FIT

To eliminate glaze problems such as crazing and shivering, see Faults and Defects in this chapter (page 100).

DESIRABLE PHYSICAL CHARACTERISTICS OF GLAZES

Regardless of the firing temperature, there are certain properties that should be considered at the time of glaze formulation, which relate to the working properties. A glaze that doesn't behave reasonably well before firing is likely to cause considerable annoyance. The desirable physical properties of a glaze include good suspension and adhesion, and low fragility. Occasionally, improvements in

one or more of these areas leads to the problem of glaze fermentation, discussed below. Note that as a general rule, very small additions of corrective materials (1 to 5 percent) are ample to make a profound difference to the pleasures of working with a delinquent glaze.

SUSPENSION

Does the glaze stay in a state of suspension while in use? Or does it continually settle to a rock hard mass at the bottom of the container, steadfastly refusing to budge? Settling often happens to a glaze with little clay because the heavy particles tend to sink. It can be improved by the addition of various materials called flocculants, such as epsom salts (magnesium sulphate), water softener (such as Calgon), carageenan (a form of seaweed), Sea Spen, Setit-A, bentonite, gum arabic, gum tragacanth, and cellulose gum (such as CMC).

Some flocculants will undoubtedly alter the fired glaze, often affecting the *color potential*. Adding clay to the glaze will definitely do this. A small amount of bentonite, however, is unlikely to change the surface, although it may affect the color. Bentonite should always be added to the dry materials before adding water, otherwise it will not mix properly. A gum solution can be made by adding gum tragacanth or cellulose gum to hot water; let this sit overnight to mix thoroughly before adding to the glaze. Gum arabic needs to be mixed with alcohol to go into a properly dispersed solution. There are various proprietary brands of suspender such as Setit-A, Sea Spen and CMC gum, which should be mixed according to manufacturers' directions.

ADHESION OR COAT

The thin film of raw glaze that covers the clay object needs to be sufficiently bonded to the surface to facilitate ease of handling. Glaze flaking is usually found when the glaze has either little or no clay in it, or conversely has an overload of clay. In the first instance, the glaze will be fragile, powdery and loose. In the second, it sometimes will have a network of fine cracks where the glaze has shrunk away on drying. Adding some clay, in the first case, or removing some, in the second, should improve the situation. Using some part of the clay content in calcined form should also help. Some of the suggested additions for keeping a glaze in suspension will also help here, notably gums and Sea Spen seaweed suspender.

FRAGILITY

Glaze fragility is a concern when multiple layers of glaze are contemplated. If one intends to paint on top of the glaze, in the Majolica fashion, one needs a surface that allows the application of color without the worry of the wet brush removing the glaze at the same time as it adds the color. This can be achieved in various ways. First, the glaze needs to have at least 10 percent clay in it, so that it becomes less powdery. If this is likely to upset the desired quality of the glaze, it can instead be applied as usual, then sprayed with a thin coat of a solution of gum, honey, sugar, size or cornstarch mixed with water, before decorating. These materials may also be added directly to the glaze to form a hardening coat. This allows easier, more fluid movement of the brush, and doesn't grab and suck. Note, however, that the glaze may start to ferment with these organic materials, and a bacteriostat such as formalin will be needed.

FERMENTATION

Very occasionally, a glaze will start to ferment. As mentioned above, this may be due to some of the organic matter, such as gums, cellulose, carbonaceous matter, or wood ash, decomposing in the glaze. It is a fairly unusual occurrence, and may be remedied by drying out the glaze completely, then remixing with a small amount of formaldehyde, in the form of formalin solution added to the water. Without doing anything, the glaze will still work, but it will have a pungent aroma. This may be masked with a little oil of wintergreen, or oil of clove.

FAULTS AND DEFECTS

One person's fault is often another person's fancy! Except in those cases where a glaze needs to be faultless for some reason of hygiene, the industrial ideal of perfection has been a stultifying influence on the creative exploration of ceramic surfaces. A surface that might be considered defective on one object can be very exciting on another. It is for this reason that one should look very carefully at all aspects of glaze tests before discarding anything as worthless.

One only has to think of Chinese crackle glazes or the Shino and Nuka glazes of Japan, which show crazing, pinholing and crawling of glazes to wonderful aesthetic effect. Western civilization is unfortunately less in tune with the natural world and the serendipitous nature of the transformation process that occurs in a potter's kiln. We have not been ready to view these so-called glaze faults in such an open-minded way as the Oriental, and as a result, wares which have them usually end up without buyers. It is a sad reflection on the lack of sensitivity of the West that naturally occuring blemishes are looked on as suspect. Has one ever seen a perfect face, or perfect skin?

The ceramist generally recognizes some of the positive qualities of imperfection, but is more often than not harassed by the retailer of his work, as an intermediary with the public, into the belief that these occurences are all defects. If the ceramist is producing functional ware in which glaze faults create any kind of health hazard, the retailer may be right. However, the same qualitative judgments on glaze surfaces are often used as criticism of surfaces which have no pretense of function. It is up to the ceramist to educate the buying public to the fact that glazes do not have to be slick, sanitary and soulless; they can and should have qualities which closely relate to the imperfections of people we love.

We generally talk about pots in anthropomorphic terms, with feet, bellies, waists, shoulders, necks and lips. If we move further along these lines, we can think of the glaze of a pot as its skin. If one then thinks of all the variety of skin textures which give individuality to the human race, one can easily see the analogy.

DETERMINING THE CAUSE

The best start in the process of detecting why a fault occurs is to break a piece of the work and look at the cross section carefully. This can be done with a magnifying glass, under a microscope, or, for some faults, with the naked eye. A cross section can reveal problems quickly, and learning to read a shard is an important skill.

There are several reasons, all very logical, why a particular glaze fault may occur, but trying to deduce the cause of a fault from a single piece may prove quite difficult. When there are a number of pieces available, all of which have the same glaze and come from the same kiln load, or when there are several different glazes being used on a single clay body, the detective process becomes much easier. The following section outlines several factors which can cause faults or defects. Faults which appear to be glaze related may result not only from the composition of the glaze, but also from the improper selection and preparation of the clay body, from faulty kiln operation, or, as is often the case, from lack of skill and care in application.

GLAZE DEFECTS DUE TO THE BODY

1 A body that is too porous because of improper wedging, kneading, blunging, or pugging, may be the cause of small bubbles, beads, and pinholes forming in the glaze. As the body contracts, its gases need to escape; in some cases, they force themselves through the still porous body. I can't say that I have ever seen this, at least to be certain of the cause, but others have claimed its existence. It is said to be quite common in low temperature clays. Firing the bisque to one or two cones above the lowfire glaze temperature should resolve it.

2 An excessive amount of manganese dioxide used as a colorant in a body or slip will cause bloating of the clay, and may also cause blistering of the glaze.

3 Soluble sulfates which are contained in some clays come to the surface in drying, forming a white scum. Pinholes and bubbles are created as these sulfates react with the glaze, forming gases. This condition may be corrected by the addition, to the body, of 1–2 percent of barium carbonate. A slight reduction fire at the point at which the glaze begins to melt will reduce the sulfates, and allow the gas to pass off before the glaze develops a glassy re-

taining film. The sintering or beginning point of the glaze melt depends upon the glaze being used. In low temperature glazes, it will be at about 800–850°C.; in mid-fire glazes, it will be at about 950–1000°C.; and in high temperature glazes, about 1050–1100°C.

4 If the body is underfired in the bisque, and therefore very porous, it may absorb an excessive amount of glaze. Soluble fluxes in the glaze, because of their relatively higher rates of thermal expansion/contraction, may cause the body to crack.

GLAZE DEFECTS CAUSED THROUGH APPLICATION

1 Blisters or pinholes may occur when coarse clay bodies have air trapped in the surface pores. This can be one of the major causes of white dots appearing on the colored areas of majolica. Slight moistening of the bisque-fired clay before glazing or firing the bisque higher help to eradicate this fault.

2 Dust or oil on the surface of the bisque may cause a resist effect and the glaze will not adhere. It can also cause pinholes or a scaly surface on the glaze.

3 If the glaze is applied too heavily, it may run, obscuring the decoration, and may stick the piece to the kiln shelf.

4 In addition to flowing excessively, thickly applied glazes will usually crack on drying. Often, when these glazes are fired, the cracks will not heal up, but will pull farther apart and bead up at the edges. If the drying contraction is great enough, the adhesion of the glaze to the body will be weak, possibly causing portions to flake off during the initial period of the firing.

5 Conversely, too thin an application of glaze will result in a thin, rough surface. This is especially true of matt glazes, which generally require a slightly thicker application than gloss glazes.

6 If a second glaze coating is applied over a completely dry first coat, blisters will probably form. The wetting of the lower glaze layer causes it to expand and pull away from the body. This can cause crawling to take place during the subsequent firing.

7 If the bisque ware is considerably colder than

the glaze at the time of application, bubbles and blisters may later develop.

GLAZE DEFECTS ORIGINATING IN FIRING

1 If freshly glazed ware is placed in a kiln and fired immediately, the resulting steam can loosen the glaze from the body, causing blisters and crawling.

2 Rapid firing can inhibit the normal gases from escaping. They can form tiny seeds or bubbles in the glaze. For some especially viscous glazes, a prolonged soaking period at top temperature for 30–60 minutes is necessary to remove these gas bubbles.

3 Excessive reduction can result in black or grey spots on the body and glaze, producing a dull surface.

4 Glazes containing lead should not be fired in reducing conditions, as the lead oxides will reduce to metallic lead. Also, the sulfur content of any combustion gases will dull the glaze surfaces, and possibly form blisters and wrinkles.

DEFECTS IN GLAZE COMPOSITION

1 Glazes which are not properly adjusted to the clay body are susceptible to stresses that may cause the glaze—and the body—to crack. If the glaze contracts at a slower rate than the body in cooling, it goes into a state of compression. This causes the glaze to buckle up and separate from the body, throwing off sharp and dangerous slivers of glass material. This defect is commonly known as *shivering*, although the problem is not very common in studio pottery glazes. It is most often encountered in glazes with a high lithium content.

2 Slightly similar to shivering, and also caused by unequal contraction rates in cooling, is *crazing* of the glaze. In this case, the glaze contracts at a greater rate than the body. This state of great tension causes numerous fine cracks to form. When done intentionally for decorative effect (or sometimes rationalized by potters after the fact), glazes with this condition are called *crackle* glazes.

3 An excessive amount of refractory colorant or opacifier, such as rutile, tin, nickel or chromium,

which are relatively insoluble in the glaze melt, can cause the glaze to become dull and rough.

4 A dull surface is likely to result if the balance between silica, clays and fluxes is incorrect for the desired temperature range of the glaze.

5 High zinc "Bristol" glazes and high colemanite glazes may tend to crawl or crack, particularly at high temperatures, when not fitted properly to the body. The fit can be improved by the addition of alumina or clay.

6 Glazes ground too finely, thus releasing soluble salts from the fluxes, feldspars, and so on, can develop pinholes and bubbles.

SOLVING MAJOR GLAZE DEFECTS

Crazing *Crazing* is the most common defect, and normally the easiest to correct. In both crazing and shivering the eradication of problems relies on matching the thermal expansion characteristics of both body and glaze. In practice, the most effective ways to correct crazing are:

a increase the silica, in body or glaze
b decrease the feldspar, in body or glaze
c decrease any other material containing sodium or potassium
d increase the boron
e increase the alumina—i.e., the clay content
f increase lead oxide.

Shivering *Shivering* is the reverse of crazing; therefore, the remedies are the opposite of crazing:

a decrease the silica in either the body or the glaze
b increase the feldspar, especially sodium feldspar or nepheline syenite, or other alkaline bearing materials.

Crawling *Crawling* is caused by a high index of surface tension in the melting glaze. It is triggered by adhesion problems, often caused by bad application. It occurs where a glaze is excessively powdery, and does not fully adhere to the surface of the clay. This can be alleviated by the addition of a small amount of gum to the glaze batch. Crawling is more common in matt glazes than in fluid ones; sometimes the problems of crawling can be adjusted by the addition of a small amount of extra flux. Crawling can also occur when one glaze is applied over another, particularly if the first is allowed to dry out completely before the second application. Some fluxes, particularly zinc and magnesium, are likely to cause crawling when used in excess. Calcining part of the zinc can help this problem.

Pitting and Pinholing These are the most annoying and difficult glaze flaws to cure. They can be caused by a badly controlled firing cycle, the glaze composition, or can originate with the body, particularly highly grogged clay bodies. The following remedies should be tried to cure pinholing or pitting:

a lengthen the firing cycle
b apply the glaze less thickly
c add more flux to the glaze to make it more fluid
d decrease the content of zinc or rutile in the glaze
e where zinc is used, try calcining half of the zinc content
f increase the maturing temperature of the glaze
g hold the kiln at the glaze maturing temperature for a soaking period of up to four hours
h cool the kiln slowly.

Blisters *Blisters and blebs* are usually the result of either excessively thick application of glaze, or incomplete clay preparation, wedging, blunging, etc. Sometimes, however, these faults can be due to overfiring, or to the use of soluble fluxes in the glazes. The following fluxes might cause this problem: borax, boric acid, potassium carbonate, magnesium sulfate, and sodium carbonate. If these materials are present in a problem glaze, it would be well to replace them with other fluxing agents, or fritted materials.

Devitrification *Devitrification* is the process whereby some glazes change from an amorphous clear solution, at the point of maturity, to a crys-

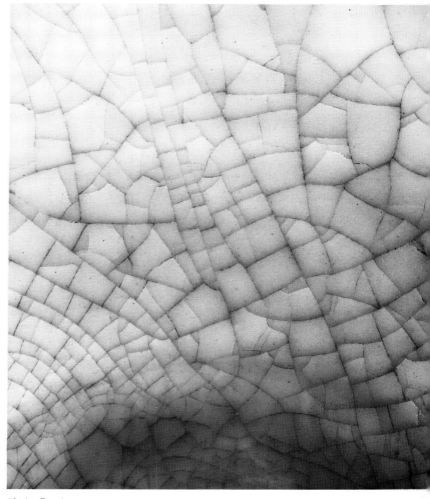

12–1. Crazing.

talline glaze, during the cooling. It is fairly common in high temperature glazes that are high in silica, clay, lime and barium; microcrystalline frosty or buttery matt surfaces develop in these glazes. Devitrification is the basis of crystalline and aventurine glazes (see chapter 13), and thus in many glazes is desirable, rather than a fault. If devitrification is occurring where it is not wanted, it is usually necessary to speed up the cooling cycle to eliminate it. If this is not possible, the crystal-forming materials—calcium, magnesium, zinc, barium, manganese, titanium and iron—will have to be partially or wholly replaced by other oxides.

Flashing *Flashing* is the name given to the habit of some materials to be volatile in the kiln.

12–2. Shivering.

12–3. Crawling.

12–4. Pinholing.

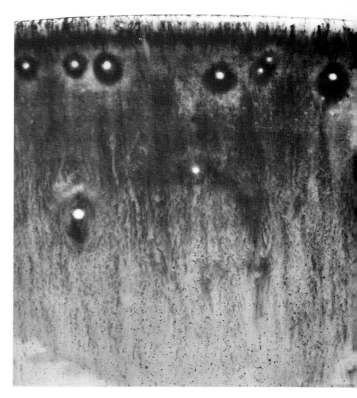

This fuming causes interesting—or annoying—effects in the color and surface of glazes. It is noticed in various ways. Volatile materials such as sodium, lead and boric acid, and to a lesser extent, barium, zinc and potassium, produce shiny glazed areas, occurring like a haze in unglazed areas of the ceramic object. The hazy surface is often an attractive toasty color on stoneware, and a pinkish blush on porcelain, and can be used for special decorative effect.

Some colorants—chromium, copper, and to a lesser extent, manganese and cobalt—are also volatile, and can distribute themselves onto other glazed pieces in the same kiln. In the case of chromium, even the kiln walls can be impregnated: The oxide can volatilize out in another firing, turning tin opacified glazes pink. These serendipitous occurrences can be encouraged, as they have been for hundreds of years. The Chinese potters of the Sung dynasty often painted the inside of saggers with copper to volatilize onto the pots, giving pink, red and blue flashing to the glazes known as Chun.

Flashing is also the name given to the surface effects of wood firing. Flames lick at the clay, creating exciting and varied surface effects. Small ash deposits graphically illustrate the movement of the fire through the kiln by the color and surface alterations which take place.

Underfiring *Underfiring* occurs when the kiln has not achieved a high enough temperature to mature the glazes properly. Underfired glazes will generally be opaque, dry surfaced, and usually quite a different color from the properly fired glaze. They will often be crawled or bubbled, in a state of arrested development. When refired to the correct maturing temperature, they should behave normally, although colors may change slightly in the process.

Overfiring *Overfiring* is usually the result of not watching the kiln closely as it approaches top temperature. Its symptoms are very glassy, sometimes blistered glazes, and often bloated clays. The solution to this is to take more care in firing. If the kiln temperature is being gauged by the usual use of three cones, the guard cone should be taken as a warning; it is wise to slow the firing at this point

to allow proper maturation to take place, without worry of overfiring. A kitchen timer can also be a useful aid.

Spluttering *Spluttering, or Spit-out,* is a defect in which small pieces of the glaze fall off the ware during firing, and are found firmly attached to the kiln shelf after firing. The glaze layer sometimes heals over, and sometimes crawls. The cause is generally from a loose glaze layer that fails to adhere during fusion. Firing ware which is still wet from the glazing process will frequently cause spluttering. It also occurs with glazes containing colemanite, which releases its chemically bonded water at around 800°C. There are two other times when this anomaly may occur. One is when the bisque fire has been very low, and has not completely burned off any carbonaceous matter in the body. Subsequently, the glaze spits off small parts as a result of gases being released. The other is when reduction may be started too early in the firing, again causing gases to spit out.

Dunting *Dunting* is a fault of irregular cracking, more related to clay than glaze, and usually caused by uneven cooling, or by cold drafts getting in the kiln. This cracking can occur from passing through the point of quartz inversion too quickly, or from compression-shattering.

Glaze dunting is most likely to occur when a piece is heavily glazed on one side only with a glaze that has high surface tension. This would typically be a high expansion glaze, possibly containing a large amount of nepheline syenite. For example, a pot made of a well vitrified stoneware clay, covered either inside or outside (but not both) with a saturated iron or temmoku glaze would be a prime candidate for dunting. With this combination, one can often find the piece splitting in half during or after cooling. The solution is to take the glaze over to the other side of the piece to relieve the tension, or to change the glaze.

If dunting does occur, it is helpful to scrutinize the piece for evidence of when the cracking occurred. If the crack formed in the heating cycle, its edges will be softened and rounded; if in the cooling cycle, the crack will leave sharp edges.

Some dunting can also occur in conjunction with black coring, particularly if the wall thickness is uneven. In this case the dunting and black core will occur in the thicker section. The crack should be examined to see if the core of the clay is black or dark grey.

Black Coring A *black core* occurs when the carbon in the body is not successfully burnt out in the bisque firing. All clays contain some carbonaceous matter, which must be completely eliminated before the completion of the bisque firing. In the process of burning out, local reduction takes place, turning the iron oxide black, possibly with some carbon. Black coring can be attributed to a lack of sufficient oxygen between 750 and 900°C., through either an unclean atmosphere or through too rapid a firing cycle. The remedy for the problem is to make certain that the atmosphere is oxidizing, and to slow the firing slightly.

13

Flashers

The last few chapters have pointed the way for flexible glaze development within a wide variety of temperatures. Many specialized glazes have already been covered, although perhaps not pointed out as such. There are some glazes, however, which would probably not be developed in the ways I have previously suggested, and the following guidelines should prove fruitful starting points for the development of suitable bases for glazes about which some mystique seems to have developed.

Once again, I am generalizing to some extent by giving the limits within which one can usually find satisfactory glazes for special effects. It would be foolish to suggest that all specialized glazes will necessarily fit into these limits, as there are always surprises and exceptions. The guidelines in this section are placed according to the general development of firing temperature.

ENAMELS

Enamels are also known as overglaze colors, onglaze colors or china paints. They are essentially a very low temperature glaze base, similar to raku glazes. Enamels are generally applied over a glaze which has already been fired, for the addition of bright touches of color. The blended or fritted enamel powders are usually mixed with an adhesive medium such as gum, linseed oil, or fat oil, although they can also be mixed with water; the oil mixtures can be thinned with turpentine if necessary. This facilitates application by such methods as spraying, air brushing, painting and stippling. They are colored with metallic oxides and/or stains. As in other glaze types, the colors are responsive to flux alteration. Because of the very low firing temperature, however, many fluxes which would

13–2. Paul Mathieu (Canada). "Tic-Tac-Toe." Slab built porcelain teapot, 10 in. high. Cone 9 oxidation. Luster decoration overglaze.

13–3. David Taylor (Canada). Vase. High fired earthenware with overglaze decoration.

otherwise control color development cannot be used in the strength which is normal for strong color. The principal fluxes used are lead, borax, boric acid and colemanite, or prepared frits. Amongst these fluxes is found enough color affecting material to produce a wide range of color.

Enamels that do not contain lead can be fired in reduction to extend the color range. Those containing lead are likely to bubble and blister in reduction firing. Enamels are usually fired at temperatures between 700 and 800°C. Most people use commercially prepared enamels, but enamels are not difficult to make from the bases given below, with the addition of colorants as suggested in chapter 15. *Any enamels containing lead are potentially hazardous. They are best used on the outside of containers, or only on decorative pieces.*

13–1. Sarah Honeyman (United Kingdom). "CLOWNS." Porcelain and T Material (proprietary white stoneware) in 50/50 blend. Reduction fired to cone 9. Subsequently fired in oxidation with overglaze enamels.

Enamel bases, cone 019–018

1 White lead, 60; any frit, 20; flint, 20
2 White lead, 30–50; any frit, 30–50; flint, 10–20
3 White lead, 40; Ferro frit 3110, 50; flint, 10
4 Ferro frit 3110, 70; cryolite, 10; feldspar, 20
5 Ferro frit 3110, 80; petalite, 20
6 White lead, 70–75; feldspar, 10–15; flint, 10–15
7 Any frit, 40; colemanite, 40; cryolite, 10; feldspar, 10
8 Any frit, 50–70; colemanite, 20–40; flint, 10–20

In doing the tests on all base glazes using lead, I have found white lead and red lead to be interchangeable without noticeable effect.

RAKU

Raku glazes are also very low temperature glazes. Any of the suggestions made for enamels

13–4. Walter Dexter (Canada). Raku lidded form, 10 in. high.
Engobe, incised and brush pattern.

may be also used for raku. They will, of course, need to be mixed with water instead of oils or gum. They can be colored in the usual ways. Sometimes they have materials such as silver nitrate, bismuth subnitrate, or copper carbonate mixed in them, to develop luster qualities during reduction firing, or in post-firing reduction. In the case of silver and bismuth, the amount of material needed for developing lusters is 1–3 percent; with copper it can be up to 20 percent. For ease of application, and also for keeping the glaze in suspension, it is helpful to have approximately 10 percent of clay in the

13–5. David Toresdahl (Canada). "Trout fishing in Victoria with a top float." Raku.

glaze. More than this is likely to make the glaze too refractory, and require a higher temperature to fuse the glaze.

Raku glaze bases

1 Lead, 65–75; flint, 25–35; kaolin, 0–10
2 Any frit, 70; colemanite, 20; kaolin, 10

13–6. Wayne Higby (U.S.A.). "Apparition Canyon." Landscape bowl, earthenware, raku technique. Thrown and corrected.

3 Any frit, 75–85; feldspar, 15–25
4 Any frit, 80; cornwall stone, 10; ball clay, 10
5 Colemanite, 50; any frit, 30; cornwall stone, 20
6 Any frit, 45; colemanite, 20; feldspar, 20; barium, 15
7 Colemanite, 65; feldspar, 25; ball clay, 5; barium, 5
8 Any frit, 40; any other frit, 40; clay, 10; feldspar, 10
9 Lead, 40; Ferro frit 3110, 50; ball clay, 10
10 Lead frit, 50; colemanite, 40; ball clay, 10

LUSTERS AND LUSTER GLAZES

There are two basic ways of obtaining lustrous, iridescent, or metallic surfaces on ceramic glazes: inglaze and onglaze.

Lowfire inglaze lusters may be developed by using any of the glaze bases suggested for either enamels or raku, particularly those which are high in alkaline materials. Add 1 to 3 percent of any silver or copper compound to the base glaze. Bismuth subnitrate at 1 percent may also help. The glaze is fired to its maturing temperature in an oxidizing atmosphere, and left to cool to approximately 650–700°C., at which point the kiln is reignited and held at the same temperature, with a heavy reduction, for between 30 and 90 minutes. The resulting sheen is likely to have many variations, and is difficult to repeat. This type of luster is sometimes called *flash luster*, and can also be created by removing the piece from the hot kiln and placing it into some combustible material to get a post-firing reduction, as in raku.

There are two methods of producing onglaze lusters. The first is generally done with industrially prepared materials. It is questionable if there is any point in trying to produce one's own lusters of this type. These commercial lusters are solutions of metallic gold, platinum or palladium, in combination with a liquid mixture consisting of nitric acid, hydrochloric acid, balsam of sulphur, tin and turpentine. The solution is usually thick and viscous, but it can be thinned with turpentine or acetone. After thinning, the lusters are painted directly onto the prefired glazed surface. They are fired to 700–750°C.

13–7. Ruth and Alan Barrett-Danes (United Kingdom). "Cabbage Kingdoms." Hand modelled and moulded porcelain. In-glaze luster oxidized to 950°C., then reduced at 800°C. for 25 minutes in the cooling cycle. The glaze is a soft alkaline frit glaze containing soluble salts of silver, bismuth, copper and cobalt for color and luster.

in an oxidizing atmosphere, where the volatile oils containing the metals burn away, creating a light local reduction and leaving a thin coating of the metal fused to the glaze. Resinate lusters may be used on top of fused glazes of any type. If they are put on high gloss glazes, a high gloss metallic surface will develop; if put on a matt glaze, a matt metallic surface will develop.

The second form of onglaze luster is also painted on prefired glazes, and is generally known as Islamic or Arabian smoked luster, after its source of development. The luster-forming materials are any silver or copper compound, or gold chloride; sometimes the addition of bismuth subnitrate will also help. Preparation consists of mixing the luster-forming materials, from as low as 2% to a high of 20% (depending on materials), into a paste with a fine red clay, ochre, or umber. This medium is then painted onto the prefired glaze surface. Vinegar should be used as the thinning medium when painting; it helps to dissolve the pigment, and gives a fine particle size. Vinegar is used because it wets the materials without causing expansion, the way water does, and thus dries with little contraction. When dry, the ware is fired at approximately 650–700°C. At the top temperature, the kiln should be reduced heavily, holding the temperature as stable as possible for three quarters of an hour. Cool fairly quickly. When the work is cold, it needs to be washed to clean off the clay binder and any residual soot, possibly using a mildly abrasive household cleaner or powdered pumice and water. The iridescent quality should have developed as a thin film of metallic luster, occasionally surrounded by a haze of other color, or by carbon trapped in the glaze. Different combinations of silver and copper will give iridescent color variations from yellow, brown and green to red, depending on the glaze base and compounds used. It is a very difficult technique to control, and a substantial amount of loss should be anticipated in the early stages of learning about it.

The most satisfactory glazes for this form of luster development are those where a lead-alkaline base is used. Glazes such as those used for majolica, or onglaze painting, and fired between cone 08 and cone 2, may also be used as a base for the overglaze luster painting. The criteria in the development of a glaze for lusterware is to make a glaze which will start to fuse at a low enough temperature that the luster will fuse to its surface, but not so low as to possibly also fuse the carrying clay or ochre. Glaze bases which will be most satisfactory are found in the following list. They can be colored in the usual ways. If copper is used as a colorant or in a mixed color, it is likely to give plum red, or even lustrous colors.

The following glazes may be used for both lusterware and majolica. It is usually better to use a glaze that combines lead and alkalines for the production of superior lusters. Glaze bases 1–5 are such glazes. However, many people do not like to use lead compounds or lead frits, and therefore glaze bases 6–10 do not contain lead; they are best used for majolica decoration on functional work.

Glaze bases for lusterware and majolica, cone 04–2

1 Any lead frit, 35; Ferro frit 3110, 40; kaolin, 15; flint, 10
2 Any lead frit, 40; any alkaline frit, 40; clay, 10; feldspar, 10
3 Any frit, 75–85; feldspar, 15–25
4 Any lead frit, 45; colemanite, 25; feldspar, 15; clay, 15
5 Any alkaline frit, 45; white lead, 25; feldspar, 15; clay, 15
6 Ferro frit 3134, 90; kaolin, 10
7 Ferro frit 3134, 80; kaolin, 10; feldspar, 10
8 Ferro frit 3134, 40; alkaline frit, 40; kaolin, 10; feldspar, 10
9 Ferro frit 3124, 60; alkaline frit, 20; kaolin, 10; feldspar, 10
10 Ferro frit 3124, 65; colemanite, 15; feldspar, 15; barium, 5

Lustrous effects can also be developed in various other ways. Spraying water solutions of stannous chloride, bismuth subnitrate or barium chloride, or throwing the dry powders of these or other soluble mineral salts directly into the kiln firebox when cooling, at about 650°C., can develop a surface luster like mother of pearl. (Better results can be obtained with stannous chloride by placing a small amount on a spoon attached to a metal rod, inserting it through a spyhole and tipping it onto a kiln shelf or a brick. If air is then introduced by using a piece of copper pipe fixed to the end of an air compressor hose and aimed at the pile of material, the fumes will coat the ware more completely with a smaller amount of stannous chloride, reducing both the cost and the potential health hazard.) Mineral salts can also be sprayed on the hot surface of raku fired work when first removed from the firing. Care should be taken when volatile materials are being used, as the chlorine gases which form when the materials fume are toxic.

When mixed together in equal parts, copper and manganese, can give a bronze gold sheen, and when used as a brushing pigment over some high-fire glazes can yield beautiful iridescent colors. With some highly feldspathic glazes fired in reduction at high temperatures, subtle pinks and red colors may haze around the pigment from the volatile copper. Glazes colored with various saturated metallic oxides are also capable of lustrous effects.

AVENTURINE GLAZES

Aventurine and crystalline glazes are similar, in that they are both caused through partial devitrification of the glaze, and the subsequent formation of crystals. Aventurine glazes are named after the gemstone aventurine, or goldstone, where myriad minute, glittering iron crystals are held in suspension in the matrix of translucent quartz.

In glazes, a similar effect may be achieved by saturating a lowfired glaze, generally a lead-borax mixture, with iron oxide to a maximum concentration of 15 percent. The glaze will need testing with increments of iron added, so that the correct amount can be determined. The glaze needs to be low in alumina, and can be colored with other metallic oxides such as chromium and uranium. Aventurine glazes should be applied fairly thickly, and fired and cooled slowly. Because of the low alumina content of the glaze, it is likely to run excessively, and pieces coated with these glazes should be fired on stands, or over crucibles which collect any runoff glaze. It is also possible to put a matt glaze on the lower portion of the piece, which will absorb some of the running glaze. Glaze bases suitable for the development of aventurine glazes follow.

Aventurine glaze bases, cone 04

1 Lead frit, 70; alkaline frit, 30
2 Lead frit, 70; colemanite, 20; feldspar, 10
3 White lead, 60; alkaline frit, 30; feldspar, 10
4 Ferro frit 3110, 60; white lead, 30; feldspar, 10
5 White lead, 50; colemanite, 40; feldspar, 10
6 High lead/zinc frit (Ferro 3300), 50; lead frit, 40; feldspar, 10

Because these glazes usually have a high lead content, they are only suitable for decorative pieces, and should not be used on the interior of functional pottery.

Aventurine glazes are normally made as low temperature glazes, but similar effects of minute crystals floating in the middle of the glaze may also be achieved in the higher temperature ranges. These glazes are usually high in alkaline materials, often in conjunction with fluoride-containing materials, such as cryolite or fluorspar, or with lithium.

High fire aventurine glaze bases, cone 6–10

1 Feldspar, 35; kaolin, 17; whiting, 12; flint, 19; colemanite, 7; cryolite, 5; fluorspar, 5
2 Soda feldspar, 35; ball clay, 17; whiting, 12; flint, 19; colemanite, 7; cryolite, 5; fluorspar, 5
3 Soda feldspar, 40; kaolin, 20; flint, 15; colemanite, 10; cryolite, 8; fluorspar, 7
4 Soda feldspar, 50; whiting, 10; red or Albany clay, 30; colemanite, 10
5 Soda feldspar, 60; whiting, 10; red or Albany clay, 20; colemanite, 10
6 Feldspar, 55; whiting, 10; red clay, 30; colemanite, 5
7 Feldspar, 50; whiting, 15; dolomite, 10; colemanite, 10; ball clay, 10; zinc, 5
8 Feldspar, 60; talc, 15; colemanite, 10; ball clay, 10; zinc, 5

The usual colorant associated with aventurine glazes is iron. It should be used in a volume of 8 to 15 percent. Other colorants, particularly rutile, may go into the microcrystalline form in these glazes.

Other highfire aventurine glazes will be found in the appendix, Oriental Iron Glazes.

CRYSTALLINE GLAZES

Crystalline glazes have many devotees and collectors, and probably just as many detractors who detest the glaze type, with its often flashy, large crystals obliterating the form with a panoply of colored snowflakes over the glaze surface. There is no doubt that they have a seductive fascination, but the forms which both they and aventurine glazes clothe are often an inadequate vehicle for ostentatious display.

Crystals, in crystalline glazes, form from the interaction of a number of minerals with silica, in the presence of a very low alumina content. The fluxes which promote crystal growth are zinc, sodium, potassium, barium, magnesium and lithium. Crystals formed through the use of these materials can vary widely in size, from tiny microcrystals, similar to aventurines, to macrocrystals which can be up to three inches across.

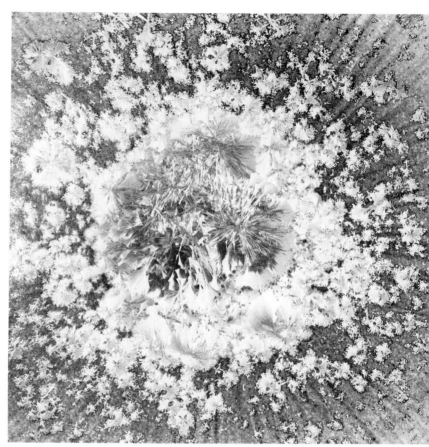

13–9. Microcrystalline formation.

13–8. Macrocrystalline formation.

The shape of the crystals can also vary widely, depending on a number of factors in the makeup of the glaze.

Crystal development occurs in the cooling stages of the firing cycle, and therefore the cooling procedures are more important than the heating. There are many schools of thought about the cooling of high- and mid-temperature crystalline glazes, but the most widespread theory revolves around an initial fast cooling to between 1000 and 1100°C., and then holding that temperature, where crystal growth is most likely to occur, for one to four hours. This period is then followed by a gentle slide in temperature to cold. Crystal glazes are usually fired in electric kilns, although crystals, particularly the smaller ones, can develop very well in reduction firing. They can be made to mature at a wide range of temperatures, depending on the desires of the

13–10. Roman Bartkiw (Canada). Porcelain vase with micro-crystalline glaze. Electric fired at cone 8. Collection of the author.

individual, the colors required, and the firing range of the kiln. Crystals which develop through the use of chromium, producing a variety of yellows, oranges and reds, are covered in the following section, but since the development of color is probably

13–11. Roman Bartkiw (Canada). Detail of vase (figure 13–10).

more important than crystal formation, it will be covered in more depth in the color section.

Glazes for chromium crystals, cone 012–010

1 Lead, 80; flint, 10; kaolin, 10
2 Lead, 80; flint, 5; soda feldspar, 10; barium, 5
3 Lead, 75; kaolin, 10; whiting, 5; flint, 5; soda ash, 5
4 Lead, 80; wollastonite, 10; feldspar, 10
5 Lead, 75; wollastonite, 15; kaolin, 10

When chromium oxide is added to the above glazes in volume up to 10 percent, a range of yellow, orange and red crystalline glazes will develop. They should not be fired above cone 09, or the reds will turn to green. In order to get the required colors from chromium, it is important that no zinc is present in the glaze, or else the color will turn muddy brown. The above glazes could substitute white lead for red lead and have Serial Numbers LCR 6–10. If uranium is used as a colorant in place of chromium in these glazes, a range of soft yellows to orange will develop, although it will not form crystals. Note that none of these glazes is suitable for functional pottery.

Lowfire crystalline glazes, cones 04–1

1 Lead frit, 70; Ferro frit 3110, 20; feldspar, 10
2 Lead frit, 70; colemanite, 15; feldspar, 15

13–12. Margarete Schott (Germany). Porcelain bowl. Copper oxide on a lithium crystalline glaze. Gas-fired reduction at 1360°C.

13–13. Monique Ferron (Canada). Raku plate, 16 in. square. Engobe, oxides and glazes, sprayed and masked on greenware.

3 White lead, 60; Ferro frit 3124, 25; feldspar, 15

4 Ferro frit 3110, 60; white lead, 25; feldspar, 15

5 White lead, 50; Ferro frit 3124, 35; feldspar, 15

6 High zinc frit (Ferro 3240), 75; frit 3124, 15; feldspar, 10

7 High zinc frit, 65; frit 3124, 25; feldspar, 10

8 High zinc frit, 85; feldspar, 15

9 High zinc frit, 70; lithium, 10; colemanite, 10; feldspar, 10

10 High zinc frit, 70; cryolite, 5; fluorspar, 10; lithium, 5; feldspar, 10

Up to 10 percent of titanium in any of the above bases will produce crystals, depending on the firing and cooling procedures. Colorants may be added.

Midfire crystalline glazes, cones 4–6

1 White lead, 50; flint, 25; kaolin, 10; zinc, 10; whiting, 5

2 Litharge, 40; flint, 25; kaolin, 15; whiting, 10; colemanite, 10

3 White lead, 45; barium, 5; zinc, 5; dolomite, 5; whiting, 5; flint, 25; kaolin, 10

4 Lead frit, 50; flint, 20; kaolin, 10; whiting, 10; lithium, 10

5 Zinc frit (Ferro 3240), 50; flint, 20; cryolite, 10; kaolin, 10; lithium, 10

6 Ferro frit 3134, 50; flint, 25; zinc, 10; cryolite, 5; kaolin, 10

7 Feldspar, 30; barium, 40; zinc, 15; lithium, 2; flint, 13

8 Feldspar, 35; barium, 20; zinc, 25; lithium, 5; flint, 15

9 Feldspar, 30; zinc, 20; barium, 30; lithium, 3; kaolin, 2; flint, 15

10 Nepheline syenite, 30; high zinc frit, 50; barium, 15; lithium, 5

Up to 10 percent of titanium dioxide in any of the above glazes will produce crystalline effects. Nickel and copper will both produce a range of interesting results, although any colorants may be added.

Highfire crystalline glazes, cones 8–10

1 Ferro frit 3124, 65; zinc oxide, 25; flint, 10

2 Ferro frit 3110, 50; zinc oxide, 25; flint, 25

3 Nepheline syenite, 50; flint, 15; barium, 15; zinc, 15; lithium, 5

   4 Frit 3110, 15; Ferro frit 3134, 40; zinc, 25; flint, 20

   5 Frit 3134, 60; zinc oxide, 20; feldspar, 20

   6 Frit 3124, 40; zinc oxide, 25; flint, 35

   7 Frit 3124, 50; zinc, 20; flint, 30

   8 High zinc frit (Ferro 3240), 50; feldspar, 25; flint, 25

   9 Frit 3110, 50; zinc, 20; flint, 20; lithium, 10

   10 Feldspar, 25; flint, 20; whiting, 15; zinc, 25; any frit, 10; lithium, 5

   11 Feldspar, 45; barium, 30; zinc, 10; lithium, 2; flint, 13

   12 Feldspar, 45; barium, 20; zinc, 20; lithium, 5; flint, 10

   13 Feldspar, 35; zinc, 20; barium, 25; lithium, 3; kaolin, 2; flint, 15

   14 Feldspar, 60; zinc, 10; barium, 20; whiting, 10

   15 Feldspar, 60; zinc, 10; barium, 30

Up to 10 percent of titanium in any of the above glazes will develop crystals, depending on firing cycles. Any colorants may be added, particularly nickel and copper, to produce colored crystals and matrixes. Chromium should not be used with glazes containing zinc, unless you want muddy brown colors.

COPPER RED GLAZES

The elusive colors produced by copper in reduction glazes have been the object of relentless searching by potters for centuries, often bringing out many of their masochistic tendencies. Colors which may be produced by reduced copper will be dealt with more fully in chapters 14 and 16. Here we are more concerned with the type of glaze which favors the development of reduced copper colors. Peach bloom, flambé, oxblood and aubergine are names which have been given to traditional Chinese glazes that use copper. Reduced copper glazes are dependent for their color on a number of variables, including the glaze formulation, application, firing schedule, initial glaze melt, sequence of reduction, degree of reduction and the reoxidation during the cooling. Is it any wonder that they can be so elusive, and so unreliable! Reduced copper glazes can

be fired in high temperature electric kilns by the addition to the glaze of 1 percent or less of 200 mesh sieved silicon carbide to promote a local reduction. Low temperature copper reds can be made by reduction of copper in the cooling cycle as low as 700°C. by relighting the kiln at this temperature and putting it into heavy reduction for approximately one hour. After this, the kiln is allowed to cool normally.

Copper reds may also be achieved by covering a glaze containing copper with another glaze sensitive to reduced copper, such as the bases mentioned below. This allows a wide range of various decorative treatments, such as wax resist between glaze coats, and glaze trailing over the copper glaze (see chapter 20).

In developing copper red glazes, the glaze base should be high in silica and alkaline fluxes and low in clay content; clay (alumina) inhibits the development of reds. The base can be fluxed with whiting, boron, frits, or combinations of any or all. Copper is an unstable material, which is likely to volatilize, or burn out. To help alleviate this problem, it is usual to add small amounts of tin, and possibly iron, as they appear to have some sort of attraction to the copper and act to keep it in a state of colloidal suspension in the glaze.

Bases for copper reduction glazes are often very complicated, unnecessarily so in my opinion. Fine glazes can be developed from the following bases, designed for firing in the cone 8 to 10 range.

Copper reduction glaze bases, cone 8–10

   1 Nepheline syenite, 65; wollastonite, 20; colemanite, 10; ball clay, 5

   2 Feldspar, 50; whiting, 20; colemanite, 10; flint, 15; kaolin, 5

   3 Feldspar, 35; cornwall stone, 35; whiting, 15; kaolin, 15

   4 Feldspar, 55; barium, 25; kaolin, 10; flint, 10

   5 Nepheline syenite, 35; flint, 30; whiting, 10; kaolin, 15; colemanite, 10

   6 Soda feldspar, 35; petalite, 5; dolomite, 15; barium, 25; kaolin, 10; flint, 10

   7 Soda feldspar, 45; borax frit, 15; whiting, 15; kaolin, 5; flint, 20

8 Feldspar, 40; flint, 20; whiting, 20; boron frit, 10; kaolin, 10

9 Feldspar, 20; colemanite, 20; whiting, 20; flint, 20; ball clay, 20

10 Feldspar, 45; flint, 20; kaolin, 10; whiting, 10; colemanite, 10; dolomite, 5

Additions of varying amounts of copper, tin and/or iron, as well as other colorants and opacifiers, will give a wide range of color potential to the listed glaze bases. Amounts of 0.5 to 2 percent of copper and up to 5 percent tin usually form the best reds. Small amounts of iron, in conjunction with the tin and copper, will give more of an orange red, while titanium (up to 5 percent), and cobalt (up to 1 percent), give purple reds. The same color reactions can be achieved with brushwork in iron, titanium, or cobalt, or other applications of these colorants over the unfired copper red glazes. When fired in oxidation, the listed glazes, colored with 5 percent tin and percentages of copper up to 5 percent, will yield soft, pale green glazes.

It should be remembered that many ceramists who work with copper reduction glazes devote considerable time to their study, often a lifetime. It is unwise to expect early control with an area which has so many variables.

PART THREE

The Development of Color

14

Materials for Color Development

Color development in ceramics can be achieved in many ways, leading to an infinite variety of results, as a visit to any museum that has a good ceramic collection will show. To the novice clay worker, the breadth of the field that ceramic history encompasses may seem too vast to cope with. It may be comforting to know, however, that everything that has been achieved has been created with comparatively few raw materials; most effects are the result of a wide variety of firing and surface enrichment techniques. All but the tiniest fraction of the world's pottery has been made with combinations of no more than a dozen materials. These materials are silica, alumina, sodium, potassium, lithium, lead, zinc, boron, calcium, magnesium, barium, and borax. They have been intermixed in an infinite variety of ways, and with added colorants have given us the ceramic spectrum that we see today.

For the glazemaker and colorist, the knowledge that the basic materials are few should open the door to their understanding. In chapter 10, I dealt with fluxes and the effect that they have in the glaze development, and also the way that colorants behave in relation to the fluxes used. Color development is not solely controlled by the fluxes, but they remain a primary influence in the search for specific color.

The potential of any individual colorant is subject to three main variables: first, the makeup of the glaze, particularly the fluxes used; second, the firing temperature; and third, the kiln atmosphere. The colorants used in ceramics come from metals such as iron, cobalt, copper, manganese, chromium and titanium. Depending on the variables of fluxes and firing, many individual colorants can produce a wide variety of color. Iron, for

14–1. Hans Coper (United Kingdom). Stoneware composite form, 11 in. high. Once-fired in oxidation at approximately cone 8. Black metallic manganese surface. Collection of the author.

instance, can produce yellow, red, green, brown, gold, blue, grey, black, pink, orange or purple. Copper is capable of producing green, red, purple, turquoise, yellow, orange, blue, grey, pink and black. Of all the colorants used in ceramics, iron and copper are perhaps the most versatile in their potential, but all materials are affected by the variables. It is the understanding of how these variables affect the color, and how to go about developing specific colors, that is the subject matter of this section of this book.

Color in glaze is developed through the use of metals in some form. These forms may be oxides,

14–2. Geoffrey Swindell (United Kingdom). Porcelain, wheelmade, 3 in. high. Oxidized at cone 9. High alumina and dolomite glaze, with copper airbrushed on.

14–3. Robin Hopper (Canada). Plate. Porcelain, 18 in. diameter. Wax resist between two glazes, a high iron content glaze below, and a thick cornwall stone glaze on top, giving rich, fluid and crystalline patterns.

carbonates, sulphates, nitrates, chlorides, or even the basic metal itself. They may be used singly, or intermixed with other raw materials, colorants, or opacifiers. Whatever the form of the unfired material, during firing it reverts to the oxide of the metal. Many metallic oxides are unstable in their oxide state, and need to be fritted (mixed and fired dry) with other materials to form reliable colors.

The ceramic industry has, over the last two hundred years, developed a wide range of fritted colors, which are called glaze stains, body stains, underglaze colors, and overglaze colors. With the exception of overglaze colors, which are essentially a very low fired colored glaze (also known as enamels), the industrially produced materials may be used for color development in glazes, alone or with

14–4. John Glick (U.S.A.). Extruded and constructed box, 9 in. long. Stoneware with multiple slips and glazes. Reduction fired at cone 10.

14–6. Peter Lane (United Kingdom). Porcelain bowl, thrown and carved. Dolomite glaze with copper carbonate airbrushed over. Oxidation fired at cone 9.

other colorants, opacifiers and so on. If the available ones do not satisfy his needs or are too expensive, the glazemaker can also create his own stains in various ways, although some are quite complex. The processes are outlined later in this chapter.

Color may also be achieved through such methods as underglaze pencils, crayons, and pastels, which may either be made by the user or pur-

chased ready-made. Unusual materials, such as good quality watercolors, household and automobile spray paints, and ordinary house paints, can all be used and fired to produce a wealth of effects. The biggest problems lie perhaps in knowing where to go and when to stop.

Basic colorants are found in the following list; the factors which either enhance or inhibit the colors that may be achieved by their use will be discussed

14–5. Karl Scheid (Germany). Vase. Hand-built stoneware form with carved decoration. High iron and manganese glaze. Reduction fired at 1360°C.

14–7. Donn Zver (Canada). Stoneware teapot, 12 in. high. Carved when leather hard, then covered with a celadon glaze, with iron and rutile in stamped decoration. Fired at cone 10 in reduction.

in chapter 16. Some colorants react in the glaze as fluxing materials, and some as refractory materials. These will be indicated by the letters (**F**) and (**R**), wherever they obviously behave in those ways. Glaze saturation with a fluxing colorant will either make the glaze run noticeably, or lower the fusion point. Refractory colorants will do the reverse. Some colorants will also produce opacity, and these will be indicated with the letter (**O**). The volume in which colorants are usually used to achieve specific colors will be discussed in the next two chapters. In most cases, the oxide form of colorant will produce stronger color, but it is usually not as finely ground as carbonate, and may cause spots and specking to develop. Most of the time, it makes little difference in the final result which form is used, since the colorant in ratio to glaze is normally small, and the differences between oxide and carbonate become insignificant.

It will be noticed that most of the materials used to develop color in clays and glazes are toxic. They should therefore be treated with due care and attention, and kept out of the range of small children. The inhalation and ingestion of metallic mineral colorants when mixing or spraying glazes should be carefully avoided through the use of a suitable mask.

BASIC COLORANT MATERIALS

ANTIMONIATE OF LEAD. $Pb_3(SbO_4)_2$. **TOXIC.** A source of yellow colors in lead glazes. Stable only up to 1050°C.

ANTIMONY OXIDE (O). Sb_3O_4. **TOXIC.** Used in low temperature glazes to produce pale yellow to cream colors. In the presence of iron it will tend to produce stronger yellow colors.

BARIUM CHROMATE (F). $BaCrO_4$. **TOXIC.** Barium chromate is used to produce bright lemon yellow, yellow green and green colors in low temperatures, particularly in overglaze enamels.

CADMIUM CARBONATE. $CdCO_3$. **CADMIUM SULFIDE.** CdS. **BOTH TOXIC.** Cadmium compounds are used in ceramic glazes and enamels to produce yellow, orange and red in low temperature glazes and enamels. They are generally combined with selenium and sulfur. Cadmium compounds are highly toxic materials, which are also likely to be soluble in glazes. They are not suitable for the inside surfaces of functional pottery, and it is questionable whether they are even safe on the outside. Colorants using cadmium-selenium have a very narrow firing range, and are subject to burning out at temperatures above cone 05. As the fumes are also extremely toxic, the kiln should be carefully vented.

CHROMIUM OXIDE (R, O). Cr_2O_3 **TOXIC.** Generally produces heavy dark green colors, which are usually opaque. In lead glazes fired below 950°C., chromium can give a range of yellows, oranges and reds. In combination with tin oxide in oxidizing atmospheres, chrome-tin pinks through to crimson may be achieved. In glazes that contain zinc, chromium will usually turn tan to brown. It can volatilize in firing, even at low temperatures, coloring adjacent pots pink, particularly those having glazes opacified with tin, or fluxed with barium. The volatilized color can also impregnate the brickwork of the kiln, releasing volatile colorant into future firings. Used in amounts over 5 percent, it may cause crawling. Chromium is also found in chromate materials such as potassium dichromate, lead chromate, barium chromate, and iron chromate, where it has a similar, but modified, effect as that expected from the oxide form. With potassium its fluxing power is increased; with lead, it also fluxes more and creates yellow-oranges; with barium, it creates yellows; and with iron, it creates greys or occasionally blues.

COBALT OXIDE (F). Co_2O_3. **COBALT CARBONATE (F).** $CoCO_3$. **BOTH TOXIC.** Cobalt compounds are the most powerful of the coloring oxides in their coloring ability. They are also strong fluxes. In glazes dominated by the color affecting fluxes, the following variations may be expected: in lead glazes, pale to dark inky blue; in barium, strontium, and alkaline glazes, brilliant ultramarine blues; in magnesium glazes, pink lilac and purple blue; in zinc glazes, soft grey blues; and in glazes containing fluoride, cerulean blues may be achieved. The carbonate form, which is more finely ground, gives a more even color. Cobalt compounds are usually mixed with other modifying colorants to eliminate some of the harshness of the purified materials. Industrially prepared colorants using cobalt are calcined with other materials to improve the color, and to eliminate specking.

COBALT SULFATE (F). $CoSO_47H_2O$. **SOLUBLE, TOXIC.** Soluble form of cobalt.

COPPERAS. See iron sulfate.

COPPER OXIDE (F). CuO Cupric. **COPPER CARBONATE (F).** $CuCO_3$. **BOTH TOXIC.** Copper compounds are capable of producing a wide range of colors, and are very responsive to atmospheric changes inside the kiln. They are active fluxes. In lead dominated glazes they usually produce grassy greens; in barium and alkaline glazes, turquoise, blue green to purple; in magnesium glazes, orange, pink and grey. In reduction a wide range of colors is possible, from lustrous metallic copper to various reds, purples and black. The carbonate form is often easier to work with. Copper compounds are subject to volatilizing action in the kiln, and may color other glazes not containing copper in the same firing.

COPPER SULFATE (F). $CuSO_45H_2O$. **TOXIC, SOLUBLE.** Blue vitriol, a soluble form of copper.

CROCUS MARTIS. See Iron.

GOLD CHLORIDE. $AuCl_3$. **TOXIC.** Gold chloride is occasionally used in the formation of pink or purple glazes. Both its use and temperature range are very limited. The high price of the raw material makes it a prohibitively expensive material for most ceramists.

ILMENITE, FERROUS-TITANATE (F). $FeO TiO_2$. A naturally occurring combination of iron and titanium, usually used to produce gold to brown glazes, although it can produce interesting blues. It is often used to produce speckles in either the glaze or the clay body. It may be purchased in either powdered or granular form. See chapter 18.

IRON. Iron is the most common as well as the most useful of the coloring oxides. All clays and many glaze materials contain traces of iron that affect the color even when iron is not added to develop a specific color. Iron is the most complex of oxides in its effect on both body and glaze color. In oxidation it produces yellow, red, brown, purple and black. In reduction it can produce blue, green, grey, yellow, purple, pink, orange and black. In both oxidation and reduction, color will be dependent mainly on the makeup of the glaze and the amount of color used. In conjunction with impregnated carbon, it will cause the development of a black body in either pit firing, or the post-firing reduction of raku. In high-fired stonewares and impure porcelains, red to brown body colors can develop during the re-oxidation of reduced ware during cooling. Iron can also produce a great variety of crystalline surface color, and inglaze crystals in the case of aventurine glazes. In oxidation, iron reacts as a refractory; in reduction, it reacts as a flux.

IRON CHROMATE (F, R). $FeCrO_4$. **TOXIC.** Ferric chromate. An iron-chromium mixture usually used to produce grey. When used in conjunction with a tin glaze in oxidation, it can develop a pink haze around the grey. It may also produce a green-blue in high boron glazes.

IRON OXIDE (BLACK) (F, R). FeO Ferrous oxide. See Iron.

IRON OXIDE (PURPLE) (F, R). Fe_2O_3 Ferric oxide—Crocus martis. See Iron.

IRON OXIDE (RED) (F, R). Fe_2O_3 Ferric Oxide. See Iron.

IRON OXIDE (MAGNETIC) (F, R). Fe_3O_4 Ferroso-ferric oxide, or iron spangles. See Iron.

IRON OXIDE (YELLOW) (F, R). Fe_2O_3 Ferric oxide. See Iron. A true iron oxide, ochre colored. The name is frequently misused to mean yellow ochre (see Ochre).

IRON SULFATE (F, R). $FeSO_47H_2O$. **SOLUBLE.** Green vitriol, copperas, a soluble form of iron.

LEAD CHROMATE (F). $PbCrO_4$. **TOXIC.** A lead-chromium compound used as a colorant.

MANGANESE CARBONATE (F). $MnCO_3$. **MANGANESE DIOXIDE (F).** MnO_2. **BOTH TOXIC.** Manganese compounds are used to develop purple in barium and low temperature alkaline glazes, and brown in lead glazes. In high temperature magnesium glazes, fawn, beige and pinky-brown may be produced. At high temperatures, used on its own and either rubbed into clay bodies or painted on them, it will form a matt to gloss, dark brown to black surface. Mixed with an equal amount of copper, it can produce bronze to gold surfaces, with some crystalline formations. Granular manganese is used in glazes and clay bodies to give specks of color, which can form attractive bleeding into the glaze. Heavy concentrations (over 4 percent) of manganese as a colorant in clay bodies are likely to cause bloating, and a low tolerance to overfiring, leading to early slumping and deformation of pieces.

MOLYBDENUM OXIDE (R). MoO_3. **TOXIC, SOLUBLE.** Little used colorant, sometimes employed to develop yellowish and yellow green colors.

NAPLES YELLOW. See Antimoniate of lead.

NICKEL CARBONATE (R). $NiCO_3$. **NICKEL OXIDE (R).** Ni_2O_3. **BOTH TOXIC.** Nickel compounds are used to produce subdued colors of green, greys, browns and blues, and also to modify other colors. In high magnesium glazes, acid greens may be developed; in high barium glazes, pink to purple. Nickel is often used in conjunction with zinc crystalline glazes to promote crystal formation; at the same time, this combination colors the glaze blue.

OCHRE. Ochre is the name given to various earthy materials consisting of hydrated ferric oxide, clay and sand. The Fe_2O_3 content of ochre is variable, but rarely more than 50 percent (see iron oxide—yellow).

POTASSIUM DICHROMATE (F). $K_2Cr_2O_7$. **TOXIC, SOLUBLE.** A chromium containing material capable of producing the usual color reactions of chromium in glazes (see Chromium). Often used to develop lowfired chrome yellow, orange and red glazes.

POTASSIUM PERMANGANATE (F). $KMnO_4$. **TOXIC, SOLUBLE.** A soluble source of manganese, which may be used for light color washes, or mixed with other soluble materials for a wider color range.

PRASEODYMIUM OXIDE (R). Pr_2O_3. **SLIGHTLY SOLUBLE.** Used in the ceramic industry to produce brilliant yellow colors when fritted with zirconium and silica. It is reasonably stable at high temperatures in both oxidation and reduction.

RUTILE (R, O). TiO_2. A natural source of titanium, usually containing some impurities in the form of iron, and occasionally chromium and vanadium. It is used to produce modified iron colors, such as yellow to brown in oxidation, and cool blues, blue-greys to streaky purple in reduction. It affects other colors strongly, turning cobalt green, iron gold, and copper yellow green. The combinations of yellow greens made with copper and rutile seem to be more or less unaffected by reduction. Rutile also produces crystalline reactions with many glaze bases, particularly those high in lithium, calcium and zinc.

SELENIUM. Se. **TOXIC.** A material used in conjunction with cadmium and sulfur to produce low temperature yellow, orange and red colors in low temperature lead glazes (see Cadmium).

SIENNA. A hydrated iron–manganese ochrous earth, similar to umber but with less manganese.

SILVER CARBONATE (F). Ag_2CO_3. **TOXIC, SOLUBLE. SILVER NITRATE (F).** $AgNO_3$. **TOXIC, SOLUBLE, CORROSIVE.** Silver compounds are rarely used in glazes because of their cost. When they are used, it is usually to produce weak yellows, or to develop iridescent lusters in reduced glazes and low-fired pigments. Mother of pearl lusters may be made with combinations of silver and bismuth. Green and yellow lusters may be made in conjunction with copper compounds. Silver compounds are likely to stain the hands with dark brown to black markings, which may take weeks to wear off. For this reason it is a good idea to wear rubber gloves when handling them.

SODIUM URANATE (F). $Na_2O\ UO_3$. **TOXIC, RADIOACTIVE.** Uranium yellow, yellow uranium oxide. It is used to develop yellow, orange and red glazes in low temperature lead-based glazes, and yellow in high temperature glazes in oxidation. In any degree of reduction it will usually turn black.

UMBER. A naturally occurring iron earth material containing significant manganese, which can be used to develop a range of brown colors that might be expected from a combination of iron and manganese. Similar to, but darker than, both ochre and sienna.

URANIUM OXIDE (F). U_3O_8. **TOXIC, RADIOACTIVE.** Black uranium oxide is a depleted nuclear fuel used to produce yellow in oxidation glazes at a variety of temperatures. It is less efficient than sodium uranate.

VANADIUM PENTOXIDE (F). V_2O_5. **SLIGHTLY SOLUBLE.** Vanadium pentoxide is used to produce yellow colors, usually in conjunction with tin. It is also used industrially to produce yellow and blue colored body stains, in conjunction with zirconium.

USING SOLUBLE COLORANTS

Many colorants may be used in their soluble form to achieve qualities quite different from the powdered oxides or carbonates of the same colorants. They can be used in a similar fashion to water color painting, either in or on the glaze or on the body. They are particularly useful for spraying color because the colorant goes into solution with water, and does not clog spray guns as other materials are prone to do. There may be a problem from the pores or the body absorbing the colorant, and possibly bloating as a result. This can usually be remedied by firing the bisque higher, and thus lowering the degree to which the body can absorb the soluble colorant. Soluble colorants are usually toxic, and therefore should be handled with care. Materials that can be used in soluble form include copper sulfate, cobalt sulfate, iron sulfate, manganese sulfate, potassium dichromate, potassium permanganate, ferric chloride and silver nitrate.

Soluble materials may be used singly or intermixed, and made into solution with water. Perhaps the easiest way to mix is to make a saturated solution by adding to water until no more is dissolved. Solubles can also be mixed as percentages of color to water. They can be used for color as described earlier. Some people find their use a little disconcerting, as the color usually disappears after application, making it difficult to remember where it has been put. Also, as a result of the absorption, it is often difficult to tell just how much color has been applied. It is possible to add a small amount of organic dye such as food coloring to the soluble colorant, to keep track of it. The dye will burn away during firing. It is not until after the work is fired to maturity that the true color of the soluble colorant becomes evident. Soluble colorants may also be sprayed onto hot pieces as they are removed

from raku firings. In this way, various colors and lustrous qualities may be produced.

WATERCOLORS

Some of the manufacturers of better quality artist's watercolors still use highly refined natural pigments in their color blending. (Some companies list the ingredients on the tube, others may produce specification sheets.) The materials that will tolerate being fired to a variety of temperatures are mostly made from mixtures of iron, cobalt, and chromium. The materials are ground far more finely than normally available ceramic materials, and consequently can give more subtle washes, sprays, and details of color, with less danger of specks forming.

The viscous color can be squeezed from the tube and mixed with water, and possibly a little sugar water solution, gum, or corn syrup, to improve flow of the material from the brush. Any of these additives will burn away during firing, leaving just the color. Application can be done on the bisque, but it is probably better on the dry greenware, where the absorption is not so acute. The colors can be brushed or sprayed onto the work.

AUTOMOBILE AND HOUSEHOLD PAINTS

As with watercolors, some manufacturers of household and automobile paints, particularly the metallic spray paints, use refined natural metallic oxide colorants which can provide the ceramist with yet another process whereby he can develop surface color in his work. Most household paints are tinted with synthetic colors that will burn away during firing, but they often use titanium as an opacifying material. Metallic spray paints such as copper and bronze contain copper in a finely ground form, which may be sprayed on the work at any stage, and will give the normal color responses to glazes and kiln atmospheres.

UNDERGLAZE COLORS, GLAZE AND BODY STAINS

Over the last two hundred or so years, the ceramic industry has developed color specialists, who produce a wide range of colors used by industrial pottery manufacturers. Research and development of ceramic color is a huge concern, and the studio potter is the lucky recipient of the wealth of knowledge on color material that results. The journals of various ceramic societies publish interesting articles on new developments, and are a very valuable source of detailed information. There are, of course, many trade secrets in such a competitive business, but color companies are generally helpful with legitimate enquiries.

Chemically, there is not much difference between underglaze colors, glaze stains, and body stains. It is their use in industrial production which has given the difference in terminology. Body stains usually contain a larger percentage of clay in relation to color, and most commercially available body stains are in pastel colors as a result. Underglaze colors and glaze stains are mixtures of materials that are processed in various ways to achieve a desired stable color. They are often fritted or calcined to remove soluble materials and to thoroughly integrate the colorants with the fluxes, clays, or silica, resulting in colors that cannot be made by the simple mixing of basic colorants.

Most ceramists use basic mineral colorants in their work, since almost any color can be obtained from them. However, in many cases, basic metal colorants are not stable enough to achieve subtle shades, and commercially prepared stains and colors are more suitable. For most people, it is not worth the time involved to produce one's own fritted colors, any more than it is worthwhile to produce one's own frits for body and glaze. Commercially made colors are available in a wide range, which can be further expanded by intermixing with basic mineral colorants and opacifiers.

Since stains and prepared colors are made from metallic oxides, carbonates, sulfates, and so on, it stands to reason that they are subject to the effects of the three variables: glaze make-up, firing temperature and atmosphere. The colors given on the industry shade cards (usually available from suppliers) should therefore be taken only as a guide to the potential color. If one produces one's own stains, they, too, will alter with the variables.

MAKING UNDERGLAZE COLORS AND GLAZE STAINS

Making one's own glaze stains and underglaze colors is a normal activity in the ceramist's life. Whenever one mixes two colorants together, such as iron and cobalt, one is, in fact, producing a simple stain. Colors and other materials are mixed to modify, soften, stabilize, opacify, crystallize, or cause to flow, according to the desired result. Most ceramists do some of this as a matter of course. There may be times when certain desired colors are elusive, or when the simple mixtures of colorants flow excessively with the glaze, making finely detailed decoration impossible. At these times it may be necessary to prepare a stain. Stains fall into two separate types: spinels, and other colored stains utilizing colorants, modifiers and fluxes.

SPINEL STAINS

A spinel is a mineral formed at temperatures in the region of 1800°C. There are naturally occurring spinels which are combinations of alkaline oxide and amphoteric oxide, usually alumina, although other metals such as manganese, chromium, and iron may be included. Real spinels are occasionally used as colorants. More often, though, spinel stains, artificially produced by the ceramic industry for use as ceramic colors, are employed for both glazes and clay bodies. These colors are stable and highly resistant to color change in glazes at a wide range of temperatures. They have the composition $RO-R_2O_3$ (R standing for a radical, O for oxygen) and are used in the following combinations to form colored stains:

Cobalt (CoO)—Alumina (Al_2O_3)	Blue
Chromium (CrO)—Alumina (Al_2O_3)	Pink
Manganese (MnO)—Alumina (Al_2O_3)	Pink
Zinc (ZnO)—Alumina (Al_2O_3)	Green
Cadmium (CdO)—Chromium (Cr_2O_3)	Green
Nickel (NiO)—Chromium (Cr_2O_3)	Green
Iron (FeO)—Chromium (Cr_2O_3)	Brown

There is little available written material on spinels,* although the color manufacturers for the ceramic industry are continually working on new spinel colors. The elevated temperatures and control required to form spinels and spinel stains are well outside the availability of most studio ceramists. A wide range of other colored stains may be developed by more practical and simpler methods.

STAIN PREPARATION

The preparation of all stains is a long procedure, requiring blending, calcination, grinding and washing before use. A stain usually consists of three components: colorants (oxides, carbonates, or salts), modifiers (opacifiers, alumina, silica, magnesium), and a flux (frits, feldspars, etc.).

Colorant

Antimony	Yellow
Cadmium	With selenium and sulfur gives reds and yellows. Extremely unstable and poisonous. Best to use commercial preparations, closely following directions, and making certain that the kiln is well vented.
Chromium	Yellow, green, red and pinks
Cobalt	Blue
Copper	Blue, green and red
Gold	Red, pink
Iron	Yellow, brown, red and green
Manganese	Brown, yellow, purple and pink
Nickel	Brown, old gold, khaki, blue and green
Platinum	Black and grey
Vanadium	Yellow, green and blue

Modifiers Some, like silica, are present in all stains, while others help to give the desired colors, Alumina Pinks with chromium and manganese.

*See *The Potter's Dictionary of Materials and Techniques* by Frank Hamer (Watson-Guptill) and *Ceramics* by Glenn C. Nelson (Holt, Rinehart and Winston) for more details.

Magnesia	Pink to purple shades with cobalt, olive green with nickel in reduction
Silica	Always present
Titanium	Yellows with iron, greens with cobalt
Tin oxide	Pinks to red with chromium and calcium
Whiting	"Victoria" greens with chromium
Zinc	Tan to brown with chromium, softens cobalt blues
Zirconium oxide	Turquoise blue with vanadium, strong yellow with praseodymium and silica
Zirconium silicate	Helps stabilize certain nickel colors

Fluxes A wide variety may be used, depending on the color required. The information given in chapter 10 on fluxes should be helpful in determining which will be most satisfactory for use.

BLENDING

Dry Blending Mixing dry materials will generally produce well integrated color. The best way to dry-blend colors is to weigh out the ingredients, place in a mortar, and grind thoroughly with a pestle. For larger amounts, a ball mill will produce a good mix. After initial grinding, the material should be dry sieved through an 80 mesh screen. After sieving, some colors may be used directly, or may need additional preparation, such as calcination.

Wet Blending This is used for materials which are in a soluble crystal form, such as copper sulfate, potassium dichromate, or other soluble salts. The soluble materials are weighed, then mixed together with a little water to a paste, which is then dried, ground and sieved. The wet process is usually used for chrome-tin pinks, vanadium stains, Victoria greens, and any other color requiring the use of soluble salts. Salts generally mix more thoroughly.

Calcination Calcining is the process of heating materials together, in the dry state, usually in some kind of crucible. The reasons for calcining the materials for ceramic stains are to develop the color in an inert, stable form, and to remove any gaseous compounds that may spoil the ware. The material should be placed in a covered crucible of unglazed, bisque-fired porcelain or stoneware, which has been washed in a solution of one part flint, three parts water, to seal the pores. The materials are calcined at a variety of temperatures, from cone 04 to 8, depending on the materials being used. Copper red and iron blue stains should be calcined in reduction.

Grinding After the material has been calcined, it should be chipped out of the crucible. It may be necessary to pound it with a mallet to break it into small enough pieces for hand grinding in a mortar. It can also be ball milled. Whatever method is used, the resulting material should be ground finely enough to pass through a 200 mesh screen.

Washing After grinding, the blend must be washed by levigation (put the blend in water, let it settle, decant, stir, repeat) to remove any remaining soluble salts and to separate the fine grains, which you want, from the coarse, which you do not. When dry, it is ready for use.

Since the number of people who are prepared to go through this process is probably quite small, I can do no better at this point than to refer potential stain makers to Kenneth Shaw's excellent book, *Ceramic Colors and Pottery Decoration* (see bibliography). Stains, whether homemade or commercially prepared, are usually mixed with water and possibly a little gum, and applied by brush or spray, either under or over the glaze. When applied over the glaze the color will usually be stronger. They can also be mixed directly into the clay or glaze batch for an overall effect. Some stain recipes are given in the appendix, page 217.

MAKING UNDERGLAZE PENCILS, PASTELS, AND WATERCOLORS

I wish to thank Jeanne Otis for her research, and Arizona State University for permission to re-state their work in the following section on making underglaze pencils, pastels and watercolors.

To make underglaze pencils and pastels, use a porcelain type slip with 50 percent white firing ball clay or plastic kaolin. For dry strength in the green state, 3 percent macaloid or 5 percent bentonite should be added. A suitable recipe for such a slip is the following:

White firing ball clay	50
Potash feldspar	25
Flint	25
Total	100

Macaloid (or 5% bentonite)	3
Colorant (maximum)	15

The material, including colorants, should be dry sieved through an 80 mesh screen to assure thorough blending. For color you can use mineral oxides, carbonates, and stains. A variety of combinations will produce a wide range of colors, although it is important that colorants be selected which will not burn out at high temperatures (not many will, but cadmium-selenium and potassium dichromate are likely to). The amount of colorant can be up to 15 percent; more than that will cause loss of plasticity in the raw state, making it difficult to form the pencils. The more colorant used, the more intense the color of the pencils or pastels will be.

The dry materials are then mixed with approximately 45 percent water, to which 1 cubic centimeter of sodium silicate per 100 grams of dry material mix has been added. This will slightly deflocculate the slip, giving additional green strength, while also intensifying some of the colorants.

The pencils can be formed by drying the colored slip to a plastic state, and then either rolling out coils or extruding lengths of the desired thickness. These can then be left as pencil lengths, or cut into shorter (1–2 inch) lengths. When dry, the pencils may be fired to between 800 and 950°C., depending on the desired hardness. The short lengths can be placed in a claw grip drafting pencil for use. The Koh-I-Noor #48 drafting pencil can hold "leads" up to ¼ inch in diameter.

Pastels and "watercolors" are used from the greenware state, and are not prefired. To make pastels, use the basic recipe as above, and simply form the clay into coils of extrusions the desired size for use. If they prove to be too fragile, they may be fired to between 600 and 800°C, without making them excessively hard. Watercolor cakes may be made by forming rounds or squares of the colored slip and letting them dry. They may then be used like ordinary school box watercolors, by wetting the surface with water, and applying with a brush.

To make crayons, use the dry recipe, and mix with ordinary commercial wax resist. Form the crayon and let it dry. Since the crayon will contain some latex, it will also have a slight resist effect on the work, particularly when used on bisque-fired ware.

15

Color Testing: Mixing and Blending

There are many methods of color mixing to develop colored glazes, or to observe the reactions of colorants with glazes. The simplest I have found for the purposes of quickly testing colorants in small batches of glaze is to use test tiles divided into six sections.

1   In a bowl, mix 100 grams of base glaze with water to a normal brushable consistency or glaze thickness.
2   Weigh out 10 grams of colorant (oxide, carbonate, or stain), and place it on a clean glossy surface (tile or paper). Flatten the color into a square or rectangular shape, using the side of a pallette knife. Divide the material in half, and then into quarters. Divide one quarter into two, and then one of these portions into

two. All divisions can be done visually. The final sectioned pile of color should look like Figure 15–1.
3   Use test tiles of bisque-fired clay, with commonly used slips, if desired, to observe a wide range of effects. Serially number the test tiles, as per instructions in chapter 4.
4   Brush the base glaze tile on the control.
5   Add pile (A) of the colorant to the base glaze, mix thoroughly, and apply to tile #1.
6   Add pile (B) of the colorant to the mix, mix thoroughly, and apply to tile #2.
7   Add pile (C) to the mix, stir well, and apply to tile #3.
8   Add pile (D) to the mix, stir well, and apply to tile #4.
9   Add pile (E) to the mix, stir well, and apply to tile #5.

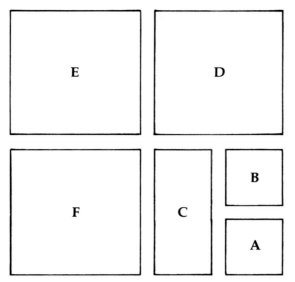

15–1. Colorant mixing diagram.

10 Add pile (F) to the mix, stir well, and apply to tile #6.

11 Fire to the required temperature, and record your results and observations.

The approximate degree of saturation of colorant in the glaze will be this:

Control tile = Base glaze only.
Tile #1 = Base glaze plus 0.625% color (Pile A).
Tile #2 = Base glaze plus 1.25% color (Pile A + B).
Tile #3 = Base glaze plus 2.5% color (Pile A + B + C).
Tile #4 = Base glaze plus 5.0% color (Pile A + B + C + D).
Tile #5 = Base glaze plus 7.5% color (Pile A + B + C + D + E).
Tile #6 = Base glaze plus 10.0% color (Pile A + B + C + D + E + F).

Although not scientifically accurate, this test method provides a good guide to the probable final color, and can be the basis for further experiment of a more specific nature. For some colors, such as copper reds, 10 percent of colorant will be far too much to produce reds, and the saturation will invariably turn to metallic black. However, there are often instances where unusual and interesting color variants develop only when there is a high satu-

ration of color. For some other colorants, even 10 percent may not be enough to give the desired color strength, and up to 20 percent may be needed.

To get less or more colorant into the glaze, you can use the above system, but instead of 10 grams of color to 100 grams of base glaze, use either 5 grams or 20 grams of color to 100 grams of glaze. All of the glaze guidelines in this book are written in a "parts by weight" system. The materials are therefore in ratio to each other and it makes no difference how much glaze is being made. As long as the ratio is kept correct when the glazes are made up into a batch, the units of weight can be ounces, grams, pounds or tons.

COLOR CROSS-BLENDING

The mixture of various colorants can give a wide range of hues, similar to those found on charts in a paint store. The following diagram shows one way of mixing two or more colorants together.

Cross-blend number	1	2	3	4	5	6
Colorant X	10	8	6	4	2	0
Colorant Y	0	2	4	6	8	10
Total	10	10	10	10	10	10

The total of the mix again adds up to 10; it should be mixed together dry before mixing into the liquid glaze base. Dry-mixing of small amounts of material can be done through a small kitchen strainer. When the dry colorants are thoroughly blended, proceed with the testing as outlined at the beginning of this chapter. If one is cross-blending colors in this way, using a ratio of either 2% or 4% of colorant X, and 8% or 6% of colorant Y, to total 10%, the following diagrams show approximately how much of each colorant will be in the various cut sections of the color pie. For the ratios 6:4% and 8:2%, just use the same process, but exchange X and Y materials.

Color-Blending Ratios, 2:8 and 8:2 (total amount of color in glaze)

Colorant or Opacifier	Ratio	Tile 1 0.625%	Tile 2 1.25%	Tile 3 2.5%	Tile 4 5%	Tile 5 7.5%	Tile 6 10%
Colorant X	2	0.125	0.25	0.5	1.0	1.25	2.0
Colorant Y	8	0.5	1.0	2.0	4.0	6.0	8.0

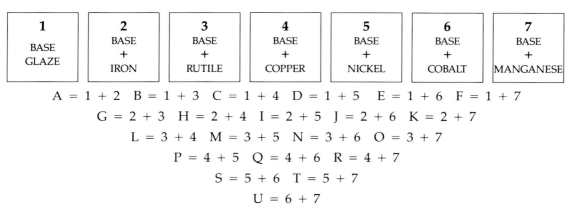

1	2	3	4	5	6	7
BASE GLAZE	BASE + IRON	BASE + RUTILE	BASE + COPPER	BASE + NICKEL	BASE + COBALT	BASE + MANGANESE

A = 1 + 2   B = 1 + 3   C = 1 + 4   D = 1 + 5   E = 1 + 6   F = 1 + 7

G = 2 + 3   H = 2 + 4   I = 2 + 5   J = 2 + 6   K = 2 + 7

L = 3 + 4   M = 3 + 5   N = 3 + 6   O = 3 + 7

P = 4 + 5   Q = 4 + 6   R = 4 + 7

S = 5 + 6   T = 5 + 7

U = 6 + 7

15–2. Glaze cross-blending and variations.

Cross-Blending Colors, 4:6 and 6:4 (total amount of color in glaze)

Colorant or Opacifier	Ratio	Tile 1 0.625%	Tile 2 1.25%	Tile 3 2.5%	Tile 4 5%	Tile 5 7.5%	Tile 6 10%
Colorant X	4	0.25	0.5	1.0	2.0	3.0	4.0
Colorant Y	6	0.375	0.75	1.5	3.0	4.5	6.0

For lighter or darker colors, the colorant volume may be halved or doubled, as suggested above. For the development of pastel colors, colorants and opacifiers may be mixed in the same way.

The cross-blending of two colorants (or colorant and opacifier), if done with the above mixtures, will give 36 color variations from two materials. There will be 6 variations of material X, 6 of material Y, and 24 of the two together. Working in this way, one can achieve very subtle gradations, and it becomes much easier to select exactly what one wants. The number of color variations which may be achieved from just one glaze is infinite.

GLAZE CROSS-BLENDING

Glaze blending can be done by line blends or triaxial blends, as explained in chapters 7 and 8, using glazes instead of single materials. Another convenient way of blending glazes which have the same base is through glaze cross-blending. This process begins with one base glaze and six colorants, as shown in Figure 15–2. Glaze numbers 2–7 can either have the same amount of color, say 5 percent, or can have random amounts as desired, or as determined by experience.

To do this series of tests, it is necessary to weigh out 700 grams of any glaze, and dry sieve it well. Then divide this into seven bowls of 100 grams each. Mark each bowl with the number of the variation, 1 to 7. Add the color to the individual variation, as in Figure 15–2, and dry sieve again. Make a small amount of each mix into a brushable consistency, and apply to tiles numbered 1–7, as a record of the base glaze variations. Weigh out 10 grams from bowl no. 1, and 10 grams from bowl no. 2, mix together with water to normal glaze consistency, and either dip or brush onto a test tile, with thick and thin variations. Call this mix A, then carry on with the same procedure through all of the mixtures from A to U.

This process will give 28 color variations from (and including) the basic seven found in the boxes. Any colorants or opacifiers may be used in this way, in place of those suggested in the boxes. If you are extremely well organized, you could also use different glaze bases, although it sometimes becomes difficult to work out just what the final glaze consists of. However, it is not impossible to come up with the correct proportions or percentages of materials.

16

The Ceramic Spectrum

Squeezing paint out of tubes and mixing desired colors by sight is a simple luxury not available to the ceramist. The glaze maker only sees what he has mixed when the glaze emerges from the kiln in its incredible metamorphosed beauty. There are methods available, however, that enable the ceramist to narrow the margin for error somewhat and approach the problem of color development with reasonable confidence. The lists on the next few pages suggest ways of developing specific colors with references to those factors which enhance or inhibit the process.

SPECIFIC COLOR DEVELOPMENT: 42 COLORS, 134 VARIATIONS

There is a vast array of commercially available underglaze colors and glaze stains. The ceramist who is aiming for a difficult color or color range—red, orange, yellow, or purple—might be well advised to look among the available preparations to minimize the difficulty of searching for his own. Commercial products will almost certainly be more expensive, but if the desired result is achieved, the expense is probably more than justified.

Commerically prepared stains are so varied that it is difficult to predict the specific colors that might result from their use. The basic metallic colorants are usually more readily available and less expensive than stains; thus, I have concentrated on the colors which may be obtained from them. It would be quite impossible to cover all of the variables involved in color development and list all the materials available, but the color list should give a good idea of where to begin, and what factors control the end result.

It should be remembered that prepared colors, whether commercially produced or home-made, are subject to the same influences of glaze makeup, temperature and atmosphere as any other colorant. Most color producing companies will give listings of the colorants used in their stains. If these are checked against the lists for colorants in chapter 14, for fluxes in chapter 10, and for colors in this chapter, it should not be too difficult to tell if any given glaze is likely to produce the desired result.

The color listings follow a spectrum sequence. I have listed 42 colors, following as closely as possible the format and color descriptions shown on the average watercolor, oil or acrylic paint color chart, for ease of reference and color expectation. Since people see color differently, I have made no attempt to point out on the color photographs of individual colorants those colors which to my eye would be the precise dark red, burgundy, maroon

and so on. It is probably more accurate for the individual to look at a paint chart and make his own comparisons.

There are some references in the list to the glaze bases found in the appendix, page 215. There are also references to some specific colored glaze sections such as copper reds in chapter 13. Colors are listed with the colorants needed to obtain them, approximate temperatures, atmosphere, amount of colorant needed, and comments on enhancing or inhibiting factors in their development. Because of the widely variable nature of glaze and color development there are many generalities. Where the word "vary" occurs in the column under "cone," it signifies that the intended results could be expected most of the time at various points up to cone 10 on the temperature scale. For a comparison between cones and temperatures, see appendix 1, page 200.

Color	Colorant Needed	Cone	Atmos	%	Comments
Dark red	Chromium	012–010	Ox.	5–10	In low-fired lead-based glazes containing no zinc.
	Copper	Vary	Red.	0.5–5	Best in glazes containing less than 10% clay content, and a high alkaline content. Needs good reduction. In low temperature glazes it can be reduced during cooling. Good reds as low as cone 018 this way.
	Cadmium–selenium stains	010–05	Ox.	1–10%	Glazes need to be formulated from special frits for best results (see appendix 4). Lead glazes can also be used. Do not over-fire. Use and fire only in well ventilated areas, as even the kiln fumes are highly toxic.
	Iron	Vary	Both	5–10%	Good in many glaze bases at all temperatures. Can be improved by addition of 2–5% tin.
Burgundy	Iron				See dark red, Iron.
	Copper				See dark red, Copper. Owing to the unstable nature of copper, this colorant can produce a wide range of results.
Maroon	Chromium–tin stains	Vary	Ox.	1–5%	Use in glazes containing calcium—no zinc. Sometimes burns out at high temperatures. All chrome-tin stains must have calcium in the glaze to develop satisfactory colors.
	Copper	Vary	Red	1–5%	Best in high alkaline glazes. See copper red section, chapter 13.
Crimson	Chromium–tin stains				See maroon-chrome-tin stains.
	Copper with titanium	8–10	Red.	1–5%	Titanium 2–5%. See copper, chapter 14, and copper reds, chapter 13.

Color	Colorant Needed	Cone	Atmos	%	Comments
Crimson (continued)	Cadmium–selenium	010–05	Ox.	0.5–5%	Best with special frits Ferro 3548 and 3278. Zirconium opacifier helps.
Vermilion and scarlet	Chromium	018–010	Ox.	2–5%	High lead glaze with no zinc.
	Cadmium–selenium	010–05	Ox.	1–2%	See Crimson, cadmium selenium.
	Uranium	010–05	Ox.	0–10%	High lead glaze needed. Strict oxidation.
Indian red	Iron	Vary	Both	5–10%	Best in high calcium glazes; bone ash helps. Tin addition up to 5% also helps. Also in ash glazes.
Brick red	Iron	Vary	Both	5–10%	Similar to Indian red. Tin to 2% helps.
Orange brown	Iron 8% + rutile 2%	Vary	Both	1–10%	Good with most glazes for soft warm colors.
	Iron 8% + tin 2%	Vary	Both	1–5%	Good with most glazes. Creamier than above.
	Uranium	010–05	Ox.	2–10%	Needs high lead glazes. An addition of iron 2% helps.
Orange red	Chromium	018–010	Ox.	2–5%	High lead glazes—no zinc.
	Uranium	010–05	Ox.	5–10%	High lead glazes.
	Cadmium–selenium	012–05	Ox.	1–4%	Best with special frits Ferro 3548 or Ferro 3278 or both. Zirconium opacifier helps.
Orange	Chromium				See orange-red.
	Uranium				See orange-red.
	Cadmium–selenium				See orange-red.
	Iron	Vary	Both	0–5%	In tin or titanium opacified glazes.
	Rutile	Vary	Both	5–10%	In many glaze types, particularly alkaline.
	Copper	8–10	Both	1–2%	High alumina or magnesia glazes (See chapter 12, Alterations.
Orange yellow	Chromium		Ox.	1–2%	See orange red.
	Uranium		Ox.	2–5%	See orange red
	Iron	Vary	Both	2–5%	With tin or titanium opacified glazes.
	Rutile	Vary	Ox.	1–10%	Best with alkaline glazes.
Yellow ochre	Rutile				See orange yellow.
	Iron	Vary	Both	1–5%	In high barium, strontium, or zinc glazes.
	Iron 5% + tin 2%	Vary	Ox.	1–5%	Various mixtures in many glaze bases.
	Iron 5% + rutile 5%	Vary	Both	1–5%	Various mixtures in many glaze bases.
	Vanadium–zirconium stain	Vary	Ox.	5–10%	Various mixtures in many glaze bases.
Chrome yellow	Chromium	018–010	Ox.	1–3%	High lead glazes.
	Uranium	010–05	Ox.	1–3%	High lead glazes.
	Praseodymium yellow stains	Vary	Both	3–10%	Good in most glazes. Sometimes burns out in reduction firing.
Lemon yellow	Praseodymium yellow stains	Vary	Both	1–10%	Good in most glazes. Best in oxidation.
Pale yellow and cream yellow	Antimony	010–02	Ox.	5–15%	Needs high lead glazes opacified with tin.
	Iron 5% + tin 2%	Vary	Both	2–5%	High barium, strontium or zinc glazes. Titanium opacified glazes help.
	Vanadium	Vary	Both	2–5%	In glazes opacified with tin.

Color	Colorant Needed	Cone	Atmos	%	Comments
Cream Yellow (continued)	Uranium	012–12	Ox.	2–5%	In a wide variety of glaze bases.
	Rutile 5% + tin 5%	Vary	Ox.	2–5%	In a wide variety of glaze bases.
Yellow green	Almost any yellow glaze with added copper will produce yellow green.				
	Copper 2–8% + rutile 2–8%	Vary	Both	2–10%	In a wide variety of glazes, particularly those high in alkaline materials.
	Chromium	Vary	Both	0–3%	In yellow glazes without tin.
	Cobalt	Vary	Both	0–1%	In any yellow glazes.
	Chromium	018–05	Ox.	0–2%	In high alkaline glazes without tin.
Light green	Copper	Vary	Ox.	0–2.5%	In various glazes except high barium, or magnesium. Best in glazes opacified with tin or titanium.
	Cobalt	Vary	Both	0–2%	In glazes opacified with titanium, or containing rutile.
Apple green	Chromium	Vary	Both	0–2%	Various glaze bases—no zinc, no tin. Good in alkaline glazes with zirconium opacifers. Use also potassium dichromate.
	Copper				See light green; use in non-opacified glazes.
Celadon green	Iron	Vary	Red.	0.5–2%	See appendix 6. Do not use with zinc glazes. Best with high sodium, potassium and calcium glazes.
	Copper	Vary	Ox.	0.5–5%	Good in a wide range of glazes. In oxidation, copper red glazes as in chapter 13.
Grass green	Copper	010–2	Ox.	1–5%	High lead glazes, sometimes with boron.
	Chromium	018–04	Ox.	1–2%	High alkaline glazes.
Olive green	Nickel	Vary	Both	1–5%	In high magnesia glazes at various cones. Matt to shiny olive green.
	Iron	Vary	Red	3–5%	In high calcium and alkaline glazes—see appendix, Oriental Iron Glazes.
Hooker's green	Copper + cobalt mixtures	Vary	Ox.	2–5%	In wide variety of glaze bases.
	Cobalt + chromium mixtures	Vary	Both	2–5%	In wide variety of glazes—no zinc or tin. Good opacified with titanium or zirconium compounds.
Chrome green	Chromium	06–12	Both	2–5%	In most glazes—no zinc or tin.
Dark green	Copper	Vary	Ox.	5–10%	Many glaze bases, particularly high barium, strontium, or zinc, or alkaline minimum 10% kaolin.
	Cobalt + chromium mixtures	Vary	Both	5–10%	Cross-blends of these colorants will give a wide range of dark greens.
	Cobalt + rutile mixtures			5–10%	
Turquoise	Copper	Vary	Ox.	1–10%	In alkaline and high barium glazes—bluish with no clay content, greenish with added clay.
	Copper + rutile mixtures	Vary	Both	1–5%	In similar glazes to above.
	Copper + tin mixtures	Vary	Ox.	1–10%	In glazes as above.

Color	Colorant Needed	Cone	Atmos	%	Comments
Blue green	Cobalt + rutile mixtures	Vary	Both	1–5%	In a wide variety of glazes.
	Cobalt + chromium mixtures	Vary	Both	1–5%	In most glazes without tin or zinc.
Light blue	Nickel	Vary	Ox.	1–2%	In high zinc or barium glazes.
	Rutile	Vary	Red.	1–5%	In wide range of glazes; best with low (10% or less) clay content.
	Cobalt	Vary	Both	0.25–1%	In most glazes, particularly opacified with tin. Also mixed with small amounts of iron.
Celadon blue	Iron	6–10	Red.	0.5–2%	In high alkaline or calcium clear glazes. Black iron is generally preferable to red. See appendix, Oriental Iron Glazes.
Wedgwood blue	Cobalt + iron mixtures	Vary	Both	0.5–2%	In most glazes small amounts of cobalt with iron, manganese, or nickel give soft blues. Added tin gives pastel blue.
	Cobalt + manganese mixtures	Vary	Both	0.5–2%	
	Cobalt + nickel mixtures	Vary	Both	0.5–2%	
	Cobalt	4–10	Both	0.5–3%	In high zinc glazes
	Nickel	4–10	Ox.	1–3%	In high barium/zinc glazes—crystalline.
Blue grey	Nickel	Vary	Ox.	0.5–5%	In high zinc/barium glazes.
	Rutile	Vary	Red.	2–5%	In a wide variety of glazes.
	Cobalt + manganese				See Wedgwood blue.
	Cobalt	Vary	Ox.	0.5–5%	In high zinc glazes.
Ultramarine.	Cobalt	Vary	Both	0.5–5%	In high barium, colemanite and calcium glazes—no zinc or magnesium.
Cerulean blue and Peacock	Cobalt	Vary	Both	0.5–5%	In glazes containing cryolite or fluorspar.
	Cobalt 0.5–1% + chrome 1–2%	Vary	Both	2–5%	In most glaze bases, except those containing zinc or tin.
Prussian blue	Nickel	6–10	Ox.	5–10%	In high barium/zinc glazes.
	Cobalt + manganese mixtures	Vary	Both	5–10%	In most glaze bases.
	Cobalt + chromium + manganese	Vary	Both	5–10%	In most glazes—cobalt 2, manganese 2, chromium 2.
Navy blue	Cobalt	Vary	Both	5–10%	In most glazes except those high in zinc, barium or magnesium.
Indigo	Nickel	Vary	Ox.	8–10%	In high barium/zinc glazes.
	Cobalt + manganese	Vary	Both	5–10%	Cross blend mixtures in most glazes.
	Cobalt + black stain	Vary	Both	5–10%	Cross blend mixtures in most glazes. See chapter 17 for black stain.
Violet	Cobalt	Vary	Both	1–10%	In high magnesia glazes.
	Nickel	Vary	Ox.	1–10%	In some high barium glazes—see chapter 10, Flux saturations.
	Manganese	Vary	Both	1–10%	In high alkaline glazes.
	Copper	Vary	Ox.	8–10%	In some high barium glazes—see chapter 10, Flux saturations.

Color	Colorant Needed	Cone	Atmos	%	Comments
Brown	Iron	Vary	Both	3–10%	In most glazes. For high fire see appendix 6.
	Manganese	Vary	Both	2–10%	In most glazes.
	Nickel	Vary	Both	2–5%	In boron, calcium and lead glazes.
	Chromium	Vary	Both	2–5%	In high zinc glazes.
	Umber	Vary	Both	2–10%	In most glazes.
	Ilmenite	Vary	Both	2–10%	In most glazes; in high calcium can give bluish tint.
	Rutile	Vary	Both	8–10%	In most glazes—gold brown.
Pink	Cobalt	Vary	Ox.	1–5%	In high magnesium glazes. Also in very low alumina content glazes.
	Copper	Vary	Red.	0.2–2%	In conjunction with tin in copper red glazes—see chapter 13.
	Copper	6–10	Ox.	0.2–3%	In high alumina or calcium glazes.
	Chromium	Vary	Ox.	1–2%	In tin opacified glazes containing calcium.
	Iron	Vary	Ox.	1–5%	In tin opacified glazes containing calcium.
	Rutile	Vary	Both	5–10%	In high calcium and some ash glazes.
	Nickel	018–012	Ox.	1–3%	In high barium glazes, with some zinc.
	Manganese	Vary	Both	1–5%	In alkaline glazes opacified with tin or titanium. Also in high alumina glazes.
Mauve or lilac	Cobalt	Vary	Both	1–5%	In high magnesium glazes.
	Nickel	Vary	Ox.	1–5%	In high barium glazes—see chapter 10, Flux Saturations.
Purple	Copper	6–10	Both	8–10%	In high alkaline or barium/zinc glazes.
	Nickel	Vary	Ox.	5–10%	In high barium glazes—see chapter 10.
	Cobalt	Vary	Both	5–10%	In high magnesium glazes.
	Manganese	04–10	Ox.	5–10%	In high alkaline and high barium glazes.
	Iron	8–10	Red.	8–10%	In high calcium glazes—see appendix, Oriental Iron Glazes.
Grey	Iron	Vary	Red.	2–4%	In many glaze bases—grey brown.
	Iron chromate	Vary	Both	2–5%	In most glaze bases without zinc or tin.
	Nickel	Vary	Both	2–5%	In most glaze bases—grey brown.
	Copper	8–10	Both	3–10%	In high magnesium glazes—warm grey in reduction, cold grey in oxidation.
	Cobalt + nickel mixtures	Vary	Both	1–5%	Blue greys in most glazes.
	Cobalt + manganese mixtures	Vary	Both	1–5%	Blue grey to purple grey in most glazes.
	Black stain—see chapter 17	Vary	Both	1–5%	Shades of grey in most opacified glazes.
Black	Iron	Vary	Both	8–12%	In high calcium glazes—see appendix, Oriental Iron Glazes.
	Copper	Vary	Both	5–10%	In a wide range of glazes.
	Cobalt	Vary	Both	8–10	Blue black in most glazes except zinc and magnesium.
	Manganese	Vary	Both	8–15%	Brown black in most glazes.
	Copper + manganese	Vary	Both	8–10%	In most glazes—sometimes lustrous.
	Uranium	Vary	Red.	5–10%	In most glazes.
	Cobalt + iron + manganese	Vary	Both	5–10%	Cross-blended in most glaze bases.
	Iron + cobalt + chromium	Vary	Both	1–10%	Cross-blended in zinc-free glaze bases.
	Black stain—chapter 17	Vary	Both	3–10%	In most zinc-free glazes.

USING PREPARED COLORANTS

The preceding spectrum list contains 42 colors, and 134 variations on ways to achieve those colors. Some stains have been included, in order to more or less complete the spectrum where standard mineral colorants prove difficult. While it is possible to develop variations on these colors using standard mineral colorants, they are usually unreliable, and unstable. It is here that the prepared stain comes into its own. As stated earlier, it must always be remembered that the glaze makeup has a profound effect on the colors that may be obtained with any given mineral colorant, or mixture of mineral colorants.

The manufacturers of ceramic stains will provide specification sheets on the type of glaze necessary to develop the color as shown on their shade charts. Many stains have to have certain oxides in the glaze base for suitable color development. One of the more obvious examples is the range of pink to red produced through chromium-tin stains, which will not develop true color without calcium in the glaze. Also cadmium-selenium stains must be used with high lead, or special frits, and cannot be fired above cone 05 without the color starting to burn away. The specification sheets will usually state these requirements.

The color photographs of color reactions from single and mixed colorants in a wide range of glaze bases, temperatures and atmospheres are explained in appendix 5 with their glaze bases. They are written as serial numbers for ease of reference. These 288 color variations should give an idea of the controlling factors in color development. The only time that the use of stains is shown in the photographs is in the development of yellow colors with a zirconium/silica/praseodymium stain no. 14 H 236, from Blythe Colors, England. The range of yellow colors which can be developed with basic mineral colorants, and the development of stains using zirconium with praseodymium or vanadium, have greatly increased the ceramist's pallette. Prepared stains can be intermixed with other colorants to expand their range.

The color photographs of glaze tests following page 48 are a guide to the colors which can be available, and although the recipes for the glaze bases and colorants are available in the appendix, they should only be viewed as examples rather than solutions. All glaze tests will vary, depending on a number of factors: clays, differing materials, kiln atmosphere, fusing procedures, kiln types and colorants. Therefore, the colors as shown are likely to vary from one glazemaker to another.

Opacification

An opaque glaze is one where light is unable to pass through, and is reflected or refracted off the surface. In reality, opaque glazes are probably translucent, but owing to the mass of the ceramic body beneath, they appear opaque. Opacification is the process whereby a glaze, or colorant, is rendered opaque by the addition of one or more materials called opacifiers. They are mainly used in low temperature glazes. At higher temperatures, more use is made of refractory materials to create opacity. These materials, such as kaolin and ball clay, are considerably cheaper for opacification than those usually used at low temperatures. In high temperature glazes, an excess of refractory material remains suspended and unmelted in the glaze matrix, preventing light from passing through. At low temperatures this would most likely cause matt-

ness or even dryness of the glaze. In low temperature glazes, the opacifying material also remains suspended in the glaze, forming a barrier to light rays, but does not usually cause the glaze to feel dry unless used to excess.

THE CHARACTERISTICS OF OPACIFIERS

Most opacifiers perform actions in a glaze in addition to opacification, and the ceramist should take these actions into consideration. They can affect the glaze both as fluxing agents, such as zinc, and as refractories, such as kaolin, ball clay and titanium. They may also have an unexpected effect on colorants, as in the reaction between chromium and tin in oxidizing atmospheres, where pink is likely to develop; and also in the reaction between cobalt and titanium, where a pale green color will occur instead of the expected pale blue.

There are only a few opacifiers. Of these, a number are commercially produced fritted materials, such as Opax, Opazon, Superpax, Zircopax and Ultrox. They are generally used in amounts of up to 10 percent, depending on the degree of opacity desired and the efficiency of the opacifier being used. Many opacifiers are absorbed into the glaze in high temperature reduction—another reason for using refractories instead of opacifiers.

Opacifiers are found in the following list. As stated, some opacifiers react as fluxing agents, some as refractories, and some as light colorants. Where these functions are reliable and clear-cut, the name of the material will be followed by the letters **(F)**, **(R)**, or **(C)**.

ANTIMONY OXIDE (C). Sb_2O_3. **TOXIC**. Used in low temperature glazes to produce a weak white. In the presence of iron, lead, rutile, or titanium, it has a tendency to produce yellowish colors.

CALCIUM ZIRCONIUM SILICATE (F). $CaZrSiO_4$. Commercially prepared; particularly useful where both calcium and zircon may be needed in a glaze. Zircon provides opacity. Calcium provides fluxing and stabilizing action, and is particularly useful where colorants, such as chrome-tin stains, need calcium to develop properly.

CLAYS, PARTICULARLY KAOLIN (R). Clays are used to make glazes opaque, at the same time as making them more viscous. When clays are added to glazes, there is a variable point at which the glazes will not absorb any more clay into the glaze melt, depending on the glaze and its maturing temperature. After this point, it remains in suspension in the glaze matrix, in its unmelted state, forming a barrier to the passing of light rays, and thus rendering the glaze opaque.

FELDSPAR (R At low temperatures, **F** at high temperatures). Feldspar and feldspar-like materials react in low temperature glazes in much the same way as kaolin does at all temperatures. It causes opacification because it melts only partially, and stays in suspension.

OPAX (R). A fritted zirconium material, containing small amounts of titanium, sodium, potassium, and iron.

OPAZON (R). A fritted zirconium silicate, mainly used in England.

TIN OXIDE—STANNIC OXIDE (Slightly R). SnO. Tin oxide is the most widely used and the most effective opacifying agent. Tin has been used as a whitener for glazes for several hundred years. It is good at all temperatures, although in many highfired reduction glazes, particularly high gloss glazes, tin tends to get absorbed into the matrix of the glaze. Tin enhances the development of some colors, such as orange to red from iron at most temperatures, and also copper reds in high temperature reduction. Tin is a necessary ingredient in the formation of pinks and reds, in conjunction with chromium. White glazes opacified with tin are usually a warm or slightly creamy white.

TITANIUM DIOXIDE (R,C). TiO_2. Titanium produces creamy white opacification. It reacts as a refractory, often producing semi-matt surfaces. It also often produces a surface covered with microscopic crystals, especially when used in conjunction with iron. Titanium can have a strong effect on many colorants. With tin, it will give ivory; with cobalt it will give a range of soft greens. In high temperature reduction glazes it can give pale blue greys. In copper red reduction glazes, titanium can produce opalescent, purplish blue, or aubergine colors. It is a particularly useful material in electric-fired glazes at all temperatures, where a mere 2 percent addition often gives an otherwise uninteresting glaze microcrystalline formations, which can have exciting effects on added color.

ULTROX (R). A fritted zirconium silicate.

ZINC OXIDE (F). ZnO. Zinc is primarily used as a fluxing agent for mid to high temperature glazes. It can, however, perform a dual function in the production of opaque glazes. It has a strong effect on many colorants, turning iron anywhere from pale yellow to mustard brown, chromium to brown, cobalt to grey blue, and nickel to blue, green or brown.

ZIRCONIUM OXIDE (R). ZrO_2. Zirconium oxide is seldom used alone as an opacifier, but is fritted with other oxides into a more stable silicate form.

ZIRCONIUM SILICATE (F). $ZrSiO_4$. Zirconium silicate opacifiers generally produce cool white glazes and often add to the fluxing action of the glaze to some extent, particularly at the higher temperature ranges. It is often used in conjunction with tin, to cut down on the high cost of tin oxide. Zirconium compounds are more stable than tin in reducing conditions. They are widely used in the formation of underglaze colors, and glaze stains.

ADDING OPACIFIERS TO GLAZE RECIPES

These opacifiers make up the selection normally used to render glazes opaque. The decision on which to use is essentially a personal one. With the exception of where a given opacifier may detrimentally affect the color requirement, surface, or working properties of a glaze, they all have their uses.

The amount of opacifier that should be used is dependent on the desired result. Under most circumstances, a maximum of 10 percent is usually adequate. However, different opacifiers have different strengths, and to get the same degree of opacification from tin and Zircopax, for instance, approximately twice the latter would be needed. Tin is generally felt to be the best and whitest opacifier for general use, although it is usually very expensive. Its color affecting properties should be borne in mind when using it with colorants, particularly colors containing chromium.

Although we usually think of opacification as the process of making glazes white, glazes may also be made opaque by the addition of modifying or darkening agents. This is like producing shade variations in painting—the addition of black to basic colors darkens them. It is, of course, not only black which can fulfill this function. In ceramics, the modifying agents most often used to darken colors are nickel, manganese and black stains. Black stains are available commercially, or can be made easily. A good black stain can be made with equal parts of iron, manganese, cobalt, chromium and a powdered porcelain body. If no porcelain body is available, the above black stain has the following recipe:

Iron	20
Manganese	20
Cobalt	20
Chromium	20
Kaolin	8
Feldspar	8
Flint	4
Total	100

This mixture is best when ball milled for a minimum of four hours, to limit the tendency to specking, and to make certain that the color is thoroughly mixed. It can be added to glazes or other colorants to develop subtle, darker opaque colors, in an action similar to the addition of whiteners to lighten. Since the black stain is a very concentrated mixture, only small amounts will be needed to have a strong effect. A maximum of 5 percent should produce an intense black. Black and white opacifiers together will produce a range of opaque greys. These greys will, of course, be subject to the variables of glaze makeup, temperature, and kiln atmosphere.

18

Textural Variations

The ceramic surface can be made in almost any texture from ultra-smooth to extremely coarse and any quality in between. The smooth surface usually comes from a well matured glaze, or superb burnishing, or from a terra sigillata finish. The coarse surface can be physically rough from unmelted materials in the glaze or clay, or from additions of coarse materials in slips or in the glaze itself. It can have rough, agitated surfaces caused by additives that boil and bubble, leaving cratered, erupted, moonlike, or volcanic skins. It can also have coverings that may pucker and fissure during the firing process. These may be caused by firing to where the glaze has fused to the clay, but has not reached maturity. It can also happen by accidental or induced drafts during the cooling cycle. The surface may simply have granular materials within the glaze that bleed or pool during the firing, giving visual, rather than physical texture.

CLAY ADDITIVES

Additions may be in the form of either colored or non-colored material.

SAND

Colored sand, such as iron-stained sandstone, or black volcanic beach sand, as found in such places as Hawaii, the Greek islands, or other volcanic areas, can be mixed with clay, or clay slip. Sand which is larger in grain size than 50 mesh can cause problems in the clay, due to quartz inversion.

GROG

Grog can be made of different clays, brick dust, or clay slips; it can be colored with oxides, carbonates or body stains, which have been fired, broken, ground up and screened through a 30 mesh sieve. The colored grog can then be added to the clay or slip and, depending on the glaze, will bleed through giving spots of color, or, if the material melts sufficiently, create streaks and tears.

GRANULAR COLORANTS

Some colorants are commercially available in a granular form, such as rutile, ilmenite and manganese. If one is living close to a mining area, it is often possible to get mine tailings in a powdered form, which may contain very interesting mineral ores. These can all be added to clays to develop unusual effects. Surfaces reminiscent of volcanic lava flows can be developed using granular manganese. The manganese will start to become molten at about cone 4–6, and will ooze through the body. Mid to high temperature clays are needed; light stoneware, porcelain, or colored porcelain give the best contrast with the dark manganese rivulets. Care must be taken to make sure that the work

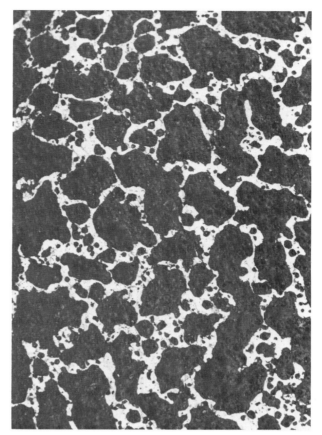

18–2. Roman Bartkiw (Canada). Detail of 18–1.

does not fuse itself to the kiln shelf, as a result of the flowing molten manganese. Setting the piece on a slice of insulating brick covered with a kiln wash, or a dusting of either flint or alumina hydrate, should eliminate this potential problem.

BURNOUT MATERIALS

Many organic materials may be put into the clay with the intention of them burning out during the firing, leaving various textures behind. Straw, coffee grounds, ground nut shells, corn husks, sawdust, and so on may be used for this purpose. Some low fusion inorganic materials, such as Perlite, expanded Vermiculite, nylon or fiberglass are also used, not only to develop texture, but also to add fibrous strength in the working stages. Fiberglass should not be used as an additive to clays which are to be thrown, as it is likely to cause lacerations to the hands during the throwing process.

18–1. Roman Bartkiw (Canada). Colored porcelain with granular manganese dioxide wedged into the clay. Oxidation fired at cone 8.

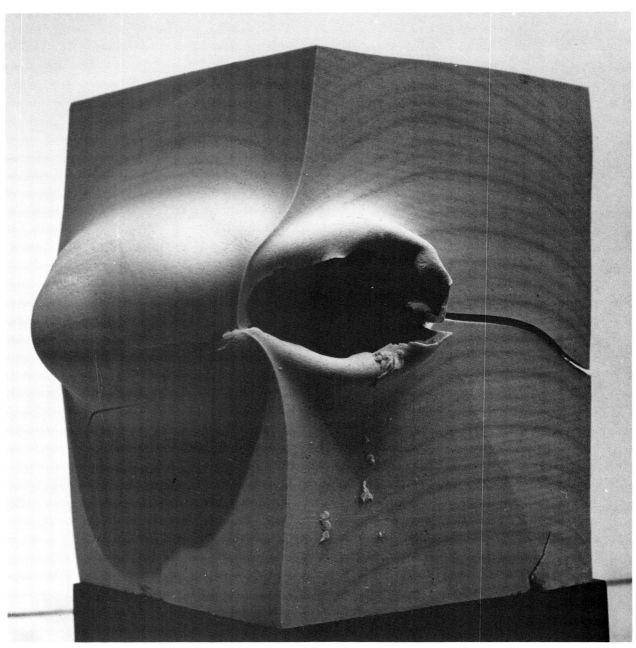

18–3. Imre Schrammel (Hungary). Porcelain cube, 9 in. high, deformed by a bullet. Cone 9 reduction.

GLAZE ADDITIVES

Many of the materials already mentioned may be used as glaze texture additives. Sands, grogs and granular colorants when added to glazes usually give quite different effects from those that occur when they are added to the clay. This is because they have a more immediate action on the glaze fusion. The volume of additive to glaze will vary, according to the desired results, but between 5 and 10 percent of most of these materials will have a marked effect.

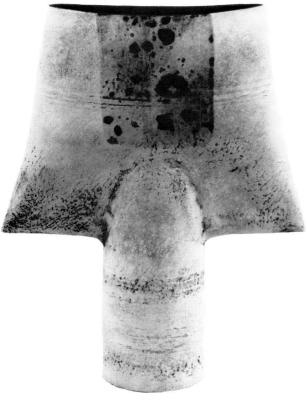

18–4. Hans Coper (United Kingdom). Envelope form vase, stoneware, 9 in. high. Once-fired, oxidation cone 8. Covered with white slip glaze, brushed on in several coats. Manganese and iron rubbed into slip texture. Reverse side of figure 11–6.

18–5. Enid Legros (Canada). "Green Burdock." Slipcast porcelain box, reduction fired to cone 11. The beaded areas are created in a third firing; crushed glass beads are applied to previously unglazed areas, then fired at a low enough heat for them to just start to melt and fuse to the surface.

18–6. Tom and Ginny Marsh (U.S.A.). Expanded spherical form. Stoneware with white Hakeme slip brushed on exterior, with trapped carbon glaze containing soluble materials that bleed through to intensify color. Reduction fired at cone 10.

18–7. Taizo Kuroda (Japan). Stoneware bowl with Hakeme slip decoration under an ash and feldspar glaze. Reduction fired at cone 9. Collection of the author.

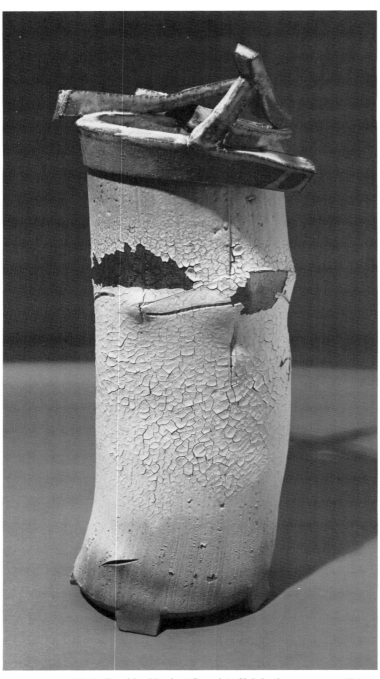

18–8. Franklin Heisler (Canada). Slab-built stoneware, 15 in. high, with white engobe over dark stoneware body. Reduction fired to cone 10.

POWDERED MATERIALS

Many materials in their powdered form may be sprinkled, heaped on, or even thrown on in a slightly moistened form, so that when the work is fired, a variety of surface enrichment takes place. Many crystalline, crackled, pooled and crawled decorative effects may be achieved in this way. Of all the materials normally used by ceramists, the most useful for powdered applications are as follows:

For crystalline effects—lithium, zinc, titanium, rutile, ilmenite and copper.

For crackled effects—nepheline syenite, lithium, borax, amblygonite and frits.

For pooled effects—frits, colemanite, cullet or broken glass, glass beads and enamelling beads.

For beaded effects—enamelling beads fired until their slumping point, and feldspar materials mixed with water and applied with a trailer.

For crawled effects—powdered clay or slip, over a high gloss glaze or zinc.

Volcanic and pitted surfaces can be developed through the addition of medium grind silicon carbon to the glaze, in additions of 3–5 percent. This will also cause some reduction to take place, even in electric kilns, and colors will be affected accordingly. Other cratered effects may be achieved by placing granular salt directly on the ware and firing to cone 8–10. This works best with high silica clay bodies, where the longer the firing, the more active the cratering. Colored cratering can be achieved by mixing common salt and soluble mineral colorants into a solution with water, spraying onto bisque or greenware, and subsequently firing to cone 8–10. Salt may be sprinkled on surfaces which are to be fired as low as cone 08 with very interesting effects.

There are many other materials which could be used. Discovering them is merely a matter of finding the time to experiment with them all.

18–9. Yvette Mintzberg (Canada). "Sinai Sand." Stoneware, slab construction with heavily grogged clay. Rutile, iron and manganese rubbed into the clay.

METALS

Some metals, such as iron, copper, brass and bronze, may be used in the form of thin sheet, wire, found objects, nails, screws and so on, and fused directly into the clay or glaze. Some deformation and decomposition will undoubtedly take place, the degree of which will be determined by the firing temperature. Much experimentation would need to be done to develop predictable results, but ex-

18-10. Ulla Viotti (Sweden). Panel, stoneware. Separate modelled figures rolled and pressed partly together. Cobalt oxide applied and rubbed off leaving deposit in the textured areas. Once-fired in oxidation to cone 9.

18-12. Dorothy Feibleman (United Kingdom). Handbuilt porcelain with fine neriage technique of colored laminated clay, using up to 40 different body stains. Oxidized at cone 7–9.

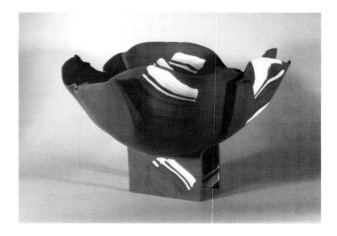

18-11. Kendra Davison (U.S.A.). Bowl, 10 in. high, 14 in. wide. Handbuilt earthenware with laminated colored clays.

tremely interesting surface and color can be developed this way. For example, a fine copper wire could be formed into shapes and fused to the surface of a tin-opacified white glaze. If the glaze is sensitive to developing high temperature copper reds in reduction, the wire can produce dark lines surrounded by red hazing. In oxidation it would most likely produce black lines with green hazing. Depending on the thickness of both the wire and the glaze, the wire may either completely disperse into the glaze or sit on top of it, giving a decomposing black line. A wide range of variations on this concept could be developed, from the impressed nails of fetish figures to fluid lines, and from silhouettes to sculptured surfaces.

18–13. Alain Tremblay (Canada). Panel. Stoneware, with refined colloidal slips, stains, and black glaze. Fired at cone 12
in oxidation.

19

Color in Clays, Slips and Engobes

Depending on the desired result, one can use stains, oxides, or carbonates, either singly or mixed together, to add color to clays. Because of the opaque nature of clays, slips and engobes, most colors will develop a pastel-like quality, and the development of pure color is extremely difficult. Commercially prepared body stains are usually made with a clay base, where the color is already diluted. They are mainly used in the sanitary ware industry for pastel colored bathroom fixtures. Other coloring materials are therefore better for the development of strong color.

MIXING COLORED CLAYS

Mixing colored clays can be done in a variety of ways, largely dependent on the volume being prepared. They can be made up in test amounts simply by weighing out the dry ingredients of both clay and colorant and soaking to a liquid slip form in a bowl. They should subsequently be dried on a plaster batt and wedged to a plastic workable state. In larger volume, they can be mixed in blungers, clay mixers, or baths, either to a liquid slip form, which generally makes for more thoroughly dispersed color, or to a plastic state, ready for working.

As with most processes that take place in the ceramist's workshop, there are a number of different ways in which clays may be prepared. Some people will suggest that the material must be ball milled, and for some colors this might be advisable. However, I have been using colored clays for at least twelve years, mixed only in the plastic state, with no problems. For those who are particularly

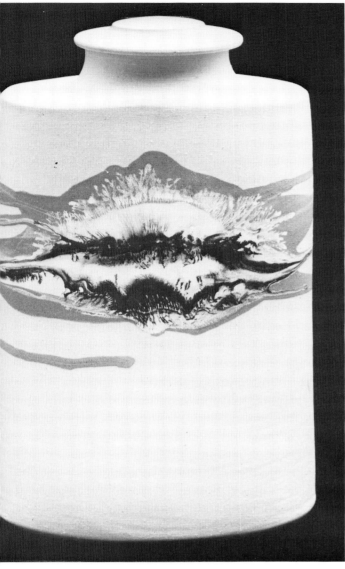

19–1. Robin Hopper (Canada). Oval lidded jar, porcelain. Mocha diffusions technique using white slip, and slip containing 10 percent rutile. Diffusions made with mild acid, mixed with yellow stain, and manganese. No glaze on exterior, oxidized at cone 9.

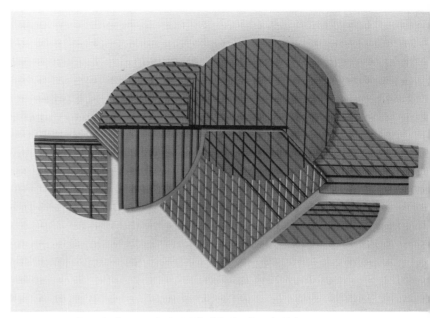

19–2. Jeanne Otis (U.S.A.). "DESERT STORM," Panel, 33 by 52 in. Porcelain with colored slips, colored porcelain clay and underglaze pencils.

19–3. Ban Kajitani (U.S.A.). Neriage laminated clays, wheel thrown and altered.

concerned about developing an absolutely flat, nonspecked clay or slip, particularly with cobalt containing materials, ball milling for several hours is probably a necessity.

Mixing color into already prepared plastic clay can be done by wedging the powdered colorant into the clay. Although many people do it this way, it is not a generally recommended process, as it is almost impossible to get the color thoroughly mixed without streaking or specking taking place. It is also difficult to be sure of an accurate percentage of colorant if any repetition of the same color is required. For small amounts it may be the only practical way to make colored clays, but for best results the color should be added to the powdered dry clay materials. The dry mix should then be made into a slip with water, sieved through a 60 mesh sieve, and allowed to soak for a few days. It should then be dried out to a workable consistency, and wedged ready for use.

The amount of colorant needed to get a par-ticular result will have to be determined through testing, as many colorants have quite different staining strengths when mixed into clay than when mixed into glazes. The type of clay will also have a profound effect on the color—white firing clays giving purer colors and darker colored clays giving more muted tones. In general, additions of $\frac{1}{2}$ to 10 percent will produce a wide range. As with the coloring of glazes, an infinite variety is possible, and the information given on color in chapter 16 is pertinent here also.

There are several techniques of working to

19–4. Robin Hopper (Canada). Agate ware lidded jar. Laminated colored clays, thrown and facetted. Clays are white, orange and black. Unglazed exterior, oxidized at cone 9.

produce decorative effects through the use of colored clays. Some are traditional to Japan, such as neriage, nerikomi and zougan, although the earliest ceramics using mixed colored clays, are almost certainly from the Tang dynasty in China. Most of the oriental colored clay techniques make use of folding and cutting of colored clays and then pressing the small cross sections of the colored clay rods into molds, to produce intricate patterns. Agate ware is the name given to the technique in Europe, after the patterned semi-precious stone. In recent years, agate ware has been produced through the throwing process, which develops spirals of color through the ware. This spiralling color can be left as it is, or glazed over, where the colorant will stain the glaze. It can also be used for many different decorative treatments, such as cutting across with wires or tools, to expose the fascinating striations.

Some colorants, particularly manganese, have a very strong fluxing effect in the body, which can cause serious bloating or bubbling. These materials can also cause the clay forms to collapse, as they have little tolerance for over-firing and will need careful watching. Work can easily be ruined through pyroplastic deformation.

Producing colored clays can be a very expensive process, given the current costs of some colorants. It is usually wise to think through the desired result thoroughly, to make certain that colored clay is the most suitable avenue for achieving that result. It is quite possible that a colored slip or engobe may be sufficient to do the job at a lower cost and with fewer potential problems.

The biggest problems that occur in developing colored clays lie in their use. Some of the colorants act as fluxes, and will cause the clay to mature at a lower temperature. Some are refractory and will raise the maturing temperature. (In chapter 14, these effects are marked as **(F)** or **(R)** next to the colorant listing.) The problems generally arise when colored clays of an opposing nature are used together. The tensions that may develop can be strong enough to split the work apart and a good

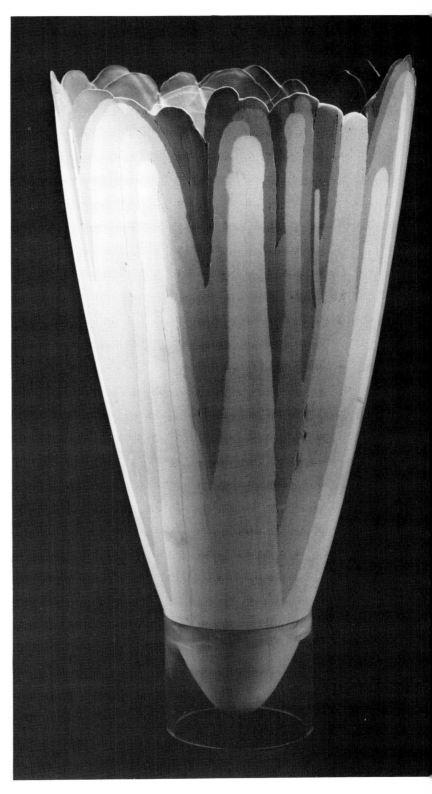

19–5. Steve Heineman (Canada). Vessel form, porcelain. Colored casting slips, poured into moulds and manipulated. Repeated layers of slip build up overlapping areas. Oxidation fired to cone 6–8.

deal of testing needs to be done to make sure that this problem doesn't arise. If it does occur, the easiest solution is to add more kaolin to the over-fluxing clay, or more feldspar or body frit to an over-refractory clay.

COLOR IN SLIPS AND ENGOBES

Slips and engobes are more or less the same thing, and some confusion exists over the use of the two words. The word "slip" is generally used to describe clays in liquid form. These clays have been mixed with pure water, or water to which 1–2 percent of a deflocculant, such as sodium carbonate (soda ash) and/or sodium silicate, has been added. Slips made with deflocculant require less water to achieve the same degree of fluidity and are usually made for casting in molds. Slips used for decorating are usually mixed with water only, unless specific qualities of fluidity or viscosity are desired. For these qualities, a flocculant such as vinegar or

19–7. Dieter Crumbiegel (Germany). Relief, constructed of thin porcelain and stoneware slabs. Ash glaze over the stoneware, porcelain unglazed. Cone 11 oxidation.

19–6. Robin Hopper (Canada). "Aurora Borealis." Porcelain bowl. Modified neriage technique done by building graphic image as a sheet with colored clays, and rolling to flatten. The completed piece is then press moulded over a hump form, with foot thrown on. Ten different colored clays. Oxidized at cone 9.

epsom salts may be used for viscosity, or a deflocculant as mentioned above for fluidity.

Decorating slips are traditionally used to coat the surface of clays in a wide variety of ways. They may be made from naturally occurring clays or from mixed materials and colorants to provide a range of decorative effects. They can be applied to wet, leather-hard, or dry clay bodies, depending on the technique being used and the dry strength of the body. The slip decoration is usually covered with a glaze after bisque firing, although many people prefer to leave the slip patterns unglazed. Slips may be used to coat another clay, to make it lighter,

19-8. Roseline Delisle (Canada). Porcelain, thrown in one piece. Decoration with vitrified engobe, fired in oxidation at cone 11.

darker, or colored. They may also be used to give a coating through which designs may be cut or scratched, or resisted with wax or latex. Slips can also be used in a number of traditional techniques for pattern making, such as combing, feathering, marbling, trailing, dotting and mocha diffusions. Where slips are stained with colorants, the color will bleed through the glaze, unless the glaze is totally opaque.

A basic creamy white slip which will fit most clays and which can be colored easily with any colorants or stains is as follows:

Ball clay	75
Kaolin	10
Flint	10
Feldspar	5
Total	100

I have used this slip for several years and have found it to be very versatile, and particularly good for traditional slipware techniques. It can be fired at any temperature from cone 04 to cone 12, in

oxidation or reduction, on most clay bodies. On some clays, however, particularly those firing at cone 2 or below, this slip may cause the covering glaze to craze. In this case more silica will be needed, and the slip can be adjusted to the following recipe:

Ball clay	40
Kaolin	20
Flint	20
Feldspar	10
Body frit (3110)	10
Total	100

The adjusted recipe should solve the crazing problem, but will also bring about a lessening in plasticity, and affect the fluid qualities necessary for use in some traditional techniques. These were previously assisted by the volume of ball clay. Some of this fluidity may be regained by adding a small amount of bentonite, gum, or deflocculant.

Colloidal slips, or terra sigillatas, are another form of liquid clay slip, but of an entirely different nature, as described in chapter 1. They produce a tough, semi-glaze-like skin, which can be polished to a high sheen before being fired, usually between cone 08 and cone 1, depending on the clays being used.

The most common forms of sigillatas are made from refined red clays, although many different clays will work very well. The type of clay will of course affect the color. Sigillatas are often reduced either during the firing or in a post-firing reduction, where the extremely thin film of slip accepts carbon very rapidly, turning to a rich black. A basic sigillata slip, white when oxidized, will usually absorb carbon and give a rich black when reduced. Such a sigillata slip is as follows:

Ball clay (Old Mine #4)	10.5 lbs. (4.77 kilograms)
Water	3 U.S. gallons (11.35 liters)
Household lye (deflocculant)	1.7 ounces (48 grams)

The weight ratio of clay to water is approximately 4 to 10. The clay and lye are poured into the water,

19–9. Tony Franks (United Kingdom). Black basalt vase, in-laid colored porcelain. Glazed inside, and oxidation fired at 1160°C.

thoroughly mixed and allowed to stand for 48 hours. (Caution: Lye is caustic soda, and should be handled with great care. Other deflocculants can be used, but lye works particularly well, and once mixed in the slip solution loses its caustic qualities.) After the material has settled, any decomposed organic matter which will possibly show up as a dark grey or black layer at the top of the solution should be removed and discarded. The thin watery slip below this will be the sigillata, and should be siphoned off, leaving heavier particles at the bottom of the container. The heavy clay material is discarded, and only the slip with ultrafine particulate used. The slip is best when sieved several times through a fine screen, up to 150 mesh, to make sure that only the finest particles of the clay are in the solution. When the slip is in the correct solution, 100 cc should weigh between 108 and 112 grams. It should be applied to bone dry greenware, by brushing, dipping or spraying. If applied to wet or leather hard work, the slip will likely run off the surface. To aid the slip in adhering to the clay, it may be helpful to lightly spray the work with water, which opens the pores and allows a better bond to take place. When the slip has lost its wet shine, but before it dries completely, it can be polished with a chamois leather or cotton material as desired.

Sigillatas may be colored by the addition of the usual coloring materials, to a maximum of 8 percent. Some colorants will likely be coarser in particle size than the slip, and may not pass through the sieve. Coarse colorants or opacifiers can be ball-

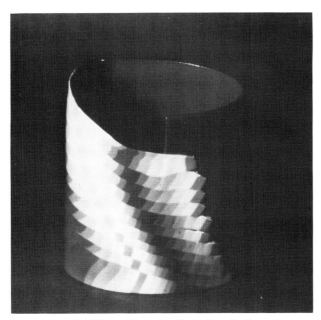

19–10. Angelo DiPetta (Canada). Vase. Handbuilt earthenware with laminated clays, made from sheets of poured colored slips, cut into strips, reassembled, and rolled. The cylindrical form is then made from this sheet. Oxidation fired at cone 04, with a clear glaze.

milled to improve the fineness of the particles. They should be sieved with the slip for thorough mixing to take place. They will also have some effect on the firing temperature, and reduction characteristics.

The above sigillata recipe is best when fired to cone 05. Sigillatas are usually fired between cone 08 and cone 1, although they can be fluxed with colemanite or lead to lower the fusion temperature. Flux additions will tend to bleach out some of the color, though, and personal decisions need to be made on the degree of compromise which is acceptable.

New or untried clay materials may be tested for potential use as sigillatas by making a few simple tests on variations of deflocculant needed to produce the finest particle size.

1 Get 5 small containers, and number them 1 through 5.
2 Into each put 100 grams of dry powdered clay and 250 milliliters (250 grams) of water.
3 Into container 1, add 0.5 gram of deflocculant (lye, soda ash, sodium silicate, or combinations of these), and mix thoroughly.
4 Into container 2 add 1 gram of deflocculant and mix thoroughly.
5 Into container 3 add 1.5 grams of deflocculant and mix thoroughly.
6 Into container 4 add 2 grams of deflocculant and mix thoroughly.
7 Into container 5 add 2.5 grams of deflocculant and mix thoroughly.
8 Let all mixtures settle for 48 hours.
9 Siphon off any clear water at the top of the container, and discard.
10 Dip a clean, dry, unfired clay test tile or other test piece into each mix. The one observed to give the greatest sheen should produce the best sigillata.

Not all clays will oblige in this process, and some might need an even smaller or larger proportion of deflocculant, but most will produce some form of usable colloidal slip. Once the more satisfactory solution has been determined, it can easily be made up into large volume, and colored or opacified as desired. Colorants and opacifiers are best added to the slip before sieving.

A true terra sigillata should develop a hard surface with a noticeable sheen. The sheen can be further developed by polishing. The application of sigillatas is usually very, very thin, as it takes only one layer of the thinnest slip to produce results. Used this way, the slip is such that it will not cover or obliterate any surface textures or imperfections on the surface of the clay, such as grog holes, scratches, or textural markings. This characteristic can be an advantage or disadvantage, depending on the desired result.

The word "engobe" is used most often in North America and describes a wider range of uses in the development of the decorative surface. Whereas the simple liquified slip is commonly used to coat greenware, an engobe may be formulated to be used at any stage, including over bisque-fired ware. Engobes are also often used without a covering glaze, giving a wider potential for experimentation with the surface. An engobe is more like a glaze in structure and may contain very little plastic clay.

Materials for engobes fall into six groups:

1 Clays—with kaolin, or calcined kaolin, usually being used in place of ball clay, to counteract shrinkage.
2 Fluxes—as used in glazes.
3 Fillers—usually flint.
4 Hardeners—borax and various gums.
5 Opacifiers—as outlined in chapter 17.
6 Colorants—as outlined in chapters 14 and 16.

The following three recipes for basic engobes should give a good starting point for further experiment:

	Cone 04–3	Cone 4–6	Cone 6–10
Kaolin	20	15	15
Calcined kaolin	10	20	35
Talc	25	10	5
Gerstley borate (or frit 3110)	15	10	—
Nepheline syenite	—	10	15
Flint	15	20	15
Borax	5	5	5
Zircopax	10	10	10
Total	100	100	100

The above engobes may be colored in any of the usual ways.

Both slips and engobes can be formulated for a wide variety of temperatures, and the higher they are fired, the more vitreous they will be. One may read of vitreous slips; these are basically combinations of clays and other materials that will become tight enough on firing to be called vitreous. They could equally well be called engobes, as they are usually halfway between slip and glaze.

The word "slip-glaze," which also brings about some confusion in terminology, refers to a glaze which is usually used for single firing. It is most often applied to those naturally occurring clays that form glazes in the higher temperature ranges, with little or no additions. Many locally found surface clays, such as those found along streams and rivers, fall into this category. Most slip glazes contain considerable iron, and therefore will be colored from yellow ochre through green to black, depending on firing conditions and additions to the makeup of the glaze. This may make it difficult to color many of them, but those that are light enough can easily be colored in the usual ways. The darker ones may be lightened with opacifiers, to produce soft, muted tones.

PART FOUR

Attacking the Surface

20

Glaze Application

No matter how eager one might be to begin splashing on one's newly concocted glazes, there are a few details that must be put in order first. The surface of the clay form must be cleaned of any dust or grease that might spoil the finished object. A large enough volume of glaze or glazes to do the job must be mixed. And decisions must be made, or will have been made earlier, on any number of issues. The type of work, clay, firing temperature and atmosphere, and pre-firing surface treatments will have been determined. So too, probably, have the type and thickness of the glaze to be used, its coloration and/or opacification, and any post-firing surface enrichment techniques.

The application of the glaze follows these decisions. They will, to some extent, have predetermined the application methods that will be used to achieve the desired result, including brushing, dipping, pouring, spraying, stippling, spattering, sponging, trailing and multiple glaze application. Many ceramists use various methods on the same piece to achieve a specific effect.

The thickness or viscosity of a glaze often gives remarkable variations in both surface and color. Diverse application methods can be used to beneficially exploit these variations. Once again, it is only by personal experiment that real understanding of the potential of any glaze can be realized. Ceramists have been known to explore the particular qualities of a single glaze for years. Certainly with many glazes, the thick and thin variables can be so extreme that, in conjunction with firing variations, a whole pallette may be made from a single glaze, in subtlety, color and surface texture. The working thickness, or specific gravity, of glazes can be monitored by the use of a simple hydrometer, if such control is required. A hydrometer can easily be made with a piece of wood dowel, or flat wood, such as a ruler, to which some form of lead weight is attached at one end. The stick can be marked with any form of calibration—inches, centimeters, or anything else—and should be varnished to facilitate washing. It is immersed, weight downwards, in the glaze, when optimum thickness has been decided upon. The thinner the glaze, the more the weight will sink into the liquid; the thicker the glaze, the less it will sink. The calibration reached on the stick should be noted beside the recipe for future reference.

BRUSHING

Brushing often develops an unevenness in the surface coat, purely due to the nature of the process. It is generally best done on unfired or greenware, as the ware is less likely to "suck" the wet glaze from the brush, which is often the case with the brushing of glazes on bisque-fired ware. For

20–1. Dora De Larios (U.S.A). Porcelain dinner plate, 11¾ in. diameter. Majolica technique of free brush glaze painting, in cobalt. Fired at cone 10. Part of a dinner set made for a White House luncheon, May 1977.

20-2. Luke Lindoe (Canada). Plate. Stoneware, cone 10 reduction. Celadon glaze with brush decoration using the same glaze, with its iron content replaced with 15 percent rutile, giving a variety of texture and color.

this reason, it is often used in the glazing of once-fired wares, or in cases where a defined brush quality is required, or where streakiness doesn't matter. Depending on the desired result and the amount of area to be covered, almost any brush may be used, from soft hair artist's watercolor brushes to various types of house painting brushes, or even homemade ones using dog or other animal hair. I know of one potter who uses the tail of a racoon which had succumbed to a passing car.

For glaze brushing where a streaky result is undesirable, Chinese brushes, which have a number of bamboo shafts joined together to make a soft brush up to 6 inches wide, are useful. This type of brush can also be cut into a variety of widths. There are also large, soft Japanese brushes called "Hake" which function in a similar fashion.

Glaze brushing is usually best done with a well charged brush, so that a maximum area can be covered in a single sweep. If it is necessary to go over an area numerous times, there will almost inevitably be a streaky result, unless the glaze itself is sufficiently fluid to disguise the brushmarks. If a flat surface is desirable, then brushing is probably not the best way of glazing the piece and one should look at other methods. Household paint rollers may be considered in this instance, as they are less likely to leave a streaky surface, although some texture will probably show.

Advantages

1 Able to cover large areas with small amounts of glaze.
2 Good for fragile items, or once-fired pieces.
3 Good for details on decorative pieces or overlapping areas.

Disadvantages

1 Likely to be streaky.
2 Bisque-fired ware "sucks" the liquid from the brush.
3 A very slow method of glazing.

DIPPING

Dipping wares into pots or buckets of glaze is probably the most common glaze application method used by ceramists. It is fast, easy, and generally gives a coating of even thickness. Dipping is the most useful glazing process for production work, where speed and efficiency are important. If the glaze runs during application, it can be removed with a knife, if necessary, to ensure a smooth coating for any further painting. Touch up the unglazed spots (from where you hold the piece) with a brush or your fingers.

Advantages

1 Ease of application.
2 Evenness of coating.
3 Speed of application.

Disadvantages

1 Large volume of glaze needed.

POURING

Pouring and dipping are often done on the same piece of work, where the inside is poured, and the outside dipped. Pouring can be done with a variety of tools, from cans, pitchers and long-spouted pots, to various forms of ladle. All pouring vessels will have their own particular quality of flow, and again, individual requirements will dic-

20–3. Sue Hopper (Canada). Porcelain box. Free brush decoration in copper, iron, and black stain on dry greenware,
with home-made brushes from dog hair. Fired in reduction at
cone 10.

20–4. Ann Cummings (Canada). Raku tray. Slab construction, slip trailed and poured glaze. Japanese Oribe influence.

tate the best tool to use for a particular job. I personally prefer an aluminum teapot with a narrow
spout, bought at the local hardware store as cheaply
as it can be obtained.

Glazes for pouring should usually be prepared a little thinner than when used for dipping,
as there is almost inevitably a certain amount of
overlap and excessive thickness can easily cause
running of the glaze.

Pouring can be used for a wide range of decorative effects, particularly when glazes of different
characters and colors are used over each other, and
the thickness variations and glaze interaction are
used to advantage.

20–5. Harrison McIntosh (U.S.A.). Lidded jar. Stoneware, cone 5. Sgraffito decoration with black, copper, and cobalt engobes, grey matt glaze.

Advantages

1 Small amounts of glaze may be used.
2 Speedy and free decoration techniques.

Disadvantages

1 Likely to be uneven, with glaze runs.

SPRAYING

Spraying is a good application method, although it usually takes quite a lot of experience to achieve even coatings and to learn to judge the thickness necessary for an adequate covering. It can be used for glazing the whole piece, or for glazing small areas.

Equipment varies from simple to very sophisticated. The simplest is the atomizer, made of two tubes fixed at right angles to each other in an

20–6. James Tower (United Kingdom). Earthenware form. Purple black glaze over white tin glaze, with sgraffito cut away areas. Fired in oxidation at 1100°C. Collection of Ruth Siegel.

L shape, and blown through by mouth. Garden insecticide sprayers can be used. There are many types of small spray units utilizing a disposable container of freon gas, with a spray nozzle attached. Some forms of vacuum cleaners have reversible air controls, where spray guns can be at-

20–7. Keith Campbell (Canada). Porcelain covered jar. Airbrushed decoration with stains, then scratched through to body. Glazed inside only. Fired to cone 10 in oxidation.

tached. There are a wide variety of spray guns of a very sophisticated nature, requiring elaborate compressors for the air control. There are also miniature spray guns, called airbrushes, which also need a compressor to function. These units are comparatively expensive, but are irreplacable for fine and detailed work, particularly with overglazes. There is a wide variety to choose from, of varying degrees of efficiency.

When spray glazing, much material is lost in the atmosphere as floating dust. It should be remembered that many glaze materials and most colorants are toxic and therefore spray glazing is best confined to a ventilated spray booth, with the glazer wearing a safety mask.

Most glaze materials are also quite abrasive, and are likely to cause severe wear to the nozzles of spray guns. To minimize this problem, carbide spray tips are available. All equipment should be carefully cleaned after every use. Glazes for spraying could also be ball milled, to ensure that the particles of material are pulverized as finely as possible. In any case, airbrushes should not be used for spraying glaze. They are better for spraying colors, lusters, or enamels, as these are more finely ground than most glaze materials and consequently are less likely to cause problems with clogging or abrasive wear.

Glazes for spraying are normally used in a much thinner consistency than for other applica-

20–8. James Tower (United Kingdom). Earthenware plate. Black and white glazes with sgraffito. Multiple firings in oxidation at 1100°C. Collection of Helmut Schiffler.

20–9. Sheila Casson (United Kingdom). Porcelain plate. Landscape decoration in paper resist and fine sgraffito through a sprayed iron slip. Reduction fired at cone 10.

20–10. David Taylor (Canada). Footed bowl. Earthenware, with black and white slips, and a white glaze fired to cone 3. Then masking tape and paper cutouts applied, and sprayed with cobalt. Refired to cone 3.

tion methods. The glaze can have a deflocculant added, such as 1 percent sodium silicate solution. This will minimize the water content, lower the likelihood of excessive wetting of the piece being sprayed, and prevent "washing" or flowing of wet glaze from the surface. Is it usual to apply several thin coatings, gradually building up the thickness to give the desired result. If the piece is to be glazed all over, particularly when an even coat is required, it is advantageous to place the pieces to be sprayed on a banding wheel.

Spraying probably wastes more material than any other glazing method. If one is doing a lot of spraying, particularly with expensive materials, some sort of waste retrieval system might be worth thinking about.

The nature of spraying usually results in a broadcast of color. If intricate patterns are desired, masking techniques such as latex, paper, or wax resist should be employed (see the discussion later in this chapter).

Advantages

1 Ease of handling, particularly for once-fired work, or work of a fragile nature.
2 Elimination of glaze runs and overlapping in the unfired glaze.
3 Ease of color gradation.

Disadvantages

1 Atmospheric pollution and health hazards.
2 Wastage of materials.
3 Cost of equipment.
4 Equipment maintenance.
5 Difficulty of spray control, except in more expensive units.
6 Difficulty in gauging correct thicknesses.
7 Need for masking in pattern control.

STIPPLING

Stippling is a form of application done with the edge or tip of a brush, or with a sponge. It is a good way of applying glaze or color, when a broken texture is wanted. The best type of brushes to use for this stippling are house painting brushes,

20–12. Eileen Lewenstein (United Kingdom). Press moulded "wave" dish. Stoneware with sprayed glazes.

20–11. Michael Casson (United Kingdom). Tall lidded jar. Stoneware, 27 in. high. Wood-fired and salt-glazed, with finger wipe decoration through slip.

or artist's bristle brushes used for oil painting. Care should be taken in the amount of glaze charged into the brush. Since stippling uses the edge or tip of the brush, it is usually held vertically. If the brush is overcharged, the glaze is likely to run out.

SPATTERING

Spattering is more or less a form of spraying, where, because of the nature of the tools used, a broken and uneven spray is achieved. Sometimes, bad, inefficient or worn out spray guns inadvertently do the same thing! The usual tool for spattering is a toothbrush, or similar form of stiff-bristled brush. The bristles are dipped into the glaze

and the brush is held near to the area to be sprayed. A knife blade is then pulled across the bristles, forcing them to bend and then spring back, releasing the glaze or color in an uneven spray. It can be a very effective way of coloring a specific area.

SPONGING

Sponges can give interesting glaze textures. Both natural and synthetic sponge can be used to soak up the glaze and apply it to the work. Synthetic sponges can be cut or burnt into patterns which may then be used to create overall repeat patterns, or patterns for simple and fast production. If the sponge is sufficiently fine grained, quite delicate patterns may be made in this way. By overlaying the sponge marks or stamps, it is possible to develop great depth in the decoration. Although the sponge will deteriorate in time, it will have quite a long life if washed carefully after use.

TRAILING

Glaze trailing is a way of drawing on the ceramic surface in a linear fashion. Like slip trailing, it can be done with a variety of tools. Almost any squeezable plastic bottle having a fine apertured tip will do well. It helps, in the cleaning, if the bottle or other tool has a removable cap or nozzle. In the Orient, trailing is done with a tool made from two pieces of bamboo. A thin length is used for the trailing end, which is joined into a short, fat, bamboo reservoir.

Glazes for trailing are best used in a thicker than normal consistency. In firing, trailed glazes will usually flatten down and spread to some extent. If a detailed drawing is required, it is often better to trail the glaze on the unfired surface, or on a bisque-fired surface before application of the main glaze. Trailed glazes that are applied over other glazes tend to be fragile during handling, as

20–13. Robin Hopper (Canada). "Night Forest Plate." Porcelain. Multiple glaze application with poured, trailed, brushed, stippled and glaze intaglio decoration. Reduction fired at cone 10. Collection of Jonathan Hopper.

20–14. Ann Mortimer (Canada). Slip cast porcelain sphere, cone 6 oxidation. Stippled and sand-blasted surface, unglazed.

result. It is usual to use similar glaze bases in multiple applications, as they melt in similar ways and are less likely to cause difficulty in application. However, it doesn't have to be done that way, and very different glaze bases applied together can provide rich results. In the application of multiple glazes it is important that the work is done in a relatively short space of time to prevent one glaze from drying out before the next is applied. If drying does occur, it is likely that the glazes will flake off, or crawl. Crawling glazes can produce interesting lizard skin patterns. They occur most often when a glaze with a high clay content is put over a glaze with a low clay content. As the second glaze dries, the clay causes greater shrinkage to occur, and the places where crawling is likely to occur are established. Glazes for multiple application are generally best used in a thinner than normal consistency, unless excessive running is desired.

Multiple glazing on vertical forms is likely to present some problems in the firing if the glazes are too thick, because they will probably run. Using thin glazes and minimizing the amount of overlapping at the lower part of the work should help to discourage runs.

GLAZE REMOVAL PROCESSES

Along with all of the variables of glaze application, there are many glaze removal processes which can add greatly to the richness and diversity of the ceramic surface. Some of these are used in conjunction with the glaze application, and some are done after the glaze firing. The processes are sgraffito, wax resist, paper resist, crayon resist, latex resist, sponge removal, finger wipe, glaze intaglio and sandblasting.

SGRAFFITO

Sgraffito, or sgrafiato, is probably the simplest form of removal, where a pigment, slip or glaze is scratched away to reveal the surface beneath. It can be done at various stages in the making and decorating processes. When done through pigment or slip on the soft or leather-hard clay, it will have a different quality than when done through

the raised portions are easily knocked off. If the drawing spreads too much in the firing, it might be a good idea to look at alternate techniques, such as brushwork or underglaze pencils, to develop the required images.

MULTIPLE GLAZE APPLICATION

Multiple glaze application is often confused with multiple firing processes. There will be an explanation of the latter at the end of this chapter.

Multiple glaze application refers to the use of two or more glazes over each other, which can be applied in a variety of ways to achieve a particular

20–15. Erik Gronborg (U.S.A.). Porcelain cup with lusters and decal overglaze.

slip on dry clay. In the first instance it will give a more fluid sharp-edged line; in the second it will usually show a broken line through the grainy quality of the clay. It can be done through once-fired glaze, cutting down into the clay, or through glaze down to bisque-fired clay. A variety of tools can be used, from sticks to knives and old dental tools. Sgraffito techniques can be compared in their visual qualities to pen and ink drawings, as both are essentially scratch processes. The fired result can have all of the expression and richness of this form of drawing.

RESIST PROCESSES

The various forms of resisting glazes, slips or colorants all do basically the same thing, although with quite different qualities. The process makes possible the removal, or resistance, of one material from another, by making some form of barrier which subsequent application of glaze or color are not able to penetrate. This can give a wide range of color, texture and glaze variation, as the resisted area will show one color and the area where the glaze or color has not been resisted will show another. Re-

sists can be done on the clay, on the bisque, or on the glaze, depending on the result required.

Wax Resist This may be done with hot paraffin wax or candle wax, or with cold latex wax or wax emulsion. In the use of hot wax, it is often a good idea to add a small quantity of kerosene or thin machine oil to make the wax melt at a lower temperature. These additions will also produce a better flow from the brush when doing resist brushwork. I prefer to heat the wax in an electric frying pan, as the temperature can more easily be controlled. If wax is overheated it can quickly ignite; thus temperature control is helpful. Overheated wax is also likely to be absorbed into the surface of the ware, losing its efficiency as a barrier. Wax may be used on the greenware, and painted over with pigments to get an underglaze decoration, after which it is then bisque fired. The wax will burn out leaving the pattern, and glaze may be applied over it. Wax may also be used on the bisque to keep glaze off entirely, to show the character of the clay body, or it may be used between layers of glaze, or between glaze and colorants. Resist processes may be used in conjunction with

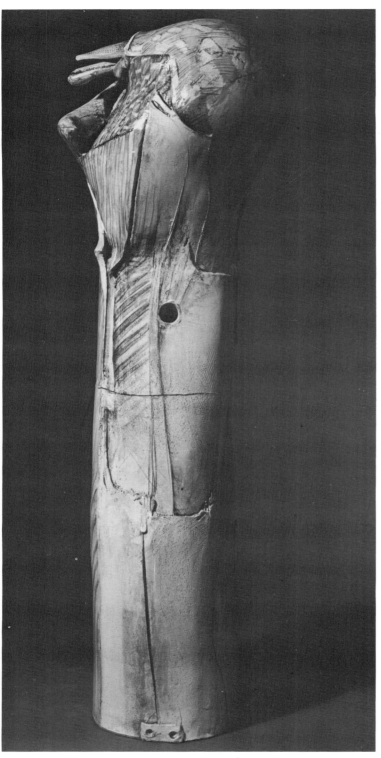

20–16. Ann Roberts (Canada). "Divine Buzzard IV." Lowfire talc body, multifired with body stains, glazes and lusters. Fired at cone 04, 06, 018.

any of the previously mentioned application processes.

Paper Resist Paper resists are usually better done on the leather-hard clay, using either slips or colorant brushed, poured, or sprayed on. Absorbent paper such as newspaper, can be applied to the piece by wetting with water, after which the slip or colorant is applied. When dry, the paper is removed leaving a positive/negative image, which can be glazed over or left as is. Masking tape also makes a good material for paper resists.

Crayon Resist The underglaze crayons described in chapter 14 may also be used to produce drawings which partially resist the glaze, depending on the thickness of both. They are best used on either bone-dry or bisque-fired clay.

Latex Resist There are various forms of latex material on the market which may be used for decorative purposes. Almost any rubberized cement or glue will do very well. Some latex materials can be thinned with water, making them more versatile. Some will dry in a sheet which can be peeled off after the desired effect has been reached, allowing further work to be done on the previously resisted areas.

Floor Wax Liquid and solid floor waxes can also be used for resists, although they are not generally as efficient as other resist materials.

SPONGE REMOVAL

Sponges can be used to produce a negative image just as well as a positive image, as described earlier. To achieve this, a damp sponge, patterned or otherwise, may be placed on the slipped or glazed area until the area softens. The sponge can then be lifted, removing the glaze or slip at the same time. Sponges can also be used freely to remove slip or glaze coatings, just by wiping the material away. The area of glaze removal can then be left as is, where the slight residual glaze will usually fuse slightly, or it can be covered with another glaze.

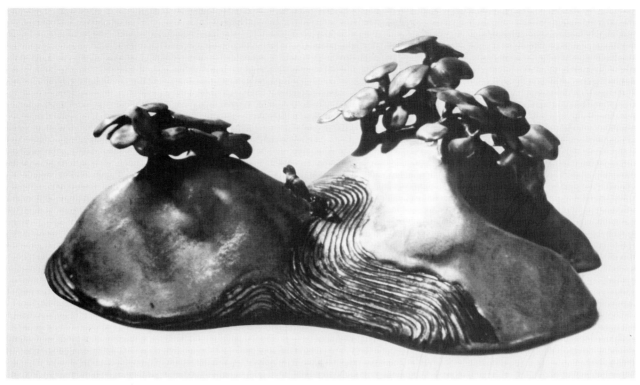

20–17. Tessa Fuchs (United Kingdom). Sculptural piece. Earthenware fired at 1100°C.

FINGER WIPE, OR COMBING

Finger wiping or combing of glaze is the reverse of finger painting. The removal of glaze produces a negative image. Combs can be made of stiff rubber, leather, or card. Wiping or combing can be done with slips or glazes, particularly glazes that contain a high clay content, in a very fluid, free movement. It should be done while the coating is still in a semi-liquid state, for best movement. The process essentially moves some of the material, rather than removing it altogether, giving a variety of thick and thin areas where concentration of glaze has one effect and thinning of glaze has another.

GLAZE INTAGLIO

Glaze intaglio is the name given when one slip or glaze is removed, by any method, and another slip or glaze is put back. It can be an extremely laborious process, but it is a way of obtaining very controlled designs in slip or glaze. It is usually done with a variety of tools, knives, needles, and so on to scratch away the material. The removal can also be effected by using a removable latex resist, or by covering an area with hot wax on top of a glaze, and removing this after subsequent application of another glaze. The resisted area can then be filled with glaze. The filling in of the glazes is best done with either brush or trailer.

SANDBLASTING

Sandblasting is a technique more often used in the decorative processes of glass then clay. It is the same process used for cleaning buildings and engraving grave markers. A high pressure jet of sand is aimed at an object, removing the surface of the object through abrasion. In clay or glass studios, sandblasting is usually done in specially designed cabinets, with glove inserts for holding the object, a window for viewing, and a nozzle for

20–18. Margaret Realica (U.S.A.). Detail of porcelain sculpture showing multiple glaze application, with high iron content bubbling through white glaze to give mottled texture. Oxidation fired at cone 10.

directing the jet of sand. Various types of sand may be used, for coarse or fine jets. The sand jet literally eats off the surface of the clay or glaze, or whatever comes in its path. Patterns are made with a resist of some sort, either a latex sheet, as used in stonemason's workshops, or with masking tape. Ordinary masking tape will withstand quite a lot of bombardment before it breaks down.

Using sandblasting, one can remove the skin of glaze or cut right down into the clay. Different qualitites can be achieved by sandblasting at different times in the making process. If it is done at the bone dry stage, the edges will be soft and rounded. When done on either bisque or glazed ware, the edges are likely to be sharp and crisp. Colored clays can produce interesting effects. For example, the unglazed surface of a porcelain clay, stained with a black stain containing cobalt and manganese, will, after a reduced firing, have a different color from that of the core of the clay. Depending on the quantity of colorant in the clay, the surface will be black, dark brown, or dark grey. The core will most likely be blue or blue grey. By sandblasting through the skin of the clay, the core is exposed, giving interesting black on blue results. Sandblasting can be used to give a delicate textured

20–19. Bryan Trueman (Australia). "Birds and Flowers." Platter (detail). Stoneware, cone 10 reduction. Glazes poured, trailed, brushed and splashed on, and wax resist.

surface when done very lightly over a glaze. It needs to be done with a great deal of care, as the process is very fast, and there is no reversing it.

MULTIPLE FIRING PROCESSES

The ceramic surface can always be altered, no matter how permanent it may seem. Sandblasting is an obvious example of this. There is also unlimited potential in post glaze-firing surface enrichment techniques, which can embellish the final result. Some of these techniques, such as lusters and overglaze enamels or china paints, have already been discussed in chapter 13.

Many of the techniques employed by the ceramic industry are generally useful for the studio potter. These include decalcomanias (decals), photo-silkscreens, acid etching, groundlaying, paste buildup, and other printing and painting processes.

Throughout the history of ceramics, many developments have occurred through the need for different expression, and the potter of today is not bound to conventions of the past. Although there are certain industrially based conventions in the normal use of ceramic techniques, the studio potter is at liberty to break all of them in his search for self-expression. The medium can be used freely, and where a result from a kiln is unsatisfactory, it can always be altered by refiring, either at its original temperature or at another. Raku glazes can be put over porcelain and refired, for example. In fact, almost anything can be explored.

There are some guidelines that can be suggested here, but they are few. Depending on the color range required in the work, it should be remembered that some colors will burn away in firings where the temperatures are too high. Many of the low temperature red producing colors, such as cadmium-selenium, chromium and uranium in lead-base glazes, are examples of color burnout, or alteration in excess heat. The usual approach in multiple firing processes is quite logical, starting with the maturation of the clay body. The glazes or overglazes can be applied in various ways, and as long as the subsequent firing is lower in temperature, the previously fired glaze will not alter much. This is also dependent on the atmospheric conditions within the kiln. Where overglaze lusters or enamels are used, these also should be fired progressively lower, until reaching the gold, silver and platinum materials.

In a simple statement, subsequent firings should work down the temperature range, from the maturity of the clay to the lowest temperature applications of precious metal solutions. Nothing much lower will melt.

PART FIVE

Portfolio

21

The Development of a Personal Idiom

The development of any form of art imposes certain traumatic constraints on the artist. Good art requires disciplines that usually take years to master, whether that art involves painting, dance, literature, or clay. Without good disciplines, and a sensitivity to the material at hand, it is unlikely that artistic excellence will occur, although some worthwhile goals may be reached.

For the ceramist, mastery means learning to live with the often unreliable responses of materials and fire, where the invisible has such a profound effect. The ceramic medium is probably the most complex of the visual art forms, and demands sympathetic treatment, which comes from intuitive understanding. It is difficult to be in control, if one ever really is. However, the clayworker generally works through, undaunted, and comes out in the

end with some sort of self-expression. How does it happen?

Ceramics is an exciting combination of art and science, mutually interdependent. It embodies geology, chemistry, physics, artistry and more than a little alchemy. It is a demanding combination of painting and sculpture, with a long history of function and non-function. The ceramist has to strike a balance for himself through this jungle. Often it is traumatic because the non-analytical soul, with which most artists seem to be endowed, is at odds with the necessary technology. Instead of learning to live with it, and enjoy it as an integral part of the creative process, the technological process is more often seen as an ogre, an intimidator of the highest order.

A lengthy look in any good museum will boggle the mind at the breadth of expressive qualities to be seen in works of clay—works which, for the most part, were made by artists and craftsmen who were not scientists or technologists, but who had probably grown up with the business of producing clay objects as part of the family ritual. They had an innate understanding of their materials. The late twentieth century ceramist, who is probably not intimately familiar with materials close at hand, is perhaps overwhelmed by the diversity of it all, and is likely to suffer ceramic indigestion. The essence of using as responsive a material as clay lies in simplification of approach. This is perhaps the most complicated and time consuming part of the process. Inspiration, divine or otherwise, seldom comes when most needed at crucial times in one's development as an artist or craftsman.

There are many avenues which one could follow. My own feelings about developing a personal idiom start with understanding oneself, and the reasons why one is involving oneself in such an incredibly difficult art or craft form. Once one has a reasonable understanding of his motives, he may then begin to understand the introspective nature of the creative act, and the catalysts that turn thought into action.

The portfolio section that follows this chapter shows the work of a number of contemporary ceramists from around the world, who have gone through the pangs of learning the techniques and technology basic to a reasonable control of the craft. They have learned them, assimilated them and probably discarded them, as one does with any form of vocabulary in the process of communication. A ceramic vocabulary improves the ability to communicate issues that deal with clay. Attention to issues beyond straight craftsmanship have led to that form of exploration which one can call inspiration, or art. Training the eye to be observant and the mind to be receptive are the core of personal artistic growth. If such a thing as genius exists in the ceramic field, it almost certainly fits in with the description suggested by inventor Thomas Edison: "Genius is one percent inspiration, and ninety-nine percent perspiration."

Observation and mind training are the background that increase potential. The more one

searches, the more one finds, the more one searches. It all becomes part of the cyclical nature of the art.

The main part of this book is devoted to pursuing and developing an intuitive approach to the study of glaze and color. This intuition comes from observation, with a selective mind. Through the preceding chapters, I hope that much that seemed confusing is now clear. However, the qualitites that artists impose on their medium should be far beyond the merely technical. Where then do ideas come from?

They usually stem from observation, whether one is aware of it or not; a fleeting glimpse of something that stirs the thought processes—a color, a form, a movement, an inspiration. Ideas come seemingly from nowhere, but stimulus is all around us, and learning how to use these stimuli is a major part of the artist's obsession. For the ceramist, analytical museum study can tell one a great deal about form, surface, color and function, as well as the cultures behind the objects. For those who can't get to museums there are many books that can help in gaining understanding. However, one should realize that historical study can become a trap, with the end result becoming no more than mere eclecticism. The same thing holds true for an oversaturation of technology. Many potters have become so caught up in the process of glaze development and technical control that they have lost sight of the reasons why they started learning the process in the first place. Technology can also become a trap and constriction to creativity.

Developing a personal idiom then becomes a striking of balances: stimulus—technique. Stimulus brings forward ideas as concept and technique puts the concept into a concrete form, as object. Self-expression in ceramics does not usually respond to imposed or forced moves; it is a natural outgrowth of the internal digestion of stimuli, and the compulsive need to express the results of that chemistry. It doesn't matter whether one is drawn to natural forms, such as shells, rocks, insects or birds, or to man-made objects such as bowls, bridges, bottles, buildings or spacecraft; the stimulus will need a response. The response may take the form of drawings, or immediate manipulation of the clay. Whatever form it takes, intuition, stimulus and response come together and result in a new expression. If one is working within a traditional framework, as in producing functional work, learn to understand the traditions but don't become entangled with them. One should have no fear of breaking traditions; that is how new ones have always started.

In dealing with the technical aspects of ceramics, and the inevitable extent of personal search that goes on, be aware that today's failure may be the beginning of a new tomorrow. The discards can breathe new life when looked at in another light. Investigate whatever and whenever possible, as this will lead to stimulation of one's own intellect, and the realization of goals. The more one learns, the more one realizes little one knows and how much more there is to learn. In response to any spark of intuition, my maxim has always been:

Try it and see!

Portfolio

This portfolio shows the work of fifty-two ceramic artists from various parts of the world. It shows some of the diversity of work being done in clay. The selection could easily have included hundreds more, but space doesn't allow for that. The intent is not to show a complete view of what is going on in contemporary ceramics on a world scale, but to show work by some people, both well known and little known, whose considerations in ceramics are heavily concerned with color and surface.

With an art form of such age and complexity, it is natural for the contemporary artist to look to the past. Within the portfolio one finds the work of many who have used the past to gain a foothold on the present, with an eye to the future. The historical references have become imbued with a new search and a new vigor, and represent a healthy exploration in form and surface development. The combination of admiration for the ancient past and the technological developments of more recent times makes this an exciting time to be producing works in clay. The opportunities for self-expression have never been greater.

The works shown here speak for themselves, but are added to by the captions, excerpted from the artists' descriptions of their methodology. It is hoped that by showing the work in this way, the student of ceramics, whether potter or collector, will gain some insight into the ceramists' thought processes and appreciate the potters' breadth of technical understanding. Ceramics is a demanding medium, where the balance between art and technology is difficult and elusive. The works shown are in a calm state of equilibrium.

John Leach (United Kingdom). Two pitchers, stoneware, wood fired at cone 9. Natural glaze from the wood ash on the exterior; interior glazed with a high iron glaze. The rim glazed with a feldspathic glaze developing iron blue colors from the combination of iron from the glaze, and phosphorous from the ash. Photograph by Ian Robson.

190

Facing page: Robin Hopper (Canada). Two footed parabolic bottles. Porcelain, taller bottle 18″. Mocha Diffusions slip decoration with two blue and one white slips, diffusions with cobalt and titanium. Unglazed outside and once-fired in oxidation at cone 9.

Right: Les Manning (Canada). Vase. Mixed clays with porcelain, and three stoneware clays varying in coarseness, sugggesting landscape features. Glazed with a celadon glaze and fired in reduction at cone 10. Photograph by Hubert F. Hohn.

Below: Sylvia Hyman (U.S.A.). Dinner ware, porcelain. Multiple overlapping glazes, six on large plate, five on the other pieces. Glazes applied by pouring and dipping. Reduction cone 10. Photograph by Larry Dixon.

Ann Mortimer (Canada). "Beyond Human Knowledge." Front wall section, 23″ × 10″ × 18″. Slab-built construction, with slips and residual salt firing at cone 03. Photograph by Courtney Frisse.

Cheri Sydor (Canada). Porcelain clay. Raku fired, 9 cm high. In-glaze luster airbrushed onto form. Fritted lead glaze containing silver nitrate and bismuth subnitrate salts. Color developed through post-firing reduction. Photograph by Brad Struble.

Laurie Rolland (Canada). Teapot. Porcelain, oxidation fired at cone 6. Pressmoulded body, with thrown spout and handbuilt handle. Hearts are stencilled slip, colored with stain. Black stain in the textured areas. Clear glaze.

Curt and Suzan Benzle (U.S.A.). "In the Mood." 5" x 6". Handbuilt porcelain with color inlay and incising. A collaborative piece, using modified millefiori techniques to develop the imagery. The piece is built in a form when the colored slabs are complete. The pieces are covered with a clear glaze and fired at cone 9. Owing to the fusible nature of the body, some pieces are fired to maturity unglazed, then later glazed at a lower temperature. Photograph by Scianablo/Benzle.

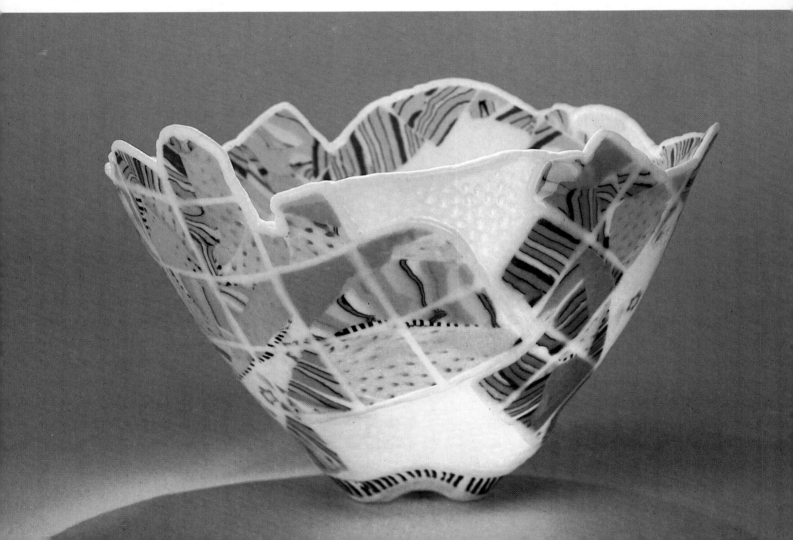

Above: Les Lawrence (U.S.A.). Six dinner plates. Porcelain, slab built and thrown. Porcelain slip with glaze stains and slip trailing. Clear glaze fired at cone 6 in oxidation.

Right: Ruth Duckworth (U.S.A.). Panel. Porcelain slabs, 19″ x 35″. Copper, iron and nickel washes sprayed on. A nepheline syenite glaze and two feldspar glazes sprayed over. Fired in oxidation at cone 9.

Far right: Ursula Scheid (Germany). Thrown bowl form. Porcelain with feldspar glaze colored with copper in the interior and lower exterior. Top exterior inlaid and polished. Fired at cone 13 in reduction. Photograph by Jochen Schade.

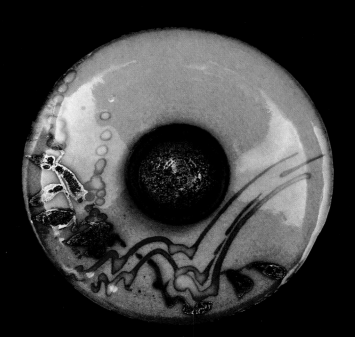

Above: Oldrich Asenbryl (United Kingdom). Porcelain plate, with a barium glaze and underglaze copper. Fired at cone 9 in reduction. Further firings for lusters, enamels and silkscreen print at 800°C, in oxidation.

Left: Sue Hopper (Canada). Shallow bowl. Porcelain with brush decoration in copper pigment, and trailed white glaze over a crackle celadon. Heavy early reduction causes carbon trapping in the white glaze. This glaze also contains tin, which encourages copper transference. Fired at cone 10.

Below: Robin Hopper (Canada). "Landscape Plate." Porcelain, 15″ diameter. Multiple glaze application, with six glazes. Poured, trailed, dipped, brushed and stippled glazes. Fired in reduction at cone 9.

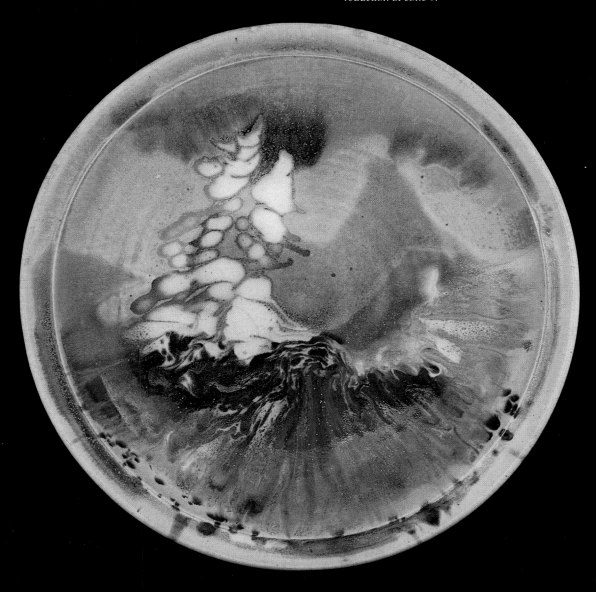

Above: Hildegard Storr-Britz (Germany). "Microbial." Glaze painting, 40cm x 45cm. Handmade stoneware tile of groggy clay body, glazed with barium glazes containing a small amount of zinc, colored with copper and nickel. Photograph by James Storr. Collection of the Museum für Moderne Keramik, Deidesheim.

Below left: Rick Hirsch (U.S.A.). "Ceremonial Cup #4." Raku, with purple and black underglazes. Base color comes from a combination of terra sigillata and underglazes. Bisque fired, then raku fired and sprayed with cupric sulfate before post-firing reduction. Photograph by Bob Aude.

Below right: Wayne Higby (U.S.A.). "Balanced Rock #2." Earthenware, raku technique. Thrown and corrected form. Partially glazed, colored with oxides, salts and stains.

Right: Ruth Gowdy McKinley (Canada). Wine server and cups. Thrown porcelain, wood fired to cone 10. Barium matt glaze colored with copper and rutile. Crystalline formation and color variation due to fly ash in the kiln. Photograph by Donald Lloyd McKinley.

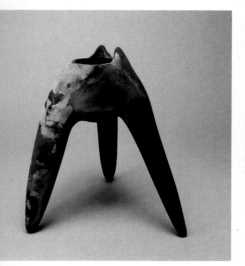

Facing page: Frank Boyden (U.S.A.). "Carp Vase." Raku, sodium fired with polished terra sigillata and sodium borate glaze. Copper, silver nitrate and iron additions to the glaze. Fired to cone 04; heavy post-firing reduction in oats. Photograph by Wood and Piper.

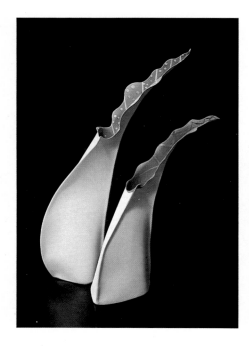

Left: Jeannie Mah (Canada). Slab-built porcelain forms, sprayed and brushed with commercial glaze stains, underglaze colors. Sprayed with light coating of glaze, and fired in oxidation at cone 6. Photograph by Ed Jones.

Below: Jane Wilson (Canada). Handbuilt bowl, 6″ x 4″ triangular form. Porcelain clay, sprayed with rutile and gerstley borate/soda ash wash with small amounts of copper and cobalt. Fired at cone 04.

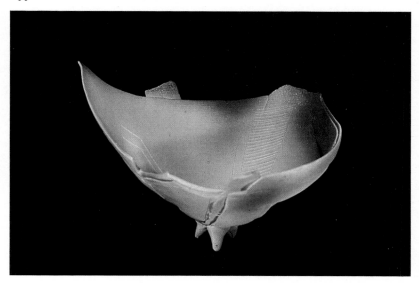

Below: Geoffrey Swindell (United Kingdom). Three thrown porcelain pots. Dolomite glaze with copper; on-glaze luster painted and air-brushed over the glaze. Fired at cone 9 in oxidation. Photograph by Bill Thomas.

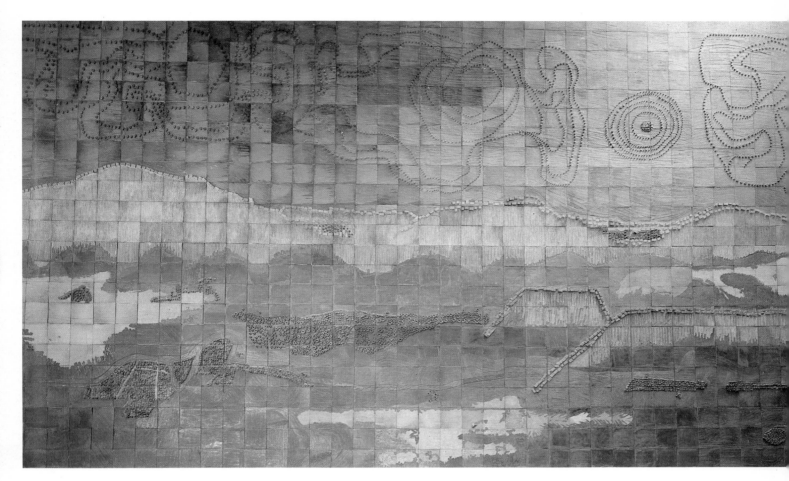

Above: Hugo Velasquez (Mexico). "Inland." Mural, 31' x 18'. Stoneware, using one engobe and two glazes, with great tonal variation through thickness variation of the glazes. Fired in reduction at cone 9.

Left: Patti Warashina (U.S.A.). "Mother Goose." Stacked and layered box. Low fired at cone 01. Underglazed with colorants and glazed. Subsequently airbrushed and handpainted with overglaze enamels, and refired. Photograph by Roger Schreiber.

Below left: Gordon Hutchens (Canada). Porcelain bowl. Slip decoration, trailed and combed, with a softwood ash glaze, fired in reduction to cone 11. Bowl interior painted with liquid bright gold, fired to 750°C, and sprayed with a liquid solution of stannous chloride, producing an array of lustrous colors, and fuming the ash glaze at the same time. Photograph by Paul Bailey.

Below right: John Chalke (Canada). Handbuilt plate, 13" square. Stoneware with multiple glaze firing, giving the surface a very complex quality. Pink chrome/tin mix brushed over a titanium white glaze. Oxidation fired at cone 6.

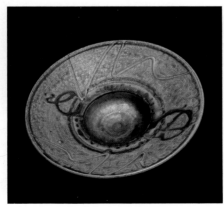

Left: Betty Woodman (U.S.A.). "Mediterranean Pillow Pitcher," 27" x 23". White earthenware, fired at cone 04, with a lead/alkaline glaze, turquoise alkaline glaze, and color from manganese copper and stains.

Facing page: Tom Turner (U.S.A.). Teapot, porcelain. Cone 9 reduction fired copper red glaze. This piece was placed in the kiln in an area which caused maroon colors to develop instead of red. Green spots from chromium. Photograph by Bill Parish.

Below left: Lou Schmidt (Switzerland). Bottle, stoneware. Wood fired in a Bizen-type firing, with heavy accumulation of ash deposit, and color coming from alternating atmospheric conditions. Fired to cone 8–9, over a 60–75 hour period.

Below right: Ken Chernavich (Canada). Slab-built cylindrical form. Casting porcelain, 24" high. After drying, the image is drawn onto the clay and airbrushed with oxides and commercial stains, using wax resist between colorants. Cone 01 oxidation.

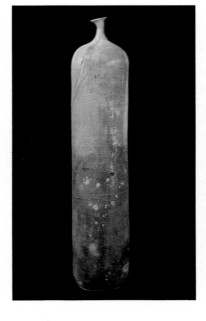

Above: Dorothy Feibleman (United Kingdom). Cylindrical form. Stained porcelain bodies, inlaid and laminated. Fired to cone 7 in oxidation. The surface is polished with fine wet and dry Carborundum paper after firing. Photograph by David Cripps.

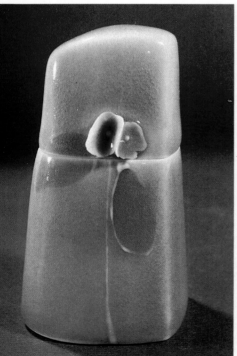

Above: Steve Heineman (Canada). Bowl, porcelain. Multiple overlapping layers of colored casting slips, poured and rolled in a plaster mould. Unglazed, fired between cone 6–8, oxidation. Photograph by James Chambers.

Below: Margarete Schott (Germany). Beaker. Thrown and faceted porcelain, 14cm high. Feldspathic glaze, with copper oxide on the surface. Reduction fired at 1350°C. Photograph by Jochen Schade.

Above left: Enid Legros (Canada). Slipcast porcelain box, 3″ high. Applied decoration with thin modelled pieces, trailed slip and blue watercolor. Copper colored "peach-bloom" glaze fired in reduction at cone 11.

Above right: Walter Ostrom (Canada). "Flower Baskets." Earthenware, white slip, tin opacified lead/alkaline glaze with oxides and stains. Oxidation fired at cone 04.

Right: Alan Kluber (U.S.A.). Handbuilt plate. Stained clays colored with commercial stains, cut and laminated into pattern form. Pressmoulded and partly thrown. Covered with a clear glaze and fired at cone 5 in oxidation. Photograph by Pete Shoemaker.

Far right: Jack Sures (Canada). "Process Piece." Detail; the last of nine porcelain tiles in a progression using a wire cut porcelain tile with varying amounts of carrot tops placed on the tiles and fired at cone 11, leaving a residual ash glaze.

Below: Lisette Savaria (Canada). "Flowers and Leaves of Bleeding Heart." Porcelain plate, thrown, carved and pierced. Glaze fired at cone 11. Overglaze decoration in enamels, with multiple firings. Photograph by Andre Couvellier.

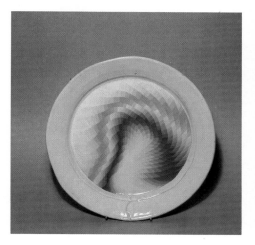

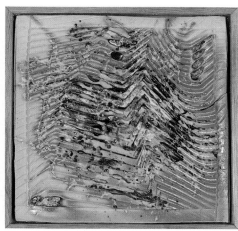

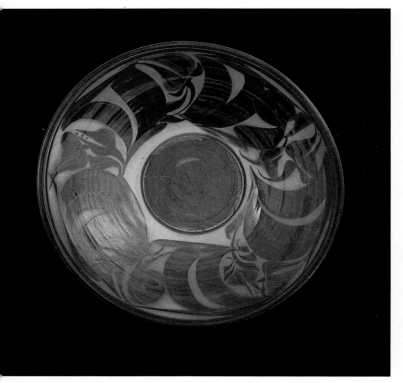

Top right: Robin Hopper (Canada). Lidded jar, earthenware. Fritted lead/alkaline glaze with copper and cobalt added. White tin glaze trailed on lid. Glaze fired to cone 2, and subsequently refired in heavy reduction at 750°C, where the white glaze becomes lustrous from the copper.

Above left: Geoffrey Eastop (United Kingdom). "The Tree IV." Earthenware plate, 21" diameter, with cadmium-selenium glazes. Red glaze applied, then design outlined with wax resist. Orange glaze painted on, with added copper green brushwork.

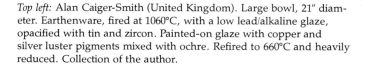

Top left: Alan Caiger-Smith (United Kingdom). Large bowl, 21" diameter. Earthenware, fired at 1060°C, with a low lead/alkaline glaze, opacified with tin and zircon. Painted-on glaze with copper and silver luster pigments mixed with ochre. Refired to 660°C and heavily reduced. Collection of the author.

Above right: David Leach (United Kingdom). Bowl, porcelain. Brush decoration and trailed red glaze over blue wash. The red glaze is a mixture of nepheline syenite and calcined red clay in equal proportions. The clay is calcined at 600°C, to remove plasticity. Not all red clays will work. Fired in reduction at cone 9.

Right: David Davison (U.S.A.). "Heart of Hearts." Soda raku, 18" × 14". Bisqued and sprayed with copper and iron wash. Fired to between 1000°C, and 1100°C, then baking soda mixed with sawdust thrown into kiln. When sodium glaze is adequate, the piece is removed from the kiln for post-firing reduction in newspaper.

Below: Tim Worthington (Canada). "House Plate," Earthenware with slips, sgraffito, and stains. Fired at cone 04 in oxidation. Photograph by Pam Birdsall.

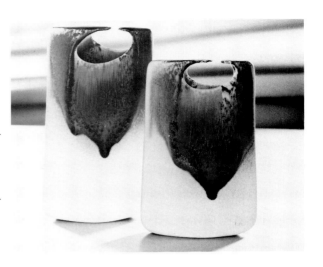

Ron Tribe (Canada). Handbuilt forms, porcelain. Multiple glazes sprayed and brushed, fired in oxidation at cone 6.

Bruce Cochrane (Canada). Lidded jar. Stoneware with thick white slip under Shino-type glaze. The color variation comes from the thickness differences of the glaze, the carbon trapped in the glaze during the early stages of firing, and the process of wood firing. Fired at cone 9–10. Photograph by Dale Pereira.

Robin Hopper (Canada). Axe Jar. Porcelain, 15 " high. Thrown, with thrown and cut handle sections. Once-fired with an alkaline slip glaze made from porcelain clay, barium and lithium, brushed on. Airbrushed with copper and rutile. Brush decoration in iron and copper. Cone 9 oxidation.

Denys James (Canada). Raku, figure slab. Incised lines, accented with slip, oxides and salt washes. Low-fire salted at cone 04.

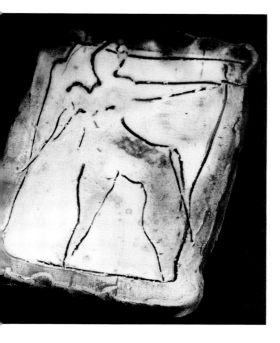

Franklin Heisler (Canada). "Cucumber's Computer Cucumber Production Unit." 24" × 28". Low fire, with commercial glazes and lusters. Multiple firings.

195

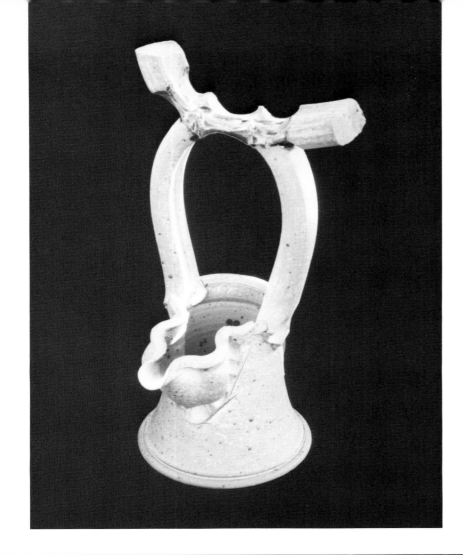

Left: Dennis Parks (U.S.A.). Pitcher, 11" high. Stoneware, glazed inside; outside has a pseudo glaze from the flashing and fuming of impurities in the sump oil used as a fuel. Photograph by V. Parks.

Below: Ian Symons (Canada). Serving platter. Red earthenware, with white slip and covered with a cone 04 clear glaze. This is then colored with cone 06 glazes and refired. A third firing at cone 019 is used for the addition of china paints. Photograph by Ron Pozniak.

Facing page: Paul Rozman (Canada). Lidded jar, 12" high. Earthenware with terra sigillata slip, applied and sgraffito decoration. Oxidation fired at cone 04. (Sigillata recipe: red art clay 20%, water 80%, Darvan (water softener) 0.5%; ball milled for six hours.)

Right: Ray Rogers (New Zealand). Pit-fired form. Placed on sawdust in pit, then firewood stacked over, and corrugated iron sheet closing over the top. Fired for 3 to 5 hours. Various oxides used on the surface. Photograph by Howard Williams.

Below: Bill Hunt (U.S.A.). Bowl. Salt-glazed stoneware, 11¼" diameter. Thrown with cut foot. Perlite added to the body for texture. Fired at cone 9.

Appendix

TABLE OF ORTON STANDARD CONES AND TEMPERATURES

Cone	Centigrade	Fahrenheit	Color	What Happens to Clay	Type of Ware and Glazes
—	0	32	—	Water freezes	—
—	100	212	—	Water boils	—
—	100–300	212–572	—	Chemical water driven off	—
—	470	878	—	Lowest point where red glow can be seen in the Dark	—
—	573	1063	—	Quartz inversion	—
022	605	1121		Lowest cone temperature	Metallic lusters (gold, platinum, etc.)
021	614	1137			
020	635	1175			
019	683	1261			Overglaze colors or enamels (China paints)
018	717	1323	Dull		
017	747	1377	Red		
016	792	1458		Organic matter in clay burns out	
015	804	1479			
014	838	1540			
013	852	1566			Inglaze lusters
012	884	1623	Cherry		
011	894	1641	Red		Raku
010	905	1661			Chromium red glazes
09	923	1693	Dark		Lowfire lead glazes
08	955	1751	Orange		Lowfired bisque
07	984	1803			Lowfire earthenware
06	999	1830			
05	1031	1888		Some red clays mature	Average bisque
04	1060	1940	Orange		
03	1101	2014			Earthenware
02	1120	2048		Buff clays mature	
01	1137	2079	Dark		
1	1154	2109	Yellow		Highfire earthenware
2	1162	2124			Semi-vitreous ware
3	1168	2134		Some red clays melt	Sanitary ware
4	1186	2167	Yellow		Bone China glazes
5	1196	2185			Lowfire stoneware
6	1222	2232	Bright	Stoneware clays mature	Salt glazes
7	1240	2264	Yellow		
8	1263	2305			Stoneware
9	1280	2336			China bodies—bisque
10	1305	2381			
11	1315	2399	White	Porcelain matures	
12	1326	2419			Porcelain
13	1346	2455			
14	1366	2491			

Note: The temperature equivalents in this table apply only to large (2½ inch) Orton Pyrometric cones when heated at the rate of 150°C. (270°F.) per hour in an air atmosphere. The above list represents the temperature range within which studio potters and ceramists generally work. For industrial and scientific purposes, higher temperatures may be needed, with cones going to cone 42, the melting point of pure silica. The color column represents the approximate color of radiant light visible in the kiln.

COMPARATIVE LIST OF COMMONLY USED FRITS

This is a list of the most commonly used frits in North America. There are a number of manufacturers who produce a staggering variety between them. Many companies produce similar frits, and each company has its own serial numbering system. For ease of reference I have separated the list into three sections, selecting the Ferro Corporation list for comparisons. The first chart presents the percentage composition of Ferro leadless frits, the second the percentage composition of Ferro lead frits, and the third cross-references the product numbers of similar frits produced by Pemco Products, and O'Hommel, Inc. This information is compiled from a variety of sources, and is therefore only as accurate as those sources. Frit 3110 is generally referred to as body frit, although it may equally well be used for glazes.

Percentage Composition, Leadless Frits

Frit #	Cone	K_2O	Na_2O	CaO	MgO	BaO	ZnO	B_2O_3	Al_2O_3	SiO_2	ZrO_2	F
3110	07	2.5	15.4	5.2	0.8	—	—	2.8	3.7	69.6	—	—
3124	05	0.6	5.6	14.5	—	—	—	12.5	10.0	56.8	—	—
3134	07	—	10.2	20.1	—	—	—	23.2	—	46.5	—	—
3195	05	—	12.7	11.3	—	—	—	15.8	12.5	47.6	—	—
3240	05	0.6	4.5	8.8	—	7.9	15.8	10.0	0.9	39.5	10.2	—
3269	07	10.0	11.2	—	—	—	—	17.1	12.8	48.9	—	—
3278	03	—	15.5	6.8	—	—	—	21.8	—	56.2	—	—
3289	07	—	5.5	—	—	27.4	—	12.4	5.4	49.3	—	—
3293	05	—	16.7	0.2	0.8	—	—	—	5.9	76.4	—	—
5301	05	5.1	19.2	2.3	—	—	—	11.7	11.3	41.8	—	8.6

Percentage Composition, Lead Frits

Frit #	Cone	K_2O	Na_2O	CaO	MgO	BaO	ZnO	PbO	B_2O_3	Al_2O_3	SiO_2	ZrO_2
3300	03	3.2	0.7	8.8	6.2	6.2	10.5	22.2	—	9.2	38.8	—
3304	07	—	2.1	—	—	—	—	52.6	—	4.8	40.5	—
3403	07	1.4	0.3	0.1	—	—	—	67.8	—	2.4	28.1	—
3417	07	1.8	1.6	4.4	—	—	—	30.4	12.6	3.1	43.1	2.4
3419	09	—	6.5	—	—	—	—	59.2	14.5	—	19.8	—
3465	03	—	14.7	6.6	—	—	—	6.6	19.3	—	52.8	—
3467	03	1.8	2.4	8.5	0.7	—	—	17.4	4.5	9.0	55.7	—
3481	03	1.4	3.1	9.9	—	—	—	23.1	6.0	7.1	49.4	—
3489	09	—	—	5.6	—	—	—	67.6	—	—	26.8	—
3493	07	1.9	1.5	4.6	—	—	—	31.3	12.9	3.1	44.7	—

Equivalent Frit Compositions, Leadless Frits

Ferro	Pemco	O'Hommel
3110	P 1505	—
3124	P 311	90
3134	P 54	14 (242)
3240	P 64	26 (69)
3269	P 25	25 (259)
3278	P 830	K3
3289	P 626	—
3293	P 283	—
5301	—	—

Equivalent Frit Compositions, Lead Frits

Ferro	Pemco	O'Hommel
3300	—	316
3304	—	61
3403	Pb 723	71 (243)
3417	Pb 63	24 (235)
3419	Pb 83	33 (240)
3465	Pb 943	18
3467	—	365
3481	—	403
3489	Pb 716	—
3493	Pb 742	373

SERIAL NUMBERS OF GLAZE BASES AND COLOR ADDITIONS

The following list of serial numbers relates to the numbering systems used in developing the glazes shown in color (Glaze Tests 1–12). This is a small selection, almost at random, from the thousands done in the preparation of this book. The numbering systems are outlined in chapters 4 and 15.

Serial Number	Glaze Base			Chapter
FS (1–15)	Flux saturations			Chapter 10
LAB	Line blend—colemanite and wood ash			Chapter 7
OIG (1–30)	Oriental iron glazes			Appendix 6
EB (1–8)	Enamel base			Chapter 13
FSS (1–6)	Flux saturations/strontium replacing barium			Chapter 10
MFV (1–25)	Matt flux variation			Chapter 10
SFV (1–25)	Shiny flux variation			Chapter 10
LM (1–10)	Lowfire majolica			Chapter 13
LTAV2	21pt Triaxial—Lowfire A = Frit 3134	40		Chapter 8
	B1 = Frit 3195	10		
	B2 = Cryolite	10		
	C1 = Colemanite	20		
	C2 = Kaolin	20		
	Total	100		
OV	Rhodes variation 1			Chapter 12
CR (1–15)	Highfire crystalline			Chapter 13
CRR (1–10)	Copper red reduction with 5% tin in base			Chapter 13
TCV2	Triaxial—Highfire A = Custer feldspar	30		Chapter 8
	B1 = Kaolin	20		
	B2 = Cornwall stone	20		
	C1 = Dolomite	15		
	C2 = Flint	15		
	Total	100		
LCR (1–5)	Lowfire chromium red bases using red lead (6–10); same base using white lead			Chapter 13
LUCR (1–5)	Lowfire chromium red bases with uranium using red lead (6–10); same base using white lead			Chapter 13

The serial numbers given to colorants throughout this book are as follows.

a = Iron
b = Cobalt
c = Copper
d = Manganese
e = Nickel
f = Rutile
g = Tin
h = Chromium
j = Yellow stain (Blythe # 14.H.236)

Thus the serial number on a test can be read as follows:

OV	Base glaze OV (Rhodes variation 1—chapter 12)
3	2.5 percent of total color (see chapter 15)
bd 2/8	Colorant mixture and ratio of mixture: cobalt 1, manganese 4
O	Fired in oxidation

Serial Numbers of Glaze and
Color Tests 1-12

Glaze Tests 1-12 appear in the color section following page 48. Numbering systems for these test are given on page 202.

FS5 3a O	LAB2 4a O	OIG.10 6a O	EB7 2a O	OIG6 1a O	FS2 5a O
1.	2.	3.	4.	5.	6.
EB7 1a O	FSS1 5a O	FSS4 5a O	OIG.17 6a R	MFV5 2a R	MFV7 6a R
7.	8.	9.	10.	11.	12.
FS6 2a R	SFV8 3a R	LM2 6a O	OIG.3 1a R	LTAV2-9 6a O	SFV9 2a R
13.	14.	15.	16.	17.	18.
MFV9 2a R	O.I.G.16 2a R	OIG.27 1a R	OIG.27 6a R	MFV5 1a R	OIG.11 6a R
19.	20.	21.	22.	23.	24.

a = IRON. Serial number references for Glaze Test 1.

Some examples of the color variation from IRON in different glaze bases and atmospheric conditions. Serial numbers are explained on page 202.

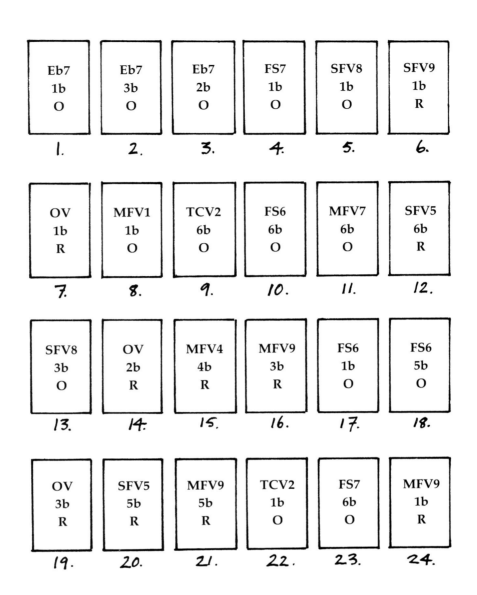

Eb7 1b O	Eb7 3b O	Eb7 2b O	FS7 1b O	SFV8 1b O	SFV9 1b R
1.	2.	3.	4.	5.	6.
OV 1b R	MFV1 1b O	TCV2 6b O	FS6 6b O	MFV7 6b O	SFV5 6b R
7.	8.	9.	10.	11.	12.
SFV8 3b O	OV 2b R	MFV4 4b R	MFV9 3b R	FS6 1b O	FS6 5b O
13.	14.	15.	16.	17.	18.
OV 3b R	SFV5 5b R	MFV9 5b R	TCV2 1b O	FS7 6b O	MFV9 1b R
19.	20.	21.	22.	23.	24.

b = COBALT. Serial number references for Glaze Test 2.

Some examples of the color variation from COBALT in different glaze bases and atmospheric conditions. Serial numbers are explained on page 202.

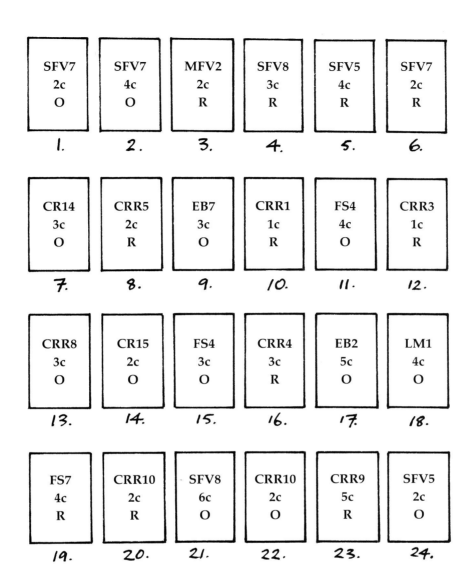

SFV7 2c O	SFV7 4c O	MFV2 2c R	SFV8 3c R	SFV5 4c R	SFV7 2c R
1.	2.	3.	4.	5.	6.
CR14 3c O	CRR5 2c R	EB7 3c O	CRR1 1c R	FS4 4c O	CRR3 1c R
7.	8.	9.	10.	11.	12.
CRR8 3c O	CR15 2c O	FS4 3c O	CRR4 3c R	EB2 5c O	LM1 4c O
13.	14.	15.	16.	17.	18.
FS7 4c R	CRR10 2c R	SFV8 6c O	CRR10 2c O	CRR9 5c R	SFV5 2c O
19.	20.	21.	22.	23.	24.

C = COPPER. Serial number references for Glaze Test 3.

Some examples of the color variation from COPPER in different glaze bases and atmospheric conditions. Serial numbers are explained on page 202.

SFV14 5d R	LM3 4d O	SFV12 6d O	SFV10 6d O	EB1 1d O	LM3 6d O
1.	2.	3.	4.	5.	6.

SFV8 3d O	SFV15 6d R	SFV14 6d R	MFV7 4d R	EB5 1d O	OV 3d O
7.	8.	9.	10.	11.	12.

OV 3d R	SFV8 6d R	LM1 6d O	SFV5 5d O	SFV5 6d R	SFV1 5d O
13.	14.	15.	16.	17.	18.

SFV10 5d O	MFV9 3d R	SFV5 4d R	MFV2 4d O	MFV6 4d R	MFV10 6d O
19.	20.	21.	22.	23.	24.

d = MANGANESE. Serial number references for Glaze Test 4.

Some examples of the color variation from MANGANESE in different glaze bases and atmospheric conditions. Serial numbers are explained on page 202.

SFV7 5e O	SFV7 6e O	LTAV2.9 6e O	CR13 3e O	CR13 1e O	CR12 1e O
1.	2.	3.	4.	5.	6.
MFV7 5e O	LTAV2.9 5e O	CR13 4e O	CR13 5e O	CR13 6e O	MFV8 6e R
7.	8.	9.	10.	11.	12.
FS5 1e O	FS5 2e O	FS5 5e O	FS6 6e O	FS6 5e O	FS6 4e O
13.	14.	15.	16.	17.	18.
FS6 1e O	FS6 2e O	FS6 3e O	EB7 1e O	EB7 2e O	EB7 3e O
19.	20.	21.	22.	23.	24.

e = NICKEL. Serial number references for Glaze Test 5.

Some examples of the color variation from NICKEL in different glaze bases and atmospheric conditions. Serial numbers are explained on page 202.

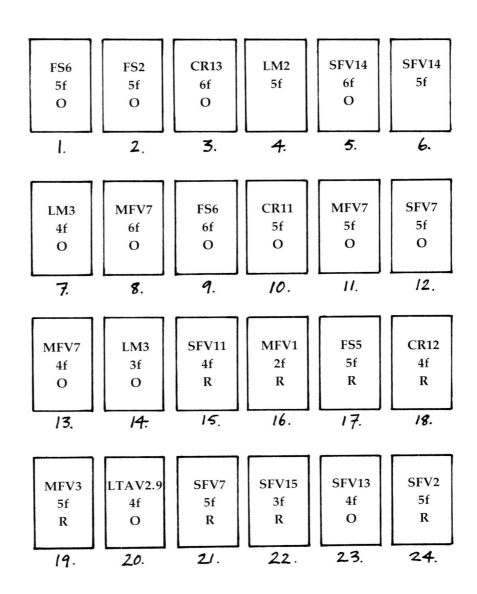

FS6 5f O	FS2 5f O	CR13 6f O	LM2 5f	SFV14 6f O	SFV14 5f
1.	2.	3.	4.	5.	6.
LM3 4f O	MFV7 6f O	FS6 6f O	CR11 5f O	MFV7 5f O	SFV7 5f O
7.	8.	9.	10.	11.	12.
MFV7 4f O	LM3 3f O	SFV11 4f R	MFV1 2f R	FS5 5f R	CR12 4f R
13.	14.	15.	16.	17.	18.
MFV3 5f R	LTAV2.9 4f O	SFV7 5f R	SFV15 3f R	SFV13 4f O	SFV2 5f R
19.	20.	21.	22.	23.	24.

f = RUTILE. Serial number references for Glaze Test 6.

Some examples of the color variation from RUTILE in different glaze bases and atmospheric conditions. Serial numbers are explained on page 202.

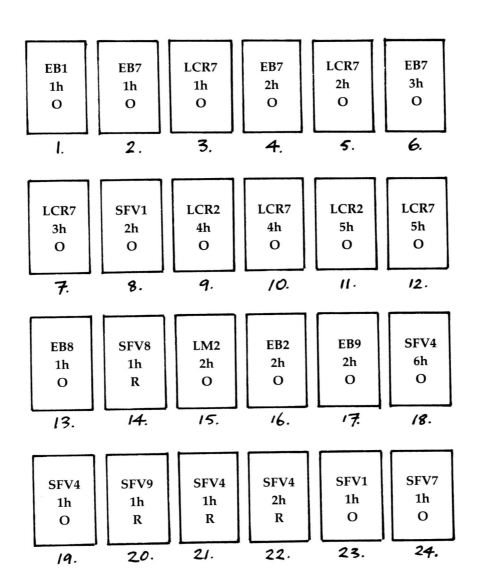

EB1 1h O	EB7 1h O	LCR7 1h O	EB7 2h O	LCR7 2h O	EB7 3h O
1.	2.	3.	4.	5.	6.
LCR7 3h O	SFV1 2h O	LCR2 4h O	LCR7 4h O	LCR2 5h O	LCR7 5h O
7.	8.	9.	10.	11.	12.
EB8 1h O	SFV8 1h R	LM2 2h O	EB2 2h O	EB9 2h O	SFV4 6h O
13.	14.	15.	16.	17.	18.
SFV4 1h O	SFV9 1h R	SFV4 1h R	SFV4 2h R	SFV1 1h O	SFV7 1h O
19.	20.	21.	22.	23.	24.

h = CHROMIUM. Serial number references for Glaze Test 7.

Some examples of the color variation from CHROMIUM in different glaze bases and atmospheric conditions. Serial numbers are explained on page 202.

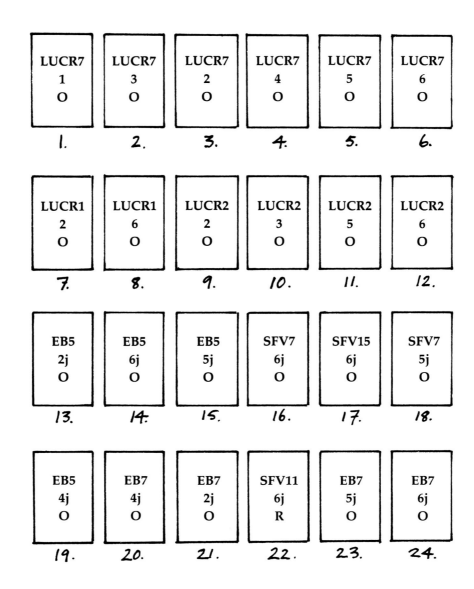

LUCR7 1 O	LUCR7 3 O	LUCR7 2 O	LUCR7 4 O	LUCR7 5 O	LUCR7 6 O
1.	2.	3.	4.	5.	6.
LUCR1 2 O	LUCR1 6 O	LUCR2 2 O	LUCR2 3 O	LUCR2 5 O	LUCR2 6 O
7.	8.	9.	10.	11.	12.
EB5 2j O	EB5 6j O	EB5 5j O	SFV7 6j O	SFV15 6j O	SFV7 5j O
13.	14.	15.	16.	17.	18.
EB5 4j O	EB7 4j O	EB7 2j O	SFV11 6j R	EB7 5j O	EB7 6j O
19.	20.	21.	22.	23.	24.

URANIUM (top 2 lines) + YELLOW GLAZE STAIN—Glaze Test 8.

Some examples of the color variation from URANIUM and YELLOW GLAZE STAIN in different glaze bases and atmospheric conditions. Serial numbers are explained on page 202.

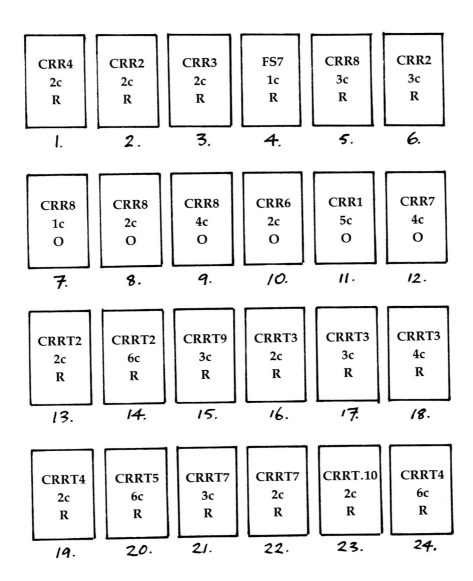

| CRR4 2c R | CRR2 2c R | CRR3 2c R | FS7 1c R | CRR8 3c R | CRR2 3c R |
| 1. | 2. | 3. | 4. | 5. | 6. |

| CRR8 1c O | CRR8 2c O | CRR8 4c O | CRR6 2c O | CRR1 5c O | CRR7 4c O |
| 7. | 8. | 9. | 10. | 11. | 12. |

| CRRT2 2c R | CRRT2 6c R | CRRT9 3c R | CRRT3 2c R | CRRT3 3c R | CRRT3 4c R |
| 13. | 14. | 15. | 16. | 17. | 18. |

| CRRT4 2c R | CRRT5 6c R | CRRT7 3c R | CRRT7 2c R | CRRT.10 2c R | CRRT4 6c R |
| 19. | 20. | 21. | 22. | 23. | 24. |

COPPER + TIN, and COPPER + TITANIUM—Glaze Test 9.

Some examples of the color variation from COPPER with tin or titanium in different glaze bases and atmospheric conditions. Serial numbers are explained on page 202.

OV $6ef\frac{4}{6}$ O	OV $5ej\frac{4}{6}$ R	OV $4eg\frac{6}{4}$ R	OV $6ej\frac{2}{8}$ O	OV $4ae\frac{4}{6}$ O	OV $2ce\frac{6}{4}$ O
1.	2.	3.	4.	5.	6.
OV $3ce\frac{4}{6}$ O	TCV2 $4ce\frac{8}{2}$ O	TCV2 $6de\frac{4}{6}$ O	TCV2 $3be\frac{4}{6}$ R	OV $1be\frac{4}{6}$ R	OV $3be\frac{2}{8}$
7.	8.	9.	10.	11.	12.
OV $5bd\frac{4}{6}$ R	LM3 $4bd\frac{2}{8}$ O	OV $3bd\frac{2}{8}$ O	TCV2 $6dg\frac{8}{2}$ O	OV $2dh\frac{8}{2}$ R	OV $3ad\frac{2}{8}$ R
13.	14.	15.	16.	17.	18.
OV $5bd\frac{8}{2}$ O	OV $4bd\frac{6}{4}$ R	LM3 $5bd\frac{4}{6}$ O	TCV2 $6df\frac{6}{4}$ O	OV $1ab\frac{4}{6}$ O	OV $3bc\frac{6}{4}$ O
19.	20.	21.	22.	23.	24.

Cross-blended colors from NICKEL, MANGANESE, and COBALT—Glaze Test 10.

Some examples of the mixed color variation in different glaze bases and atmospheric conditions. Serial numbers are explained on page 202.

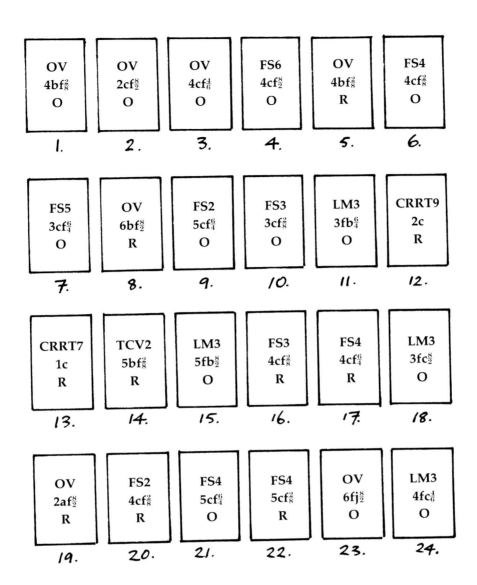

1. OV $4bf\frac{2}{8}$ O	2. OV $2cf\frac{8}{2}$ O	3. OV $4cf\frac{4}{6}$ O	4. FS6 $4cf\frac{8}{2}$ O	5. OV $4bf\frac{2}{8}$ R	6. FS4 $4cf\frac{2}{8}$ O
7. FS5 $3cf\frac{6}{4}$ O	8. OV $6bf\frac{8}{2}$ R	9. FS2 $5cf\frac{6}{4}$ O	10. FS3 $3cf\frac{2}{8}$ O	11. LM3 $3fb\frac{6}{4}$ O	12. CRRT9 $2c$ R
13. CRRT7 $1c$ R	14. TCV2 $5bf\frac{2}{8}$ R	15. LM3 $5fb\frac{8}{2}$ O	16. FS3 $4cf\frac{2}{8}$ R	17. FS4 $4cf\frac{6}{4}$ R	18. LM3 $3fc\frac{8}{2}$ O
19. OV $2af\frac{8}{2}$ R	20. FS2 $4cf\frac{2}{8}$ R	21. FS4 $5cf\frac{6}{4}$ O	22. FS4 $5cf\frac{2}{8}$ R	23. OV $6fj\frac{8}{2}$ O	24. LM3 $4fc\frac{4}{6}$ O

Cross-blended colors from RUTILE, IRON COBALT and MANGANESE— Glaze Test 11.

Some examples of the color variation in different glaze bases and atmospheric conditions. Serial numbers are explained on page 202.

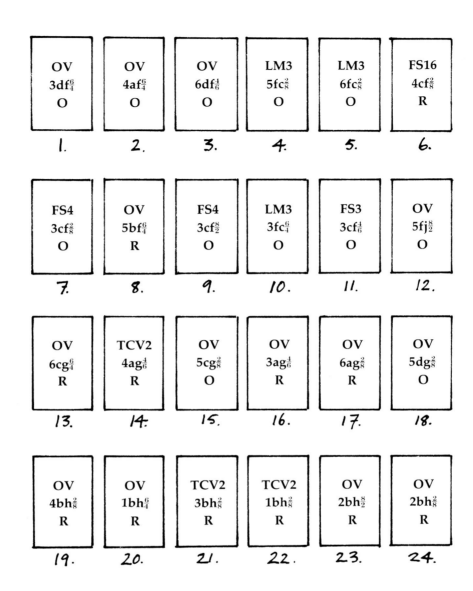

OV $3df_4^6$ O	OV $4af_4^6$ O	OV $6df_6^4$ O	LM3 $5fc_8^2$ O	LM3 $6fc_8^2$ O	FS16 $4cf_8^2$ R
1.	2.	3.	4.	5.	6.
FS4 $3cf_8^2$ O	OV $5bf_4^6$ R	FS4 $3cf_2^8$ O	LM3 $3fc_4^6$ O	FS3 $3cf_6^4$ O	OV $5fj_2^8$ O
7.	8.	9.	10.	11.	12.
OV $6cg_4^6$ R	TCV2 $4ag_6^4$ R	OV $5cg_8^2$ O	OV $3ag_6^4$ R	OV $6ag_8^2$ R	OV $5dg_8^2$ O
13.	14.	15.	16.	17.	18.
OV $4bh_8^2$ R	OV $1bh_4^6$ R	TCV2 $3bh_8^2$ R	TCV2 $1bh_8^2$ R	OV $2bh_2^8$ R	OV $2bh_8^2$ R
19.	20.	21.	22.	23.	24.

RUTILE, TIN, COPPER, MANGANESE, COBALT and CHROMIUM cross-blends—Glaze Test 12.

Some examples of the color variation in different glaze bases and atmospheric conditions. Serial numbers are explained on page 202.

EFFECTIVE FIRING RANGE OF GLAZE OXIDES

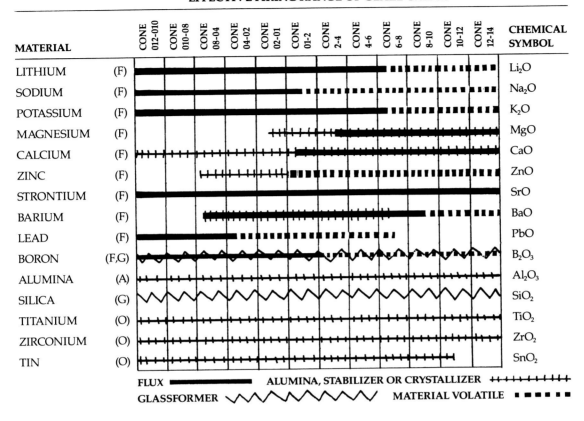

MATERIAL		CHEMICAL SYMBOL
LITHIUM	(F)	Li₂O
SODIUM	(F)	Na₂O
POTASSIUM	(F)	K₂O
MAGNESIUM	(F)	MgO
CALCIUM	(F)	CaO
ZINC	(F)	ZnO
STRONTIUM	(F)	SrO
BARIUM	(F)	BaO
LEAD	(F)	PbO
BORON	(F,G)	B₂O₃
ALUMINA	(A)	Al₂O₃
SILICA	(G)	SiO₂
TITANIUM	(O)	TiO₂
ZIRCONIUM	(O)	ZrO₂
TIN	(O)	SnO₂

Cone columns: 012-010, 010-08, 08-04, 04-02, 02-01, 01-2, 2-4, 4-6, 6-8, 8-10, 10-12, 12-14

FLUX ▬▬▬ ALUMINA, STABILIZER OR CRYSTALLIZER ++++++++
GLASSFORMER ∧∧∧∧∧ MATERIAL VOLATILE ■ ■ ■ ■ ■

ORIENTAL IRON GLAZES FOR CONE 8–10 REDUCTION

Iron oxide is the main colorant used in the great majority of early Oriental pottery. The colors that come from iron are greatly affected by small amounts of titanium, manganese and phosphorous, which may be found as impurities in many glaze ingredients. Ball clays are particularly likely to have trace amounts of titanium, an impurity which causes iron to produce green rather than blue celadon colors. Analysis sheets on clays are usually available from suppliers, and in the selection of materials for the glaze, care should be taken to use clays as free from titanium as possible, if a blue celadon is desired. Manganese will tend to make the iron colors muddy, and phosphorous, when used in conjunction with small percentages of iron, can give opalescent qualities.

The following group of glaze bases cover a wide range of Oriental glazes. With varying additions of iron oxide, generally from 0.25 to 10 percent, as suggested in the color mixing chart in chapter 15, these bases will give a range of Celadon, Temmoku, Chun, Shino, Kaki or iron red and Tessha glazes. The addition of up to 5 percent iron will give celadons from very pale green and pale blues, through grey green to olive green. Celadon glazes, when fired in oxidation, are usually pale yellow to amber. For blue celadons, fired in reduction, usually called Ying Ching, or Ying Xing, it is preferable to use black iron oxide, instead of red. For the other variations it doesn't seem to make much difference which form of iron is used, although they will all have slight variations. From 5 to 10 percent iron will give dark olive celadons to black temmoku, with characteristic orange-brown edges and thin spots. Some of them will also crystallize in finely marked aventurine patterns, and some will give deep plum reds. From 10 to 15 percent iron in those glazes containing bone ash will develop Kaki or persimmon iron red glazes. Low calcium content generally favors the development of iron orange and reds. Although most of these glazes are at their best in reduction, many of the traditional qualities, such as oil spot, hare's fur, and other specialities may be achieved in oxidation at the same temperature range. These surface effects are produced through the bubbling of the glaze, often specially developed through the use of carbonate materials such as dolomite or whiting. The oil spot, hare's fur and other traditional effects also rely on exacting kiln control, so that the rings and lines of iron crystals, formed as the bubbles burst, do not sink back into the molten glaze, but are solidified on the surface in cooling. Quick cooling of the glaze from the shutoff temperature down to 1100°C. usually helps. Because of their relatively high clay content, most of these glazes can be used for once-firing.

Oriental Iron Glazes: Serial Numbers OIG 1–30

1 Cornwall stone, 25; kaolin, 25; whiting, 25; flint, 25

2 Cornwall stone, 40; kaolin, 15; whiting, 15; zinc, 10; flint, 20

3 Cornwall stone, 40; kaolin, 15; whiting, 15; barium, 10; flint, 20

4 Porcelain body (powdered), 70; wollastonite, 30

5 Nepheline syenite, 40; whiting, 20; kaolin, 15; flint, 25

6 Nepheline syenite, 55; Albany or red clay, 30; flint, 10; talc, 5

7 Cornwall stone, 50; Albany or red clay, 20; whiting, 10; colemanite, 10; wood ash, 10

8 Cornwall stone, 20; feldspar, 20; whiting, 10; bone ash, 10; flint, 20; kaolin, 20

9 Feldspar, 30; dolomite, 15; ball clay, 20; flint, 20; bone ash, 15

10 Feldspar, 45; kaolin, 8; whiting, 7; talc, 8; flint, 20; bone ash, 12

11 Cornwall stone, 35; feldspar, 35; kaolin or ball clay, 15; whiting, 15

12 Cornwall stone, 35; feldspar, 35; Albany or red clay, 15; whiting, 15

13 Cornwall stone, 35; flint, 20; colemanite, 20; ball clay, 15; whiting, 10

14 Feldspar, 35; flint, 15; colemanite, 10; whiting, 15; ball clay, 25

15 Feldspar, 30; flint, 20; colemanite, 20; ball clay, 15; whiting, 15

16 Feldspar, 35; flint, 25; kaolin, 15; whiting, 15; talc, 10

17 Feldspar, 50; whiting, 10; Albany or red clay, 30; colemanite, 10

18 Feldspar, 22; whiting, 22; kaolin, 22; flint, 24; talc, 10

19 Feldspar, 30; whiting, 20; kaolin, 20; flint, 20; talc, 10

20 Cornwall stone, 30; dolomite, 10; colemanite, 20; red clay, 20; flint, 20

21 Feldspar, 40; Albany clay, 15; flint, 25; whiting, 15; ball clay, 5

22 Feldspar, 40; flint, 20; Albany or red clay, 20; wood ash, 20

23 Cornwall stone, 40; flint, 15; Albany or red clay, 15; wood ash, 30

24 Feldspar, 45; kaolin, 20; whiting, 10; wood ash, 25

25 Cornwall stone, 30; flint, 25; colemanite, 15; ball clay, 15; whiting, 15

26 Feldspar, 25; flint, 25; Albany or red clay, 25; wood ash, 25

27 Feldspar, 30; wood ash, 30; flint, 30; ball clay, 10

28 Feldspar, 30; wood ash, 20; flint, 30; whiting, 10; any frit, 10

29 Cornwall stone, 75; wood ash, 10; any frit, 10; talc, 5

30 Cornwall stone, 45; flint, 25; whiting, 15; talc, 5; colemanite, 5; ball clay, 5

Ceramic Stains For Underglaze or Glaze Staining

Material	#1 Red.	#2 Crimson.	#3 Orange.	#4 Yellow.	#5 Yellow.	#6 Victoria Green.	#7 Irish Green.	#8 Blue-Green.	#9 Turquoise.	#10 Ultramarine.	#11 Mazarine Blue.	#12 Canton Blue.	#13 Red-Brown.	#14 Brown.	#15 Pink.	#16 Pink.	#17 Mulberry.	#18 Black.	#19 Black.	#20 Black.
Tin Oxide.	40	45	15	20	50	—	—	—	45	—	—	—	—	—	50	50	—	—	—	—
Whiting.	30	23	—	—	—	20	—	—	—	—	10	—	—	—	25	20	—	—	—	—
Flint.	20	20	5	5	5	30	30	5	5	12	20	20	5	5	18	20	5	5	5	5
Borax.	—	—	—	—	—	—	25	—	—	—	—	—	—	—	4	—	—	—	—	—
Potassium Dichromate.	2	1.5	—	—	—	35	—	—	—	—	—	—	—	—	3	7.5	—	—	—	—
Calcium Sulfate.	—	5	—	—	—	—	—	—	—	—	—	—	—	—	—	—	—	—	—	—
Fluorspar.	10	7	—	—	—	15	—	—	—	—	—	—	—	—	—	7.5	—	—	—	—
Alumina Hydrate.	—	—	—	—	—	—	—	40	—	—	10	—	—	—	—	—	—	—	—	40
Chromium Oxide.	—	—	—	—	—	—	25	20	—	50	—	—	20	10	—	—	—	35	65	20
Cobalt Oxide.	—	—	—	—	—	—	5	40	—	38	40	40	—	—	—	—	10	5	—	40
Iron Oxide.	—	—	15	—	—	—	—	—	—	—	—	—	25	10	—	—	—	45	35	—
Manganese Dioxide.	—	—	—	—	—	—	—	—	—	—	—	—	—	—	—	—	60	15	—	—
Antimony Oxide.	—	—	30	30	25	—	—	—	—	—	—	—	—	—	—	—	—	—	—	—
Copper Phosphate.	—	—	—	—	—	—	—	—	55	—	—	—	—	—	—	—	—	—	—	—
Red Lead Oxide.	—	—	40	50	25	—	—	—	—	—	—	—	55	8	—	—	—	—	—	—
Zinc Oxide.	—	—	—	—	—	—	15	—	—	—	—	—	—	65	—	—	—	—	—	—
Boric Acid.	—	—	—	—	—	—	—	—	—	—	—	—	—	7	—	—	—	—	—	—
Feldspar.	—	—	—	—	—	—	—	—	—	—	—	30	—	—	—	—	30	—	—	—
Barium Carbonate.	—	—	—	—	—	—	—	—	—	—	—	10	—	—	—	—	—	—	—	—

Ceramic Stains.
For Preparation
Methods, See
Chapter 14.

Bibliography

BOOKS

Artigas, L. *Formulario y Practicas de Ceramica.* Barcelona: Grafos, S.A., 1968. This title is available from The Pottery Supply House, Oakville, Ontario, Canada (416) 827-1129.

Binns, C.F. *The Manual of Practical Potting.* Saint Clair Shores, MI: Scholarly Press, Inc., 1976.

Caiger-Smith, A. *Tin-Glaze Pottery.* London: Faber and Faber, 1973; Lawrence, MA: Merrimack Book Service, Inc., 1973.

Cardew, M. *Pioneer Pottery.* New York: St. Martin's Press, Inc., 1969.

Caruso, N. *Ceramica Viva.* Milan: Hoepli, 1979.

Charleston, R.J. *Roman Pottery.* London: Faber and Faber, n.d.

————, ed. *World Ceramics.* London: Paul Hamlyn, 1968.

Cooper, E., and Royle, D. *Glazes for the Studio Potter.* London: B.T. Batsford, 1979.

Cox, W.E. *The Book of Pottery and Porcelain.* New York: Crown Publishers, Inc., 1944.

Fournier, R. *Illustrated Dictionary of Practical Pottery.* New York: Von Nostrand Reinhold, 1973.

Fraser, H. *Glazes for the Craft Potter.* New York: Watson-Guptill, 1974.

Gray, B. *Early Chinese Pottery and Porcelain.* London: Faber and Faber, n.d.

Hamer, F. *The Potter's Dictionary of Materials and Techniques.* New York: Watson-Guptill, 1975.

Hamilton, D. *Manual of Pottery and Ceramics.* New York: Van Nostrand Reinhold, 1974.

Hetherington, A.L. *Chinese Ceramic Glazes.* Los Angeles, Commonwealth Press, 1948.

Jones, W.R. *Minerals in Industry.* 4th ed. London: Penguin Books, Ltd., 1963.

Kidder, J.E. *Jomon Pottery.* New York: Kodansha International, Ltd., 1968.

Koenig, J.H., and Earhart, W.H. *Literature Abstracts of Ceramic Glazes.* Ellenton, FL.: College Institute, 1951.

Lane, A. *Greek Pottery.* 3rd ed. New York: International Publications Service, 1971.

Lane, P. *Studio Ceramics.* Radnor, PA.: Chilton Book Co., forthcoming.

——— *Studio Porcelain.* Radnor, PA.: Chilton Book Co., 1980.

Lawrence, W.G., and West, R.R. *Ceramic Science for the Potter.* 2nd ed. Radnor, PA.: Chilton Book Co., 1982.

Leach, B. *A Potter's Book.* London: Faber and Faber, 1940.

Nelson, G.C. *Ceramics: A Potter's Handbook.* 4th ed. New York: Holt, Rinehart and Winston, Inc., 1978.

Norton, F.H. *Ceramics for the Artist Potter.* Reading, MA.: Addison-Wesley, 1956.

Parmelee, C.W. *Ceramic Glazes.* 3rd ed. Boston: CBI Publishing Co., Inc., 1973.

Pearl, R.M. *How to Know Minerals and Rocks.* New York: New American Library, n.d.

Press, F. and Siever, R. *Earth.* 2nd ed. San Francisco, W.H. Freeman and Co., 1978.

Rackham, B. *Medieval English Pottery.* London: Faber and Faber, 1949.

Rawson, P. *Ceramics.* London: Oxford University Press, 1971.

Rhodes, D. *Clay and Glazes for the Potter.* 2nd ed. Radnor, PA.: Chilton Book Co., 1973.

——— *Kilns.* 2nd ed. Radnor, PA., Chilton Book Co., 1981.

——— *Stoneware and Porcelain.* Radnor, PA.: Chilton Book Co., 1959.

Sanders, H. *Glazes for Special Effects.* New York: Watson-Guptill, 1974.

——— *The World of Japanese Ceramics.* New York: Kodansha International, Ltd., 1981.

Shaw, K. *Ceramic Colors and Pottery Decoration.* New York: F. Preager, 1969.

Shepard, A.O. *Ceramics for the Archaeologist.* Washington, D.C.: Carnegie Institution of Washington, 1956.

Tyler, C., and Hirsch, R. *Raku.* New York: Watson-Guptill, 1975.

Williams, G., ed. *Studio Potter Book.* New York: Van Nostrand Reinhold, 1979.

Wood, N. *Oriental Glazes.* New York: Watson-Guptill, 1978.

MAGAZINES AND JOURNALS

Ceramics Monthly. Professional Publications, Inc., Box 12448, Columbus, Ohio 43212.

Ceramic Review. Craftsmen Potters Association of Great Britain, 25 Carnaby Street, London W1V 1P1.

Journal of the American Ceramic Society, 65 Ceramic Drive, Columbus, Ohio 43214.

Journal of the British Ceramic Society, Shelton House, Stoke-on-Trent ST4 2DR.

Journal of the Canadian Ceramic Society, 2175 Sheppard Ave. E., Suite 110, Willowdale, Ontario.

Pottery in Australia. Potter's Society of Australia, 48 Burton Street, Sydney.

Raw Materials Handbook. Cahners Publishing Company, 5 S. Wabash Ave., Chicago, Illinois 60603.

Studio Potter. Box 65, Goffstown, New Hampshire 03045.

Index

Page numbers in *italics* refer to information in black and white photographs; color photographs are found in the section following the page number given for each entry.